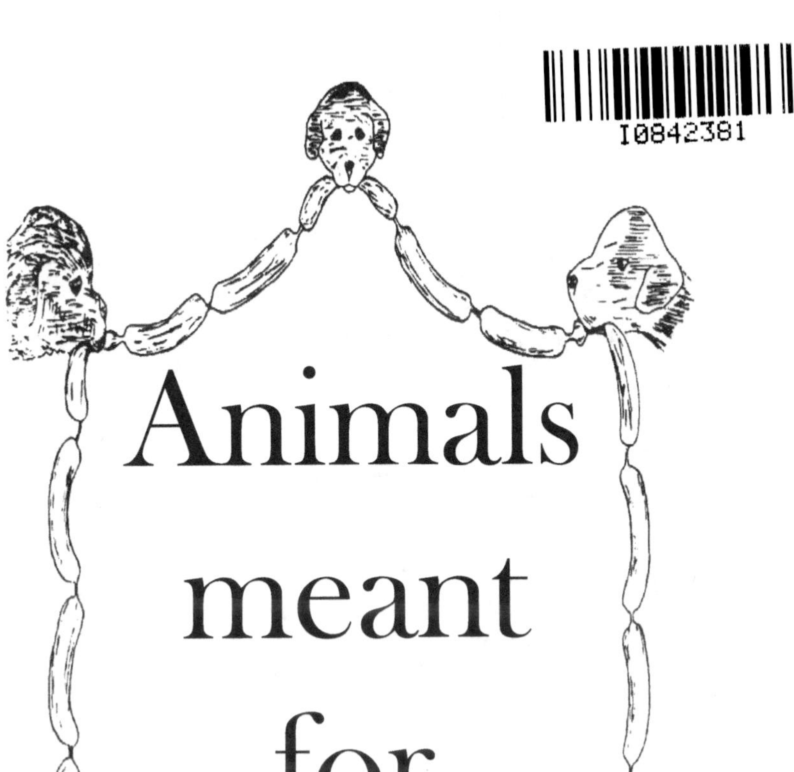

# Animals meant for coloring

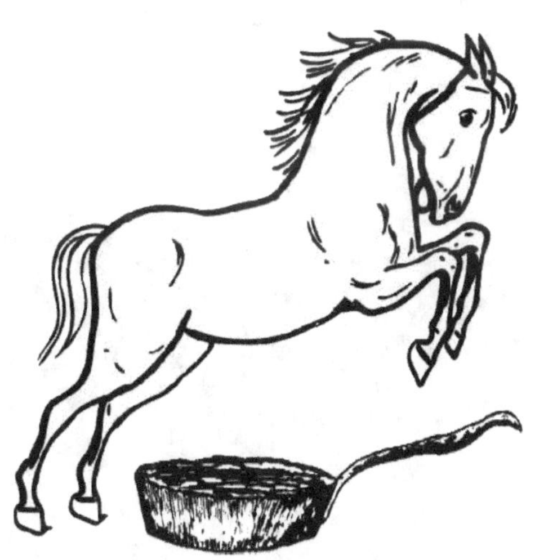

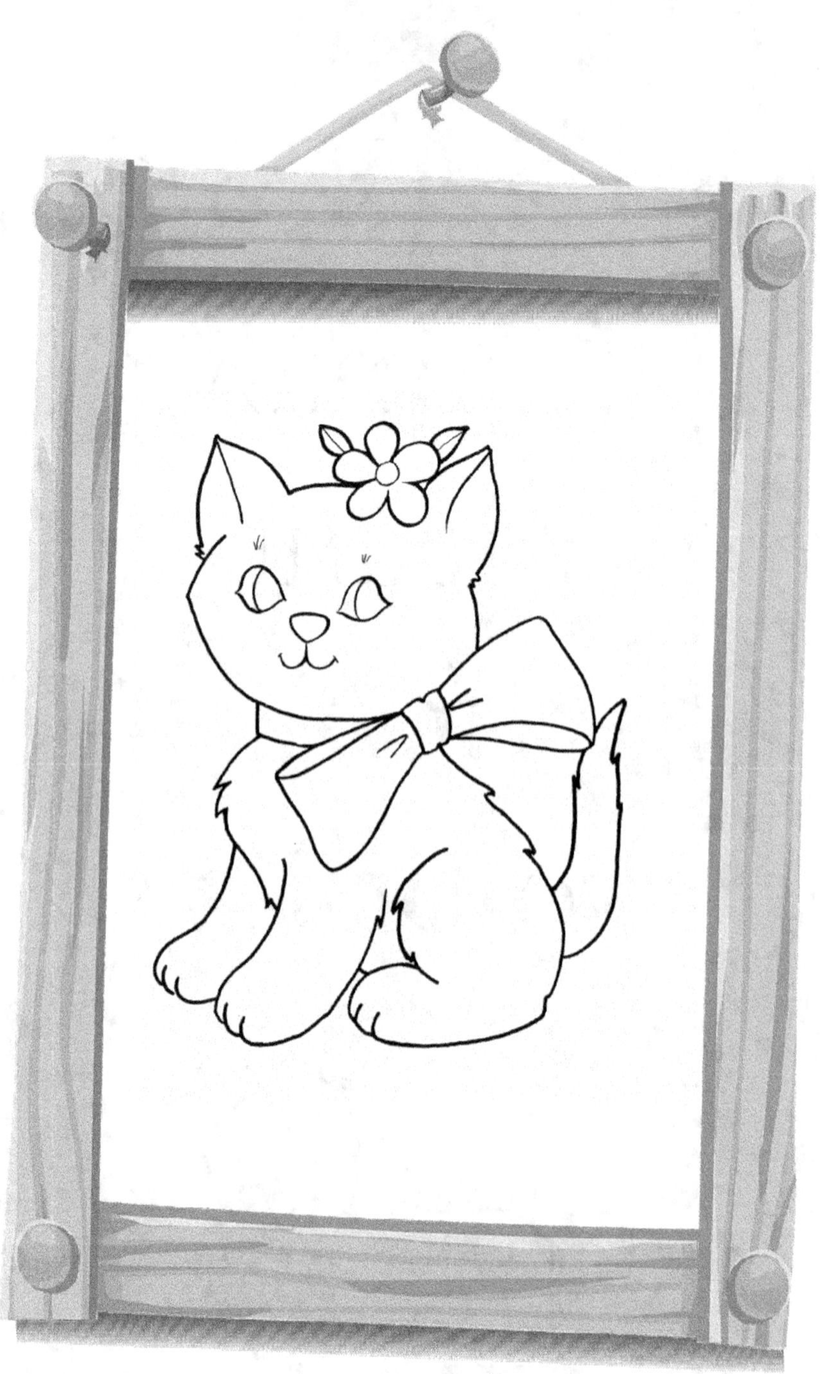

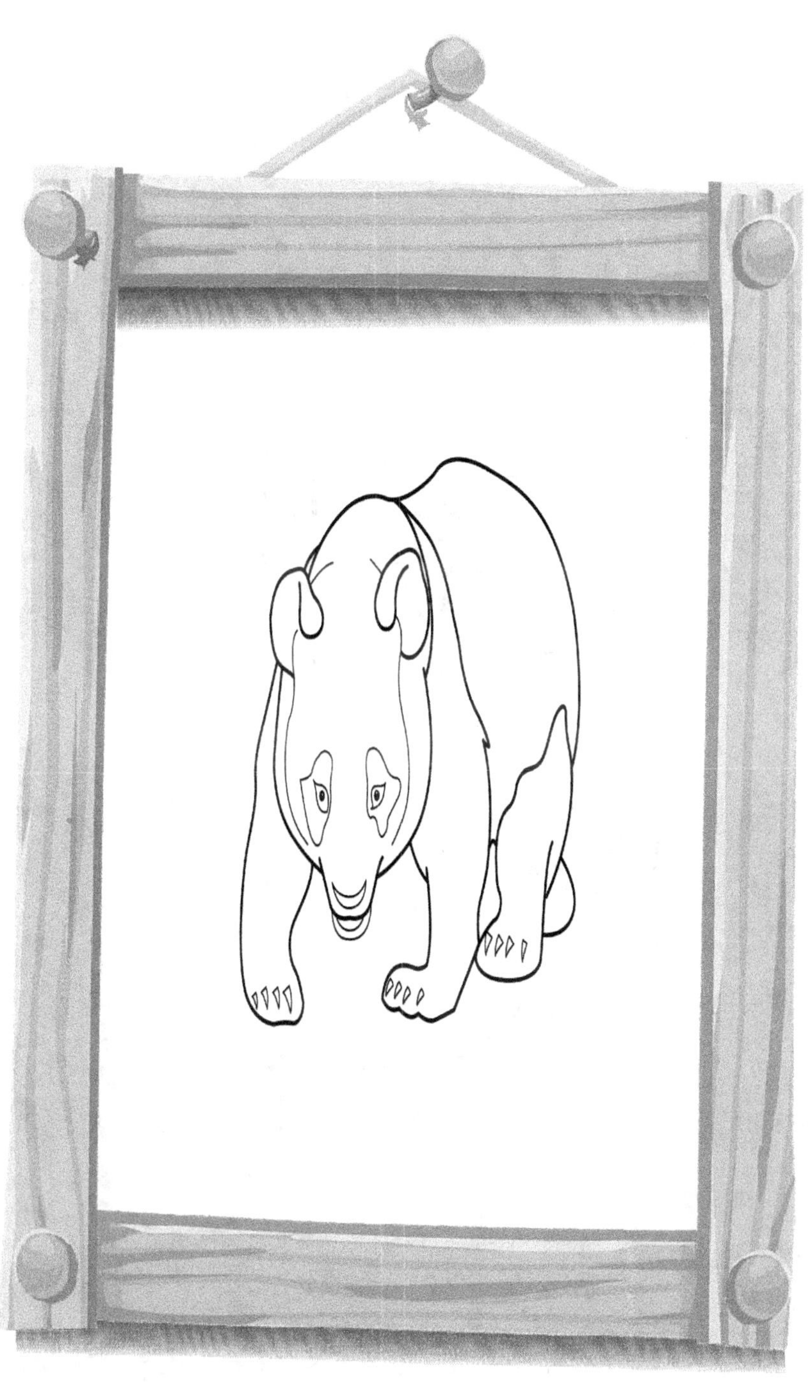

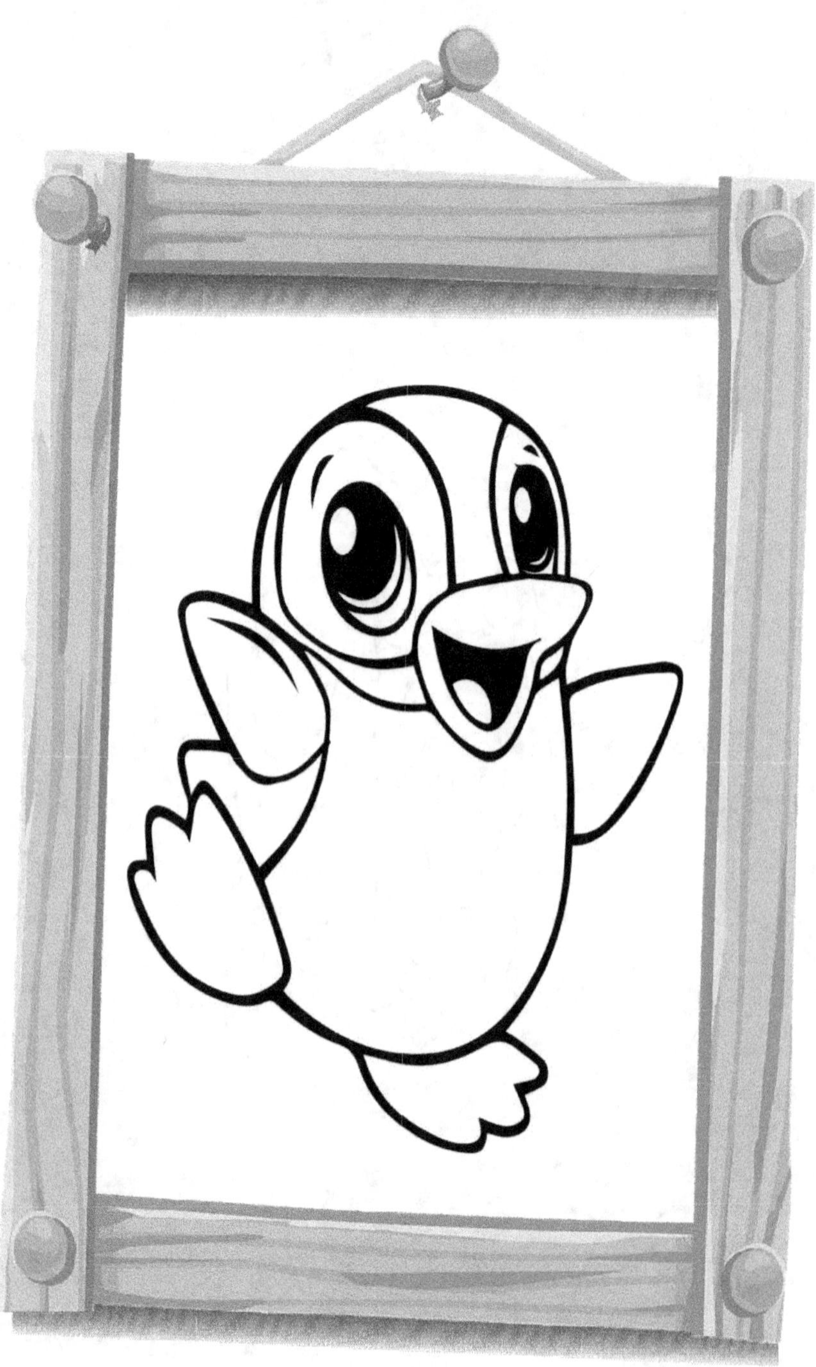

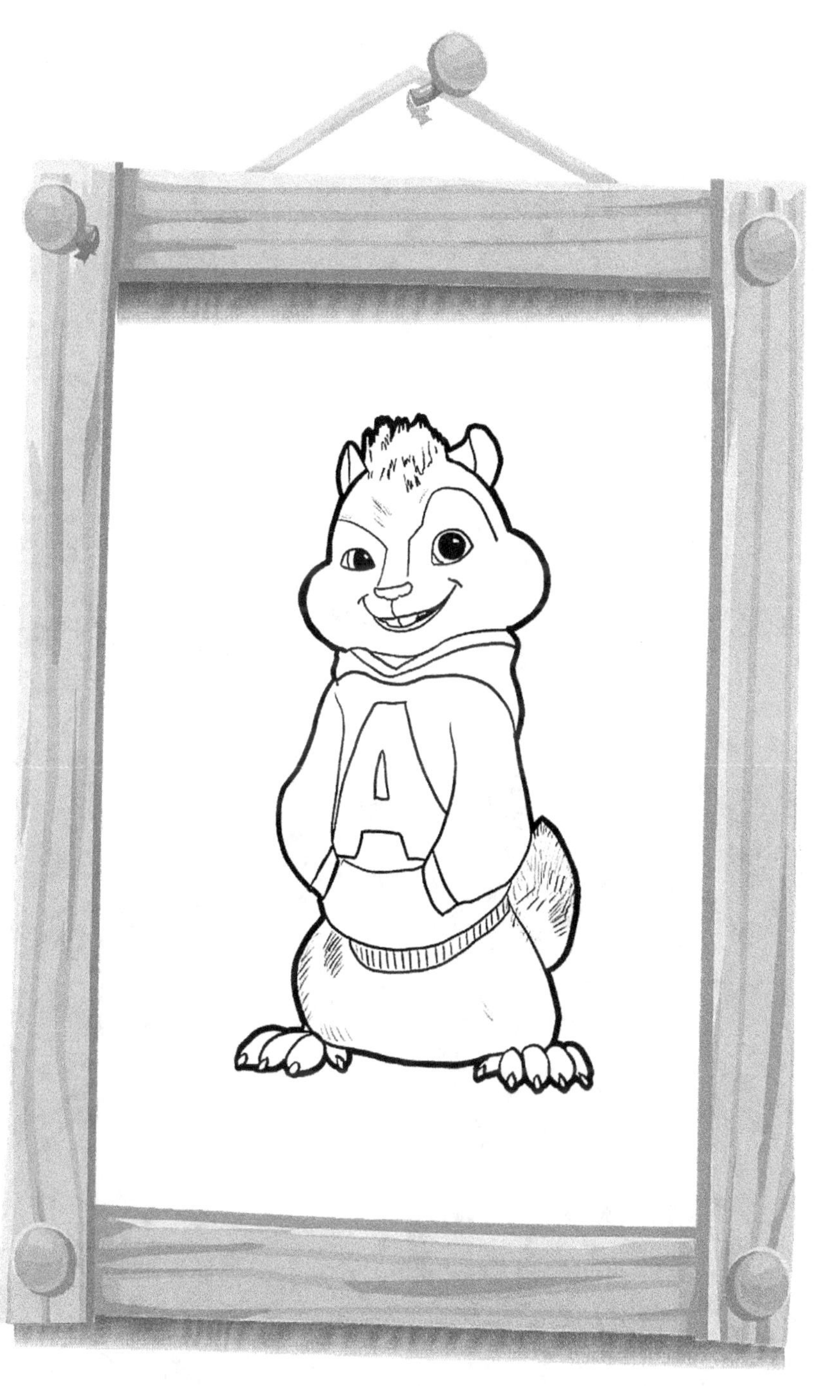

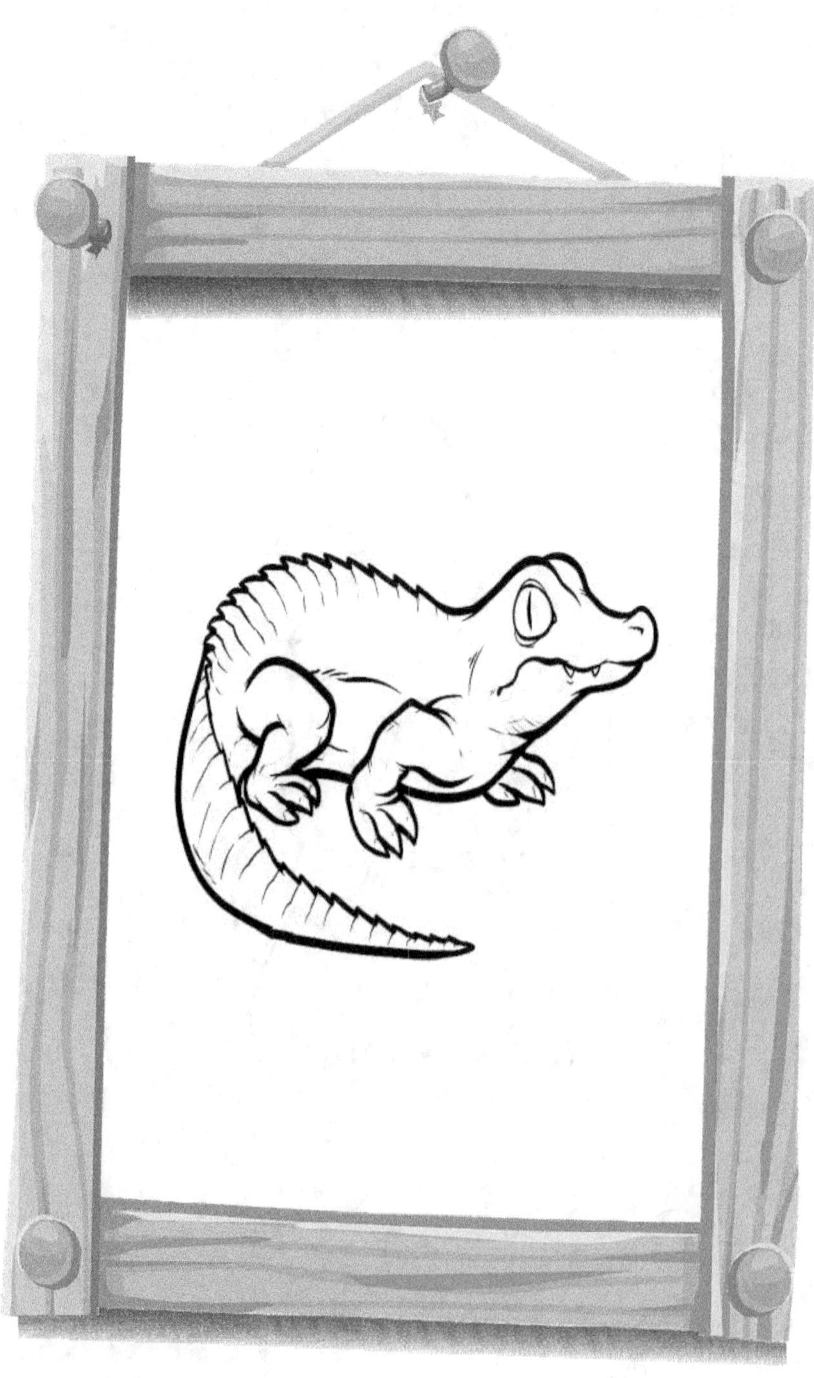

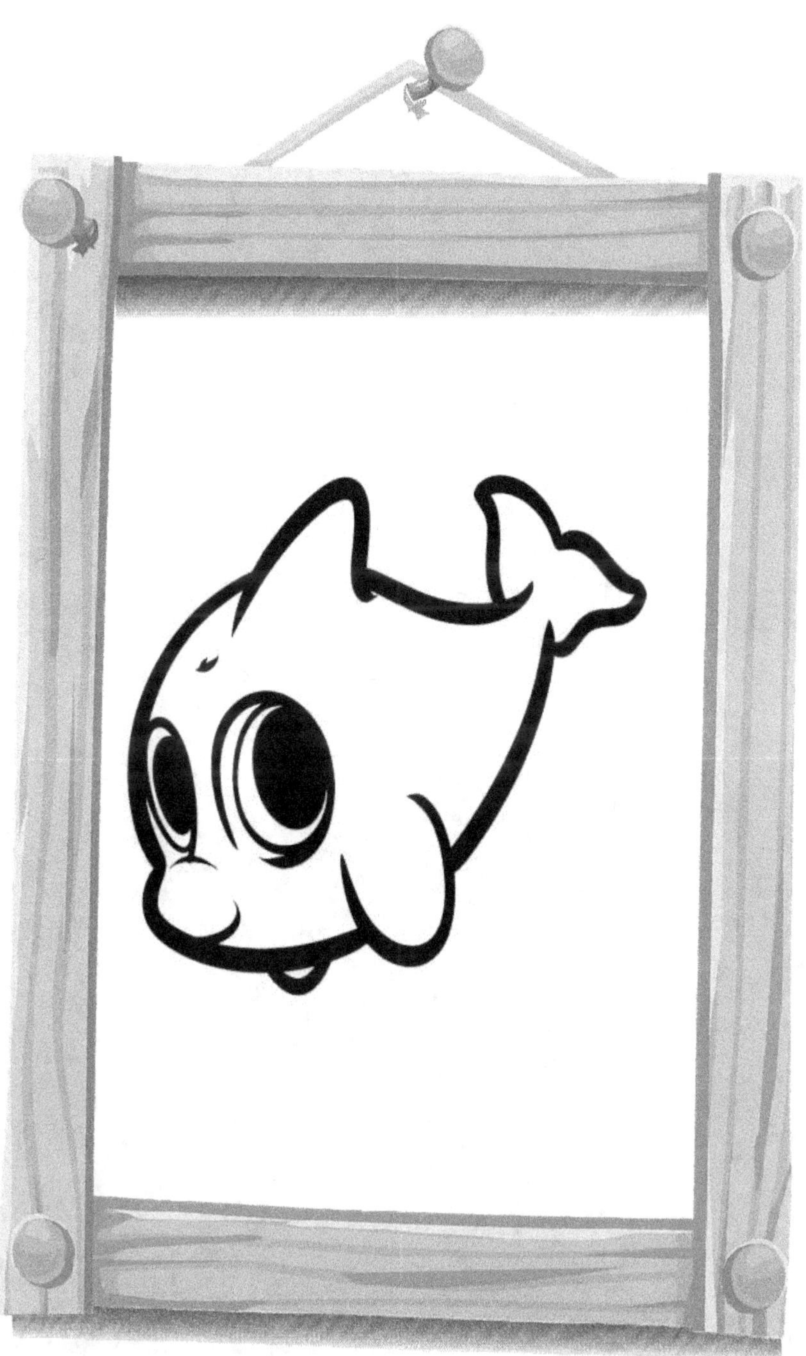

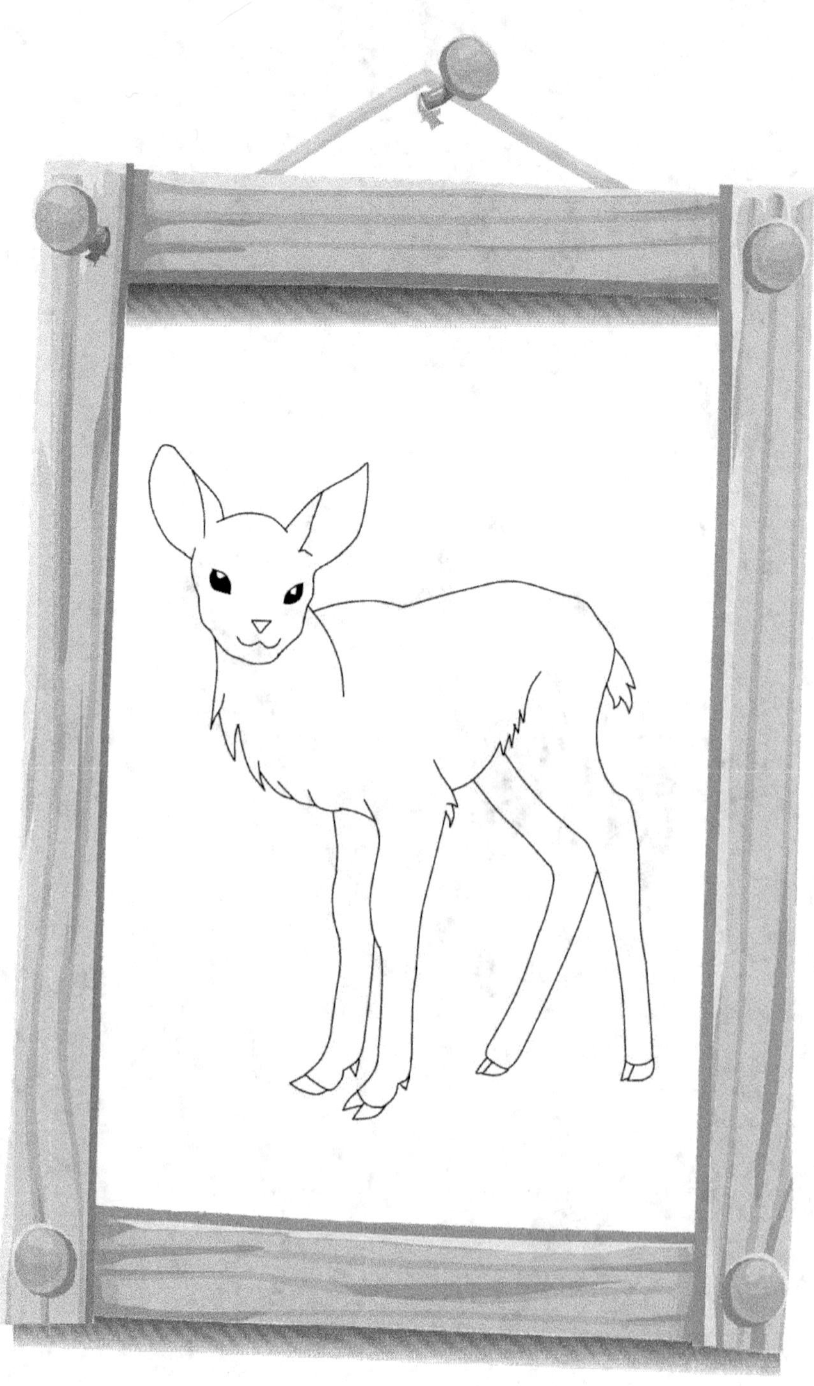

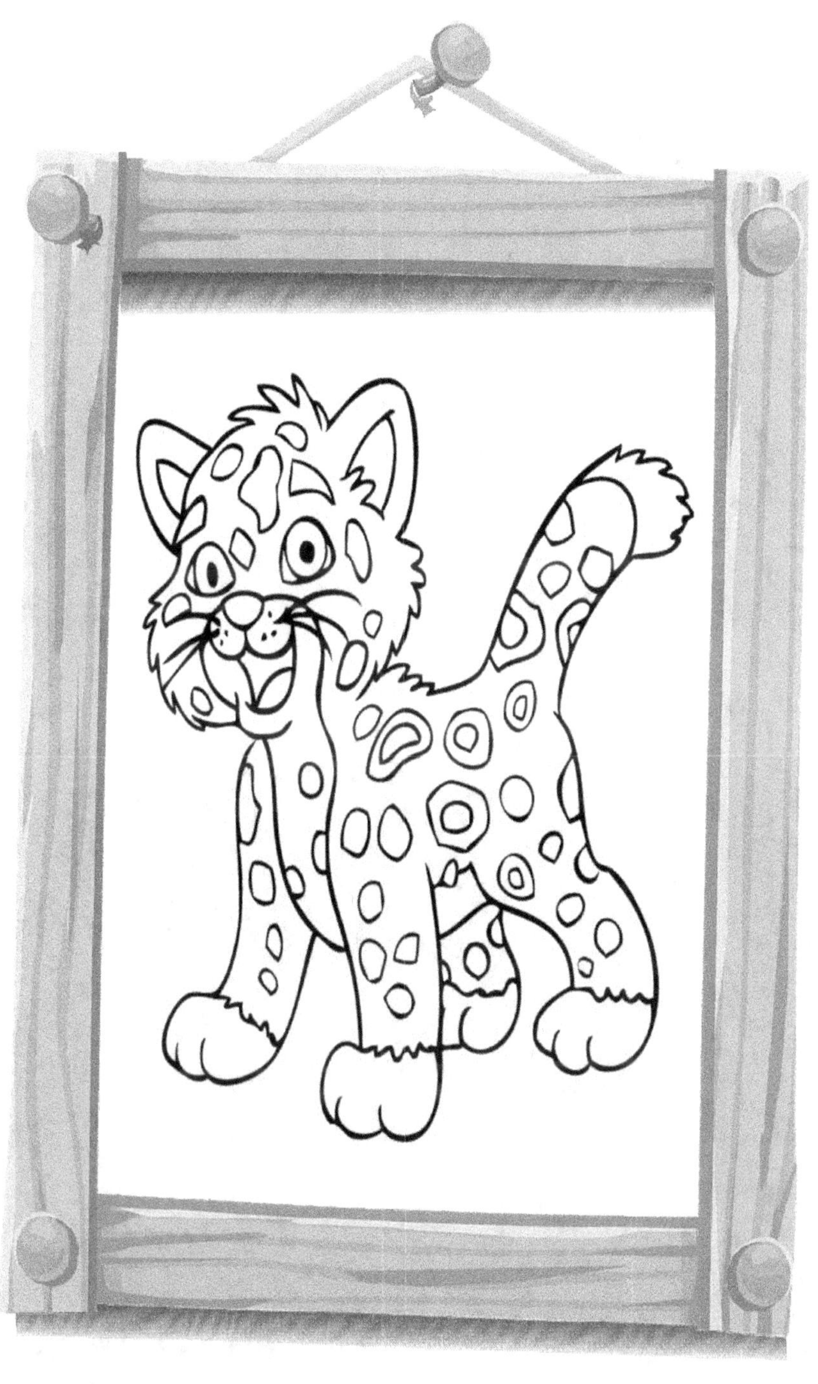

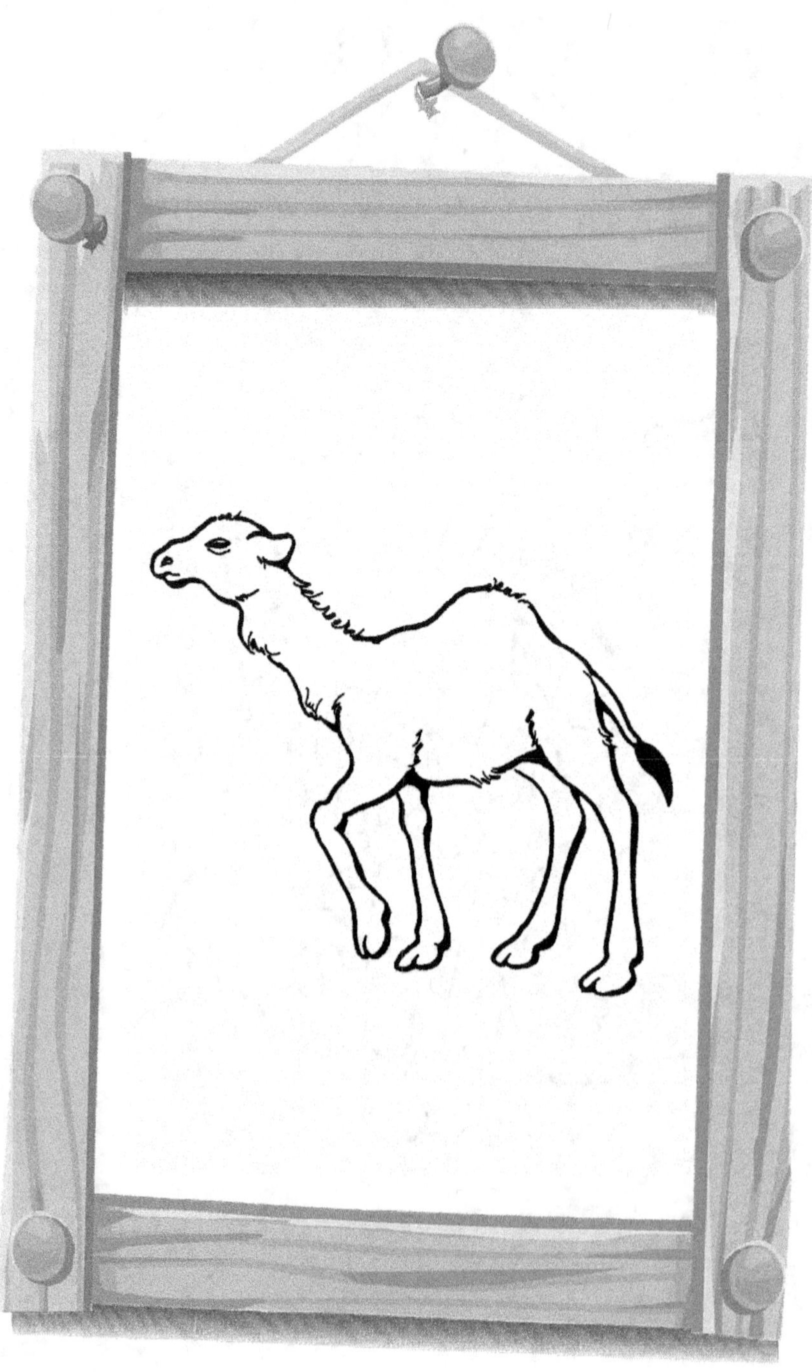

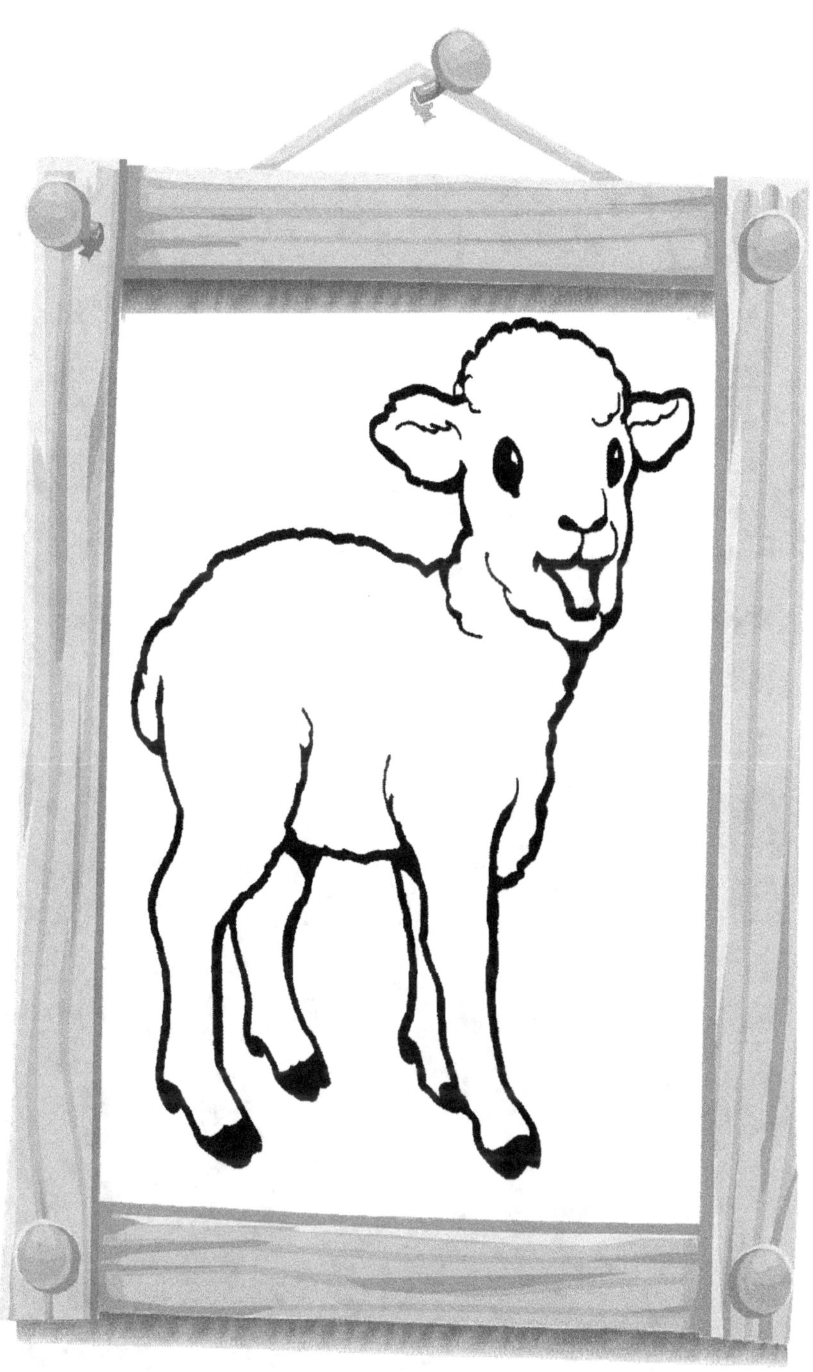

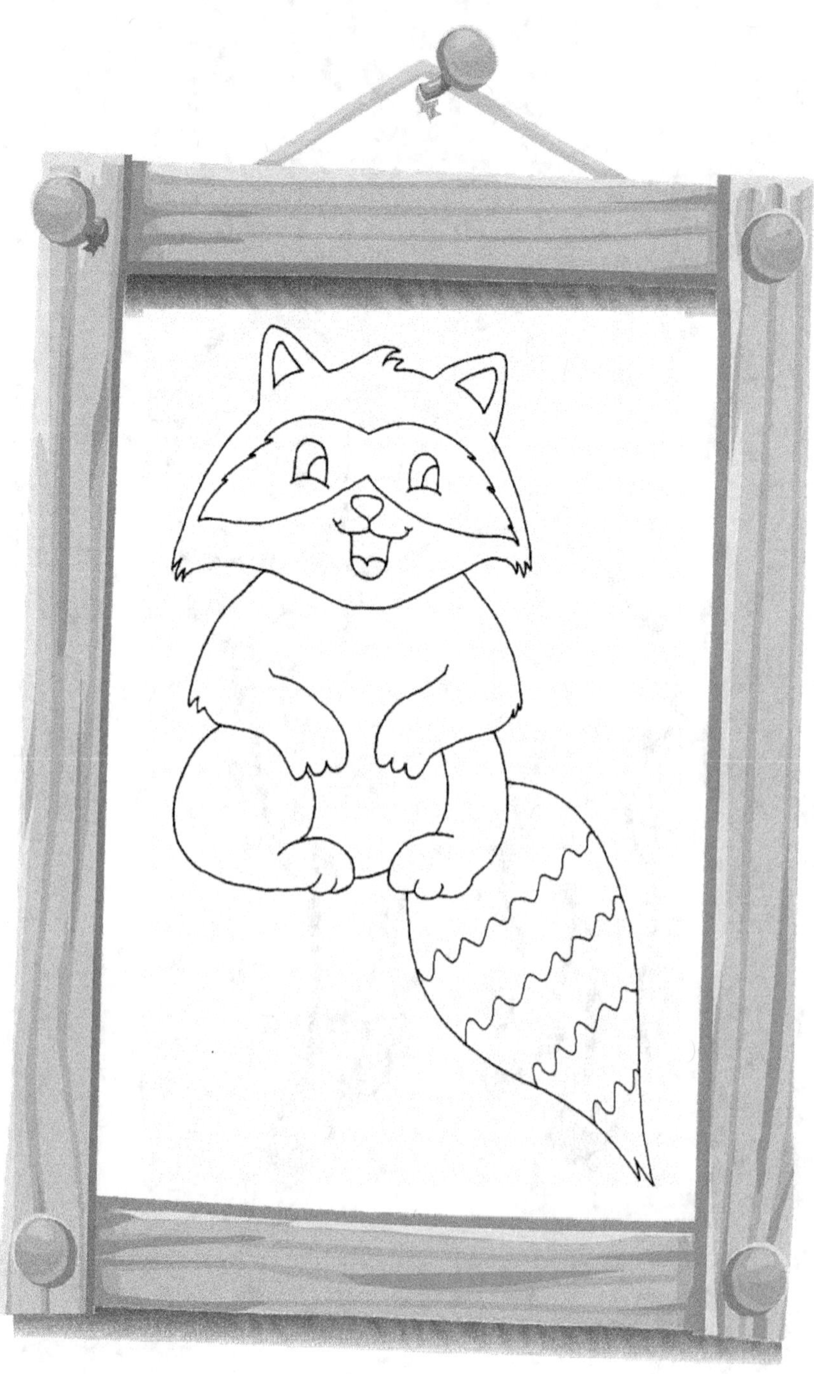

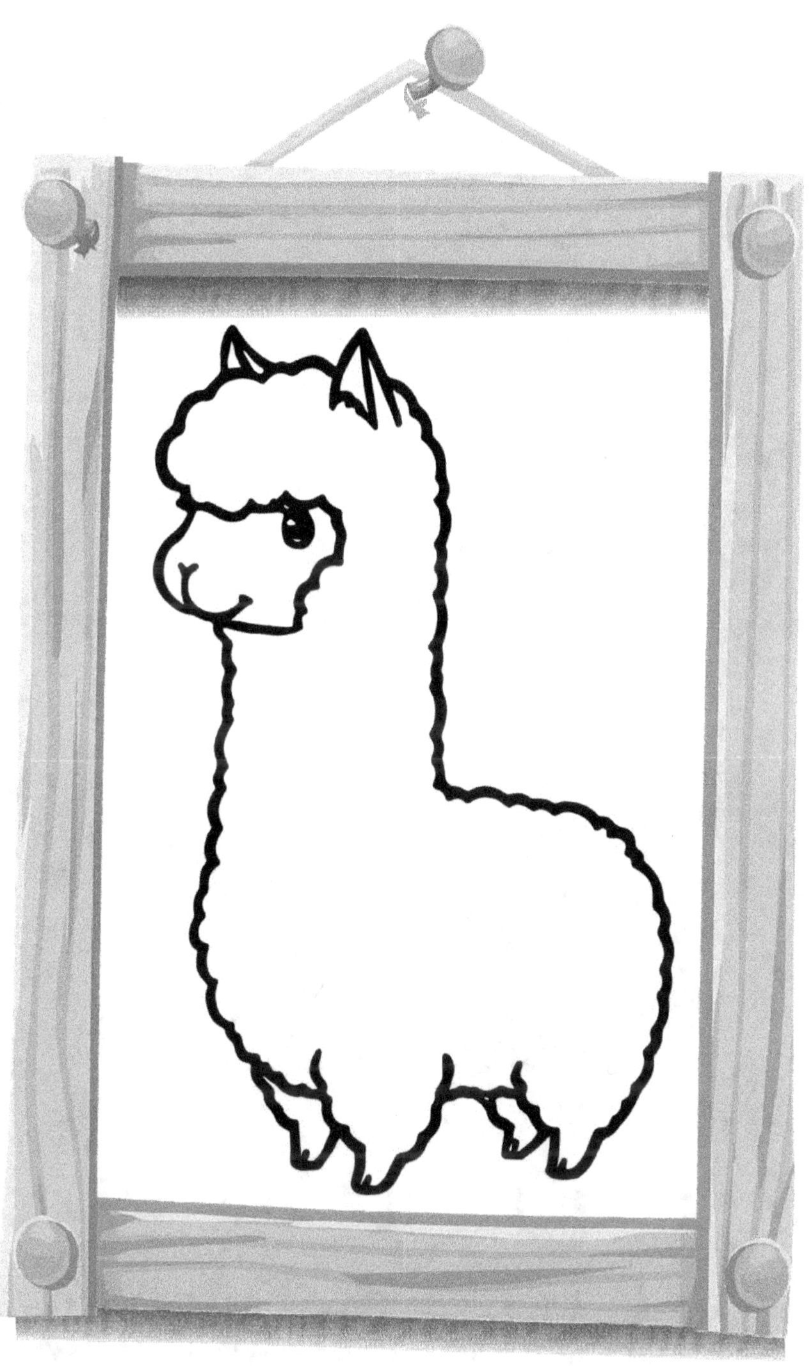

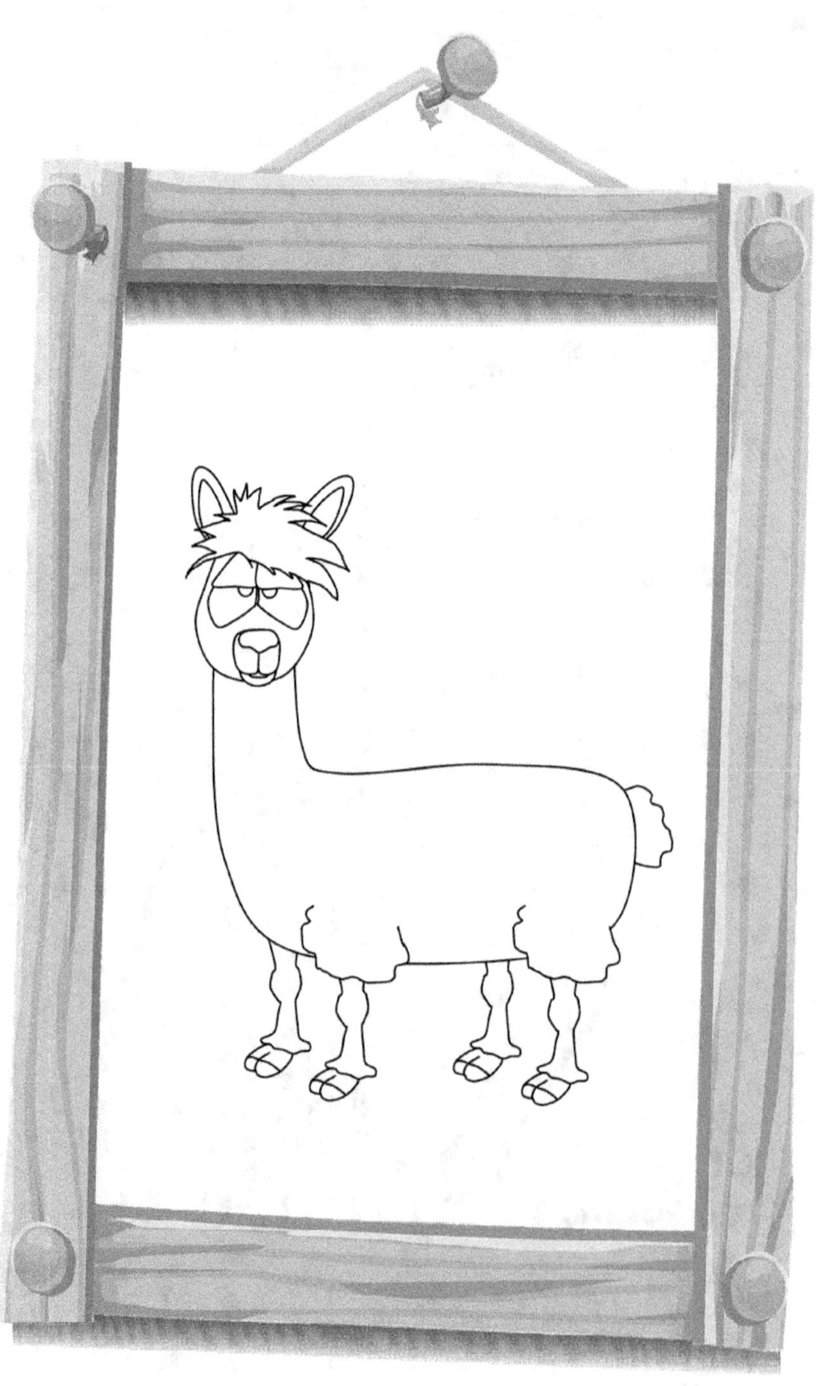

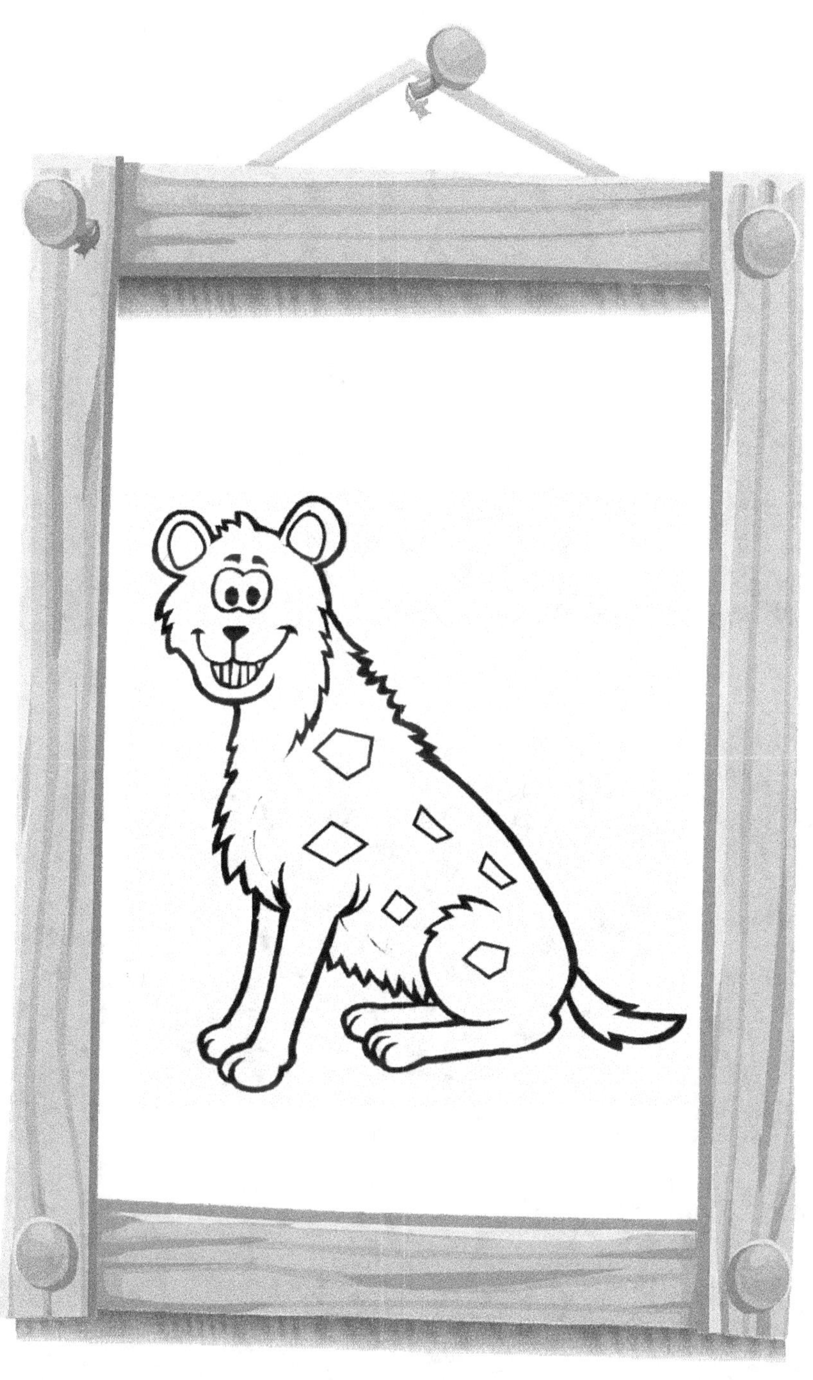

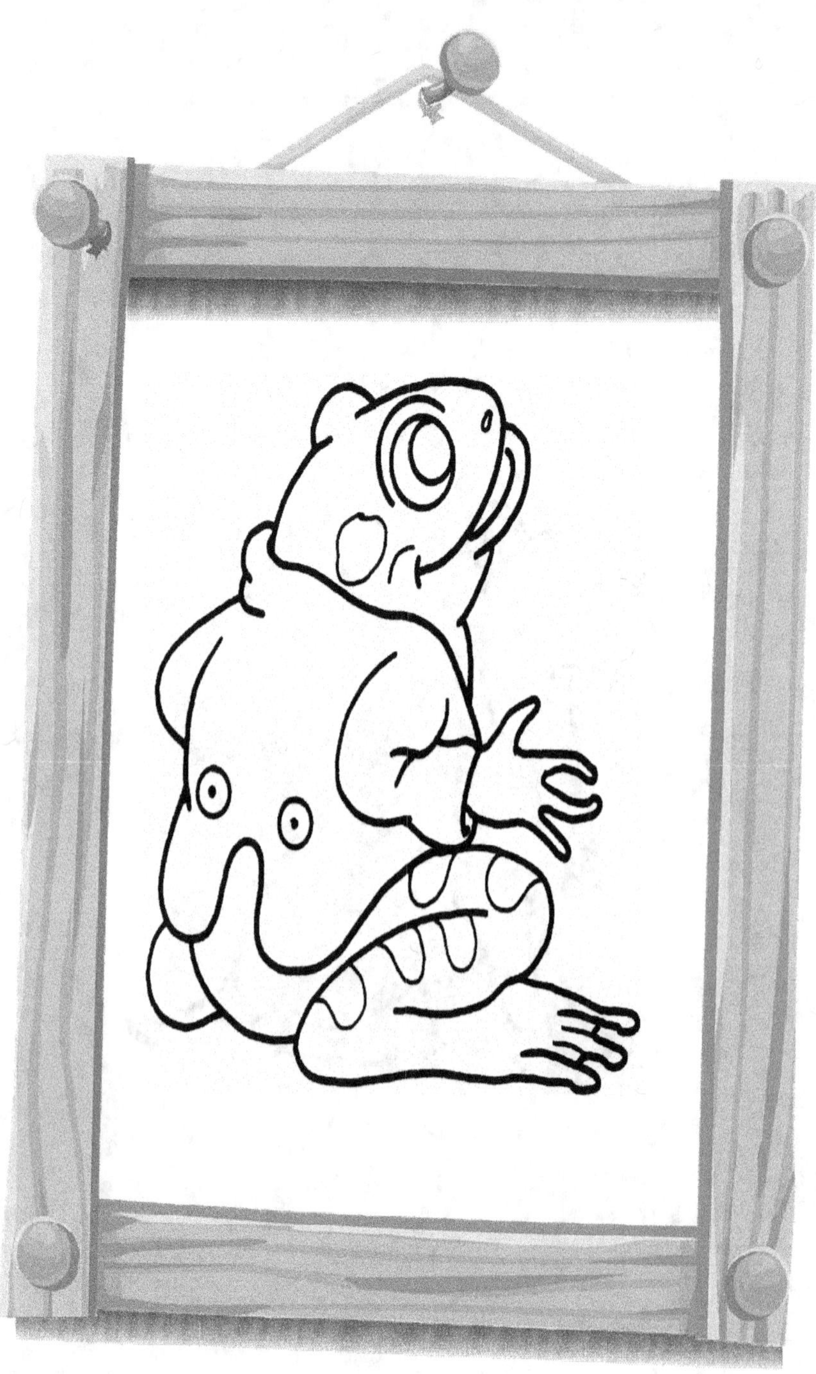

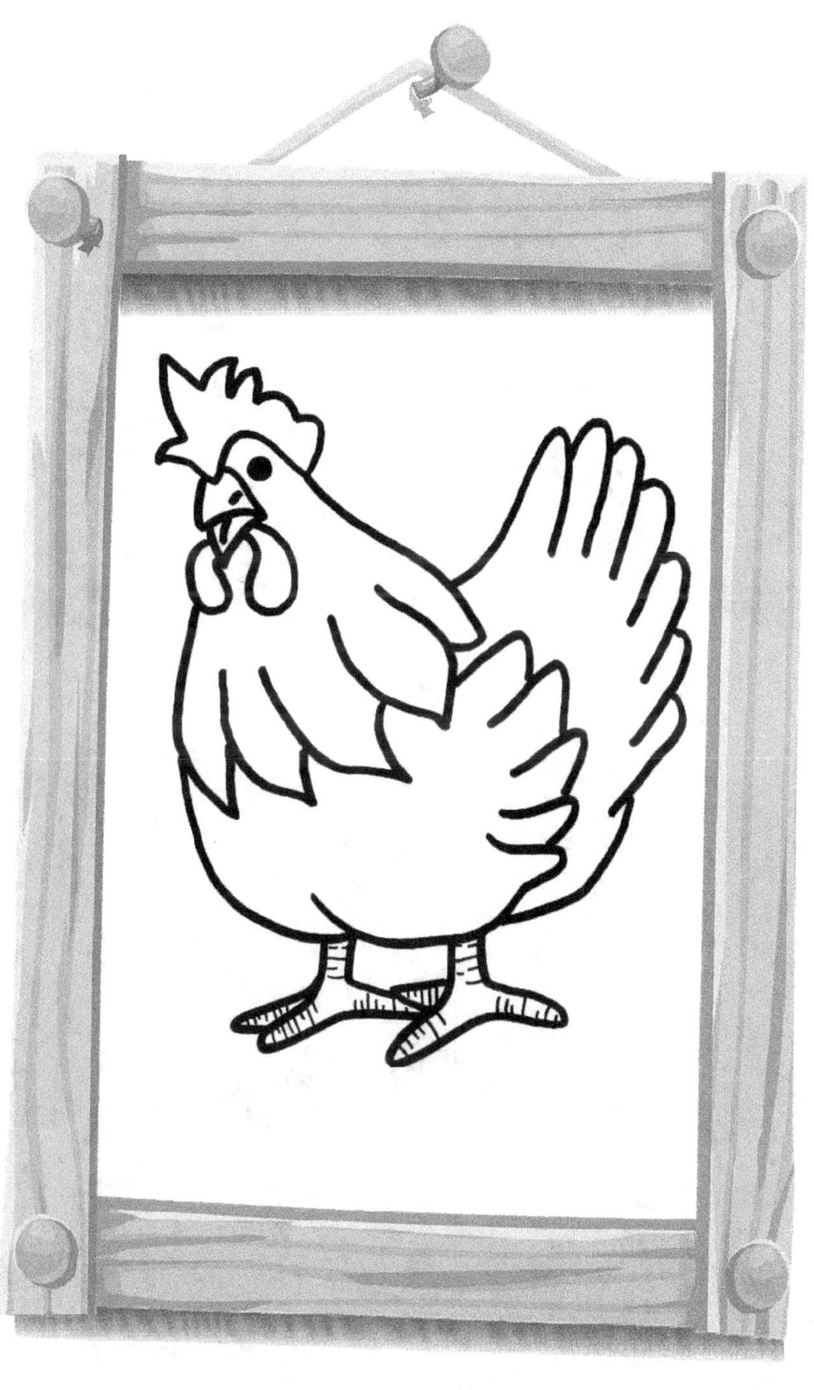

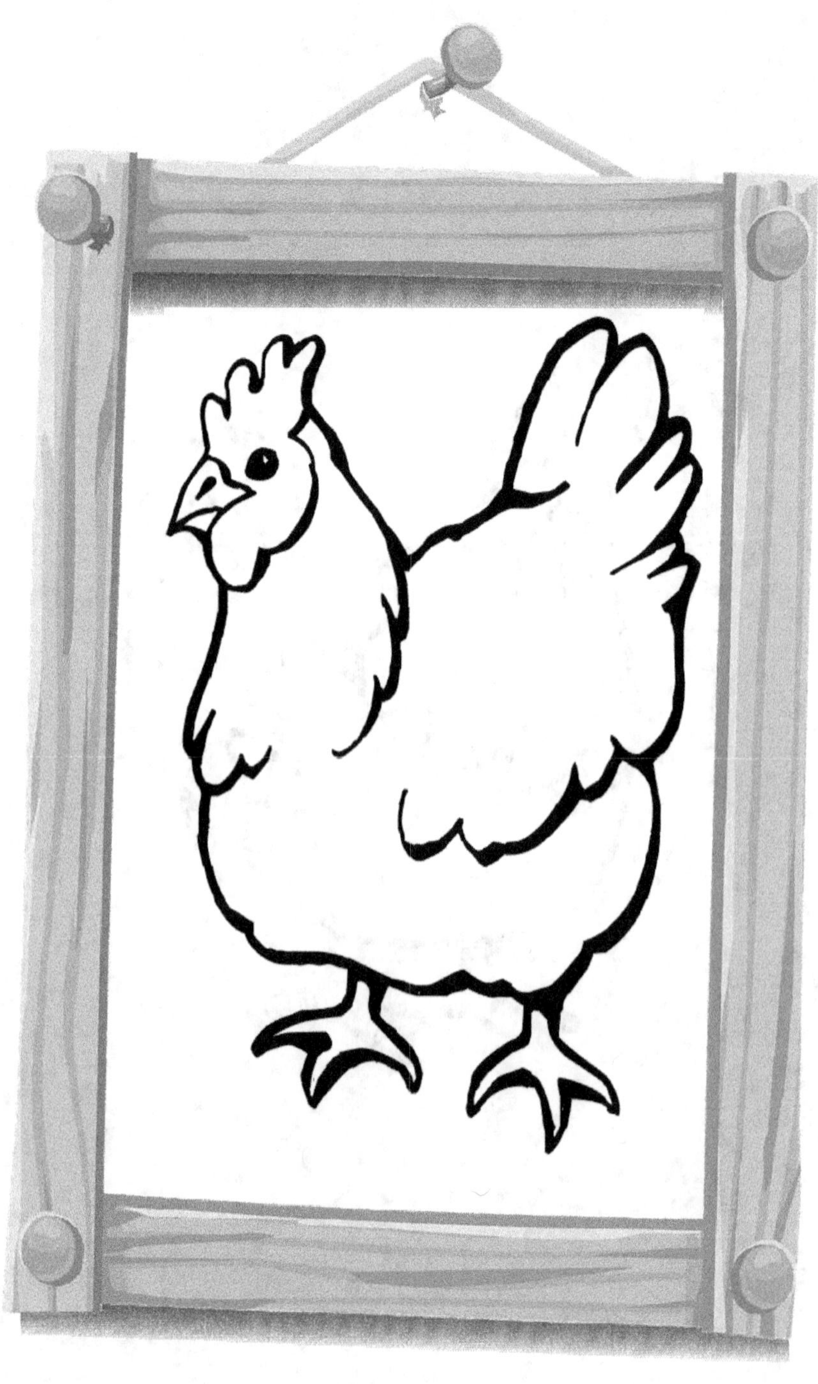

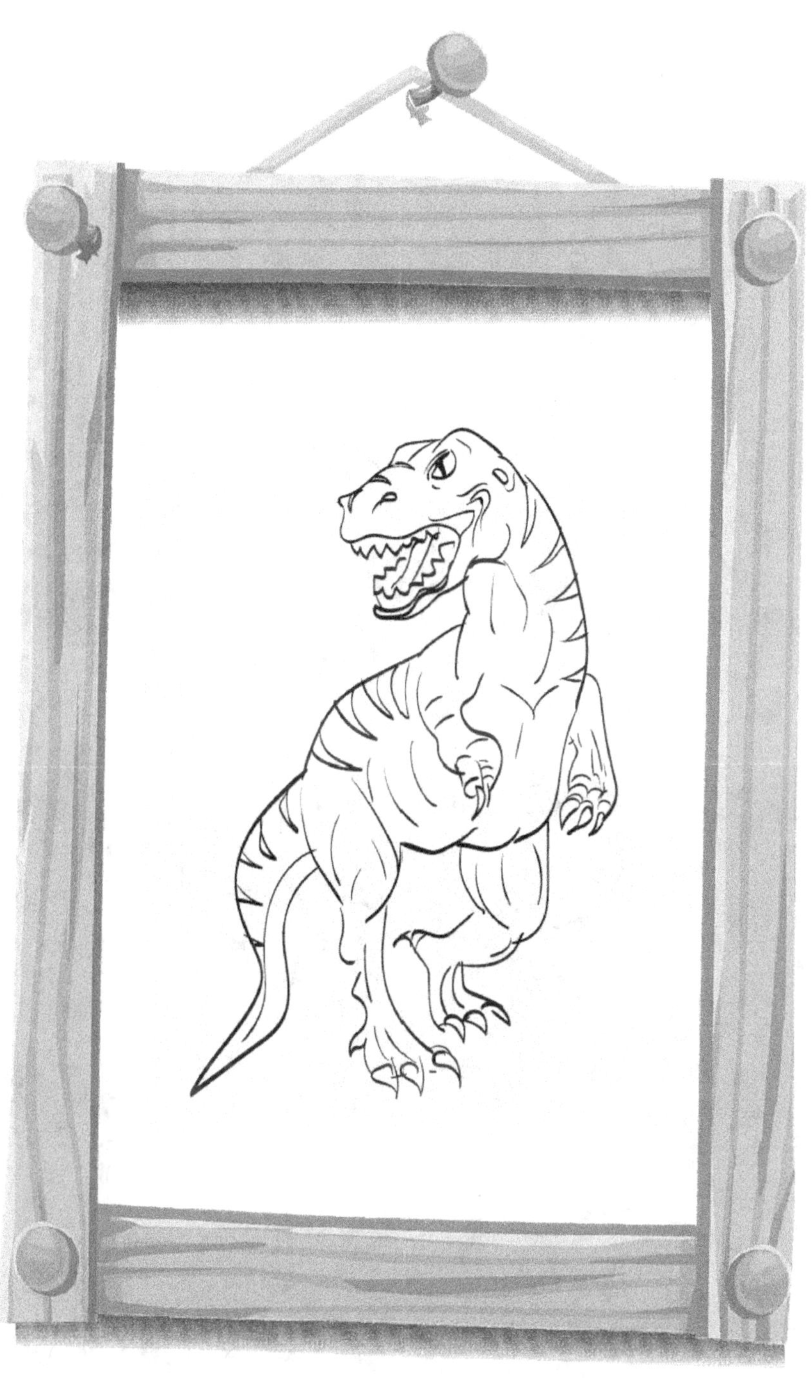

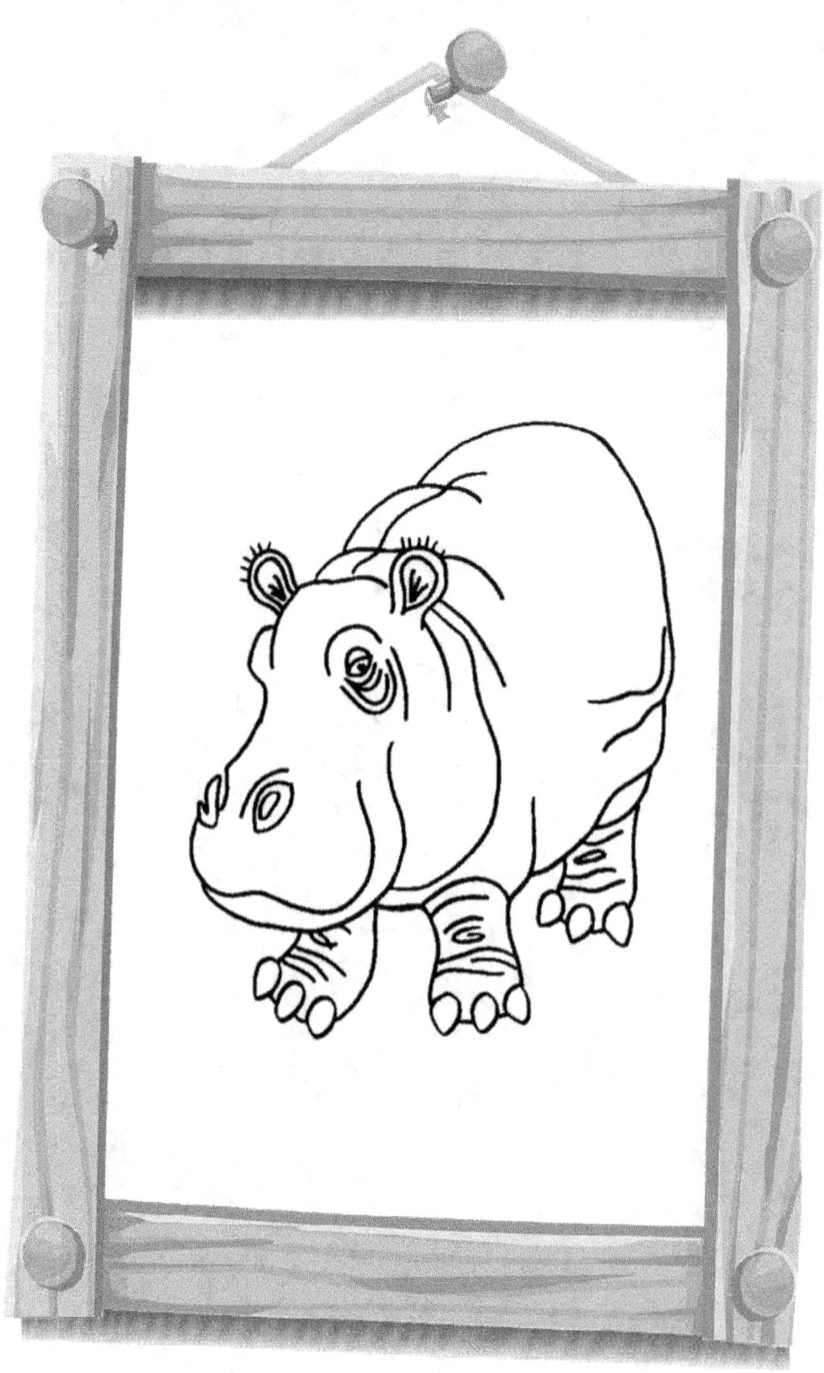

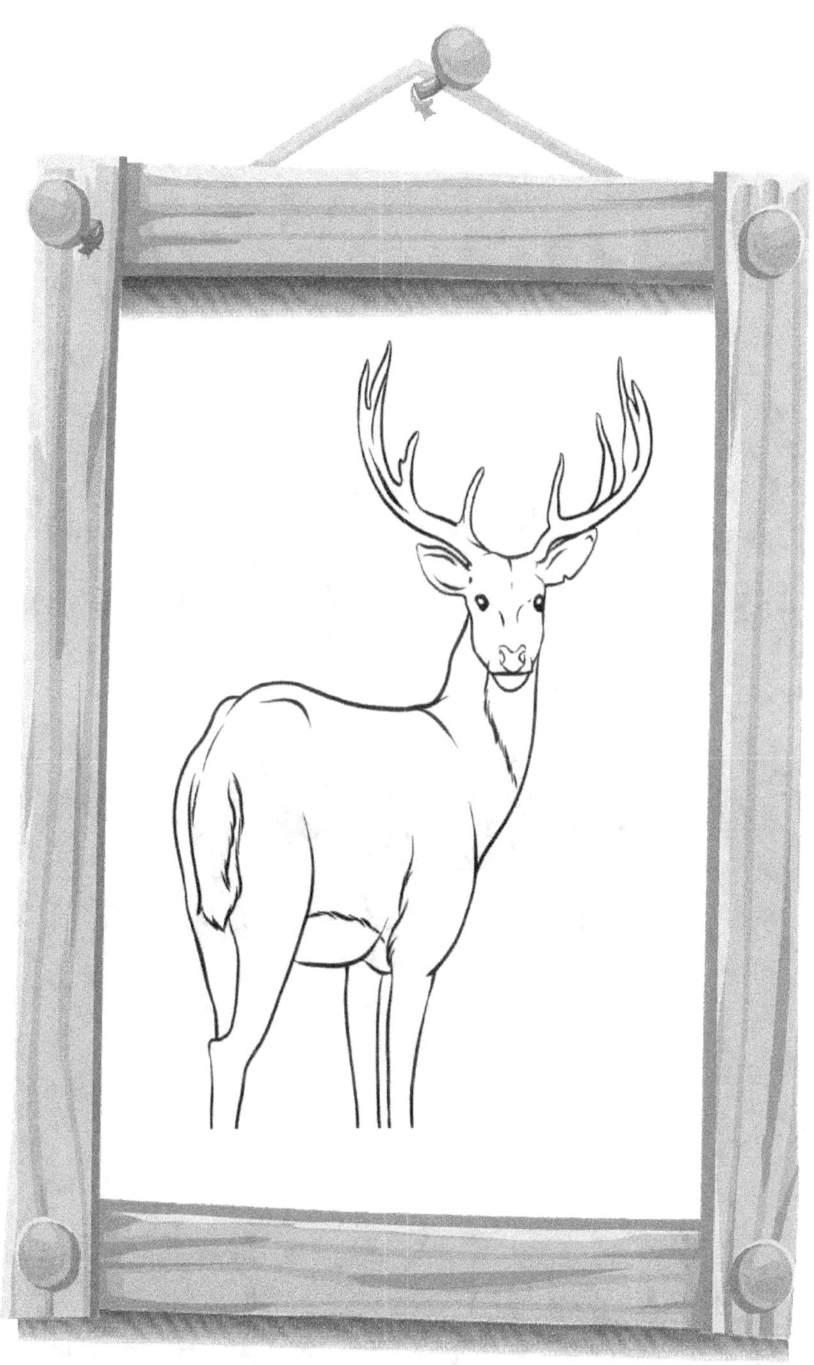

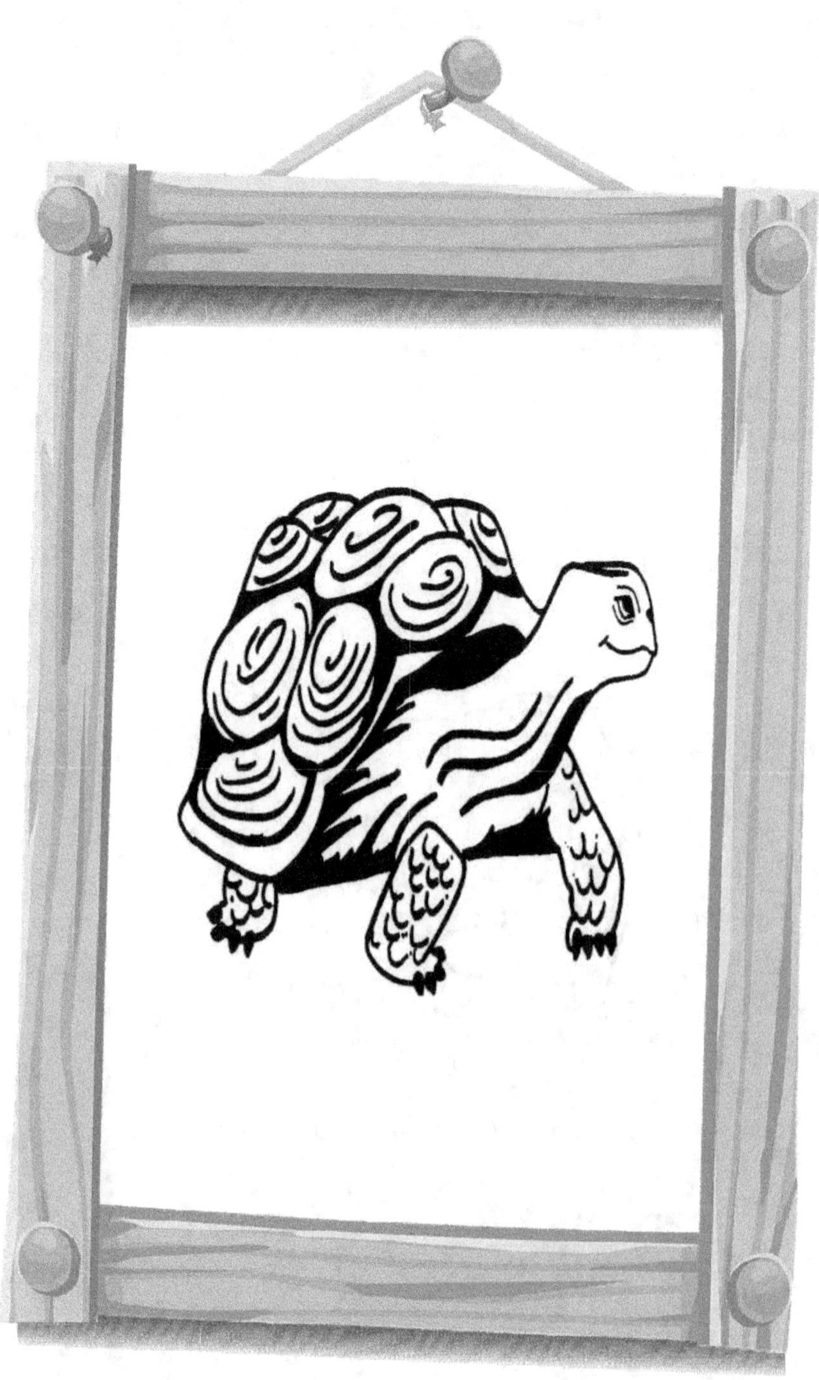

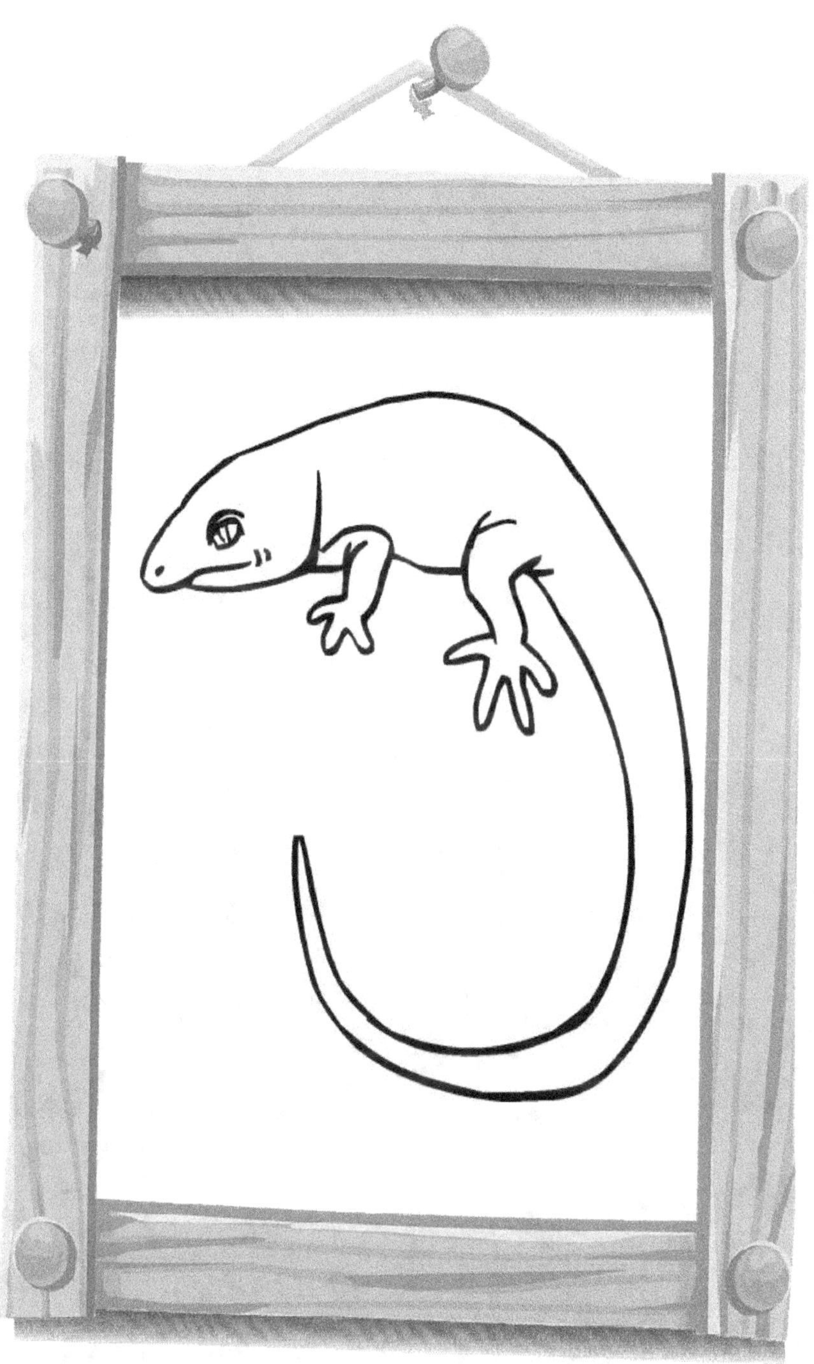

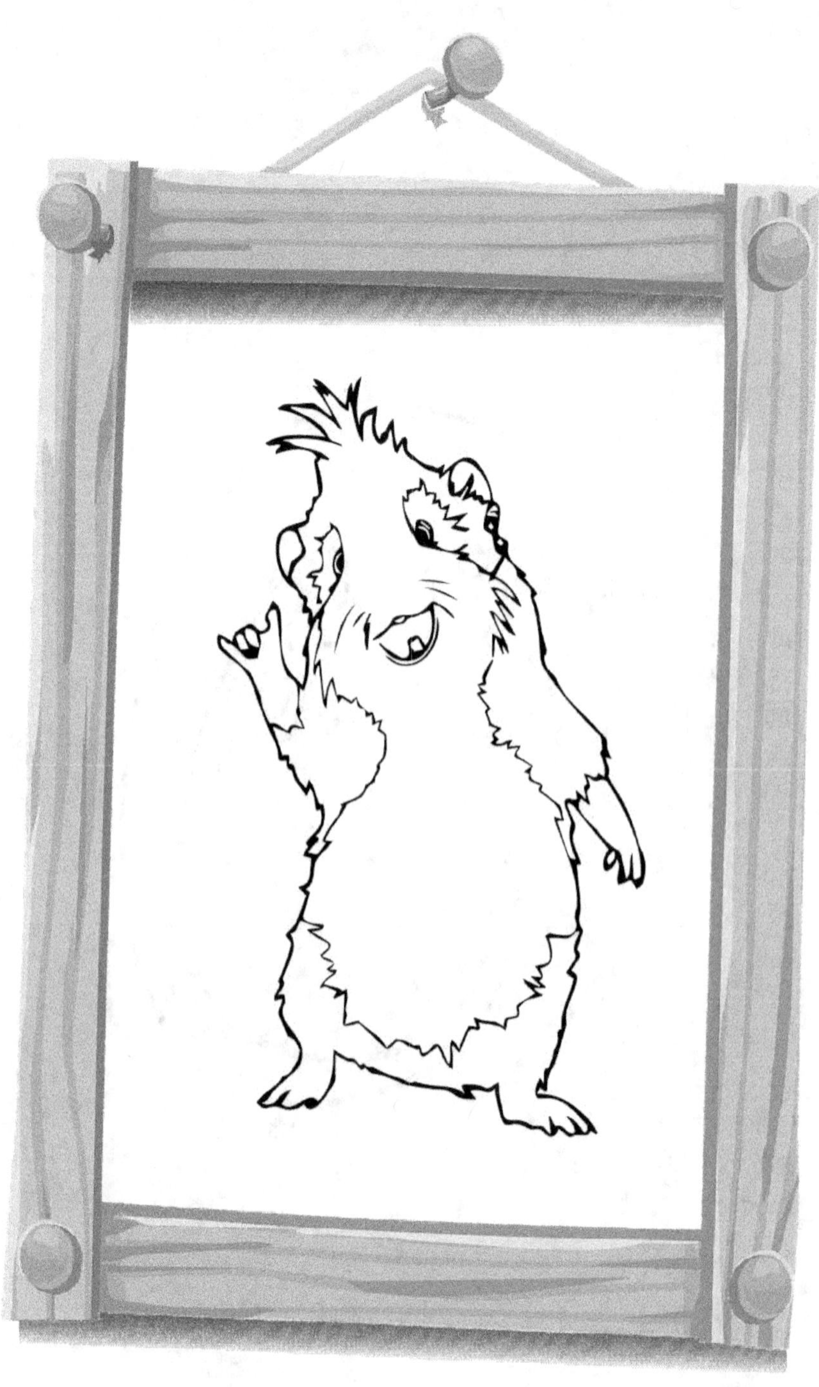

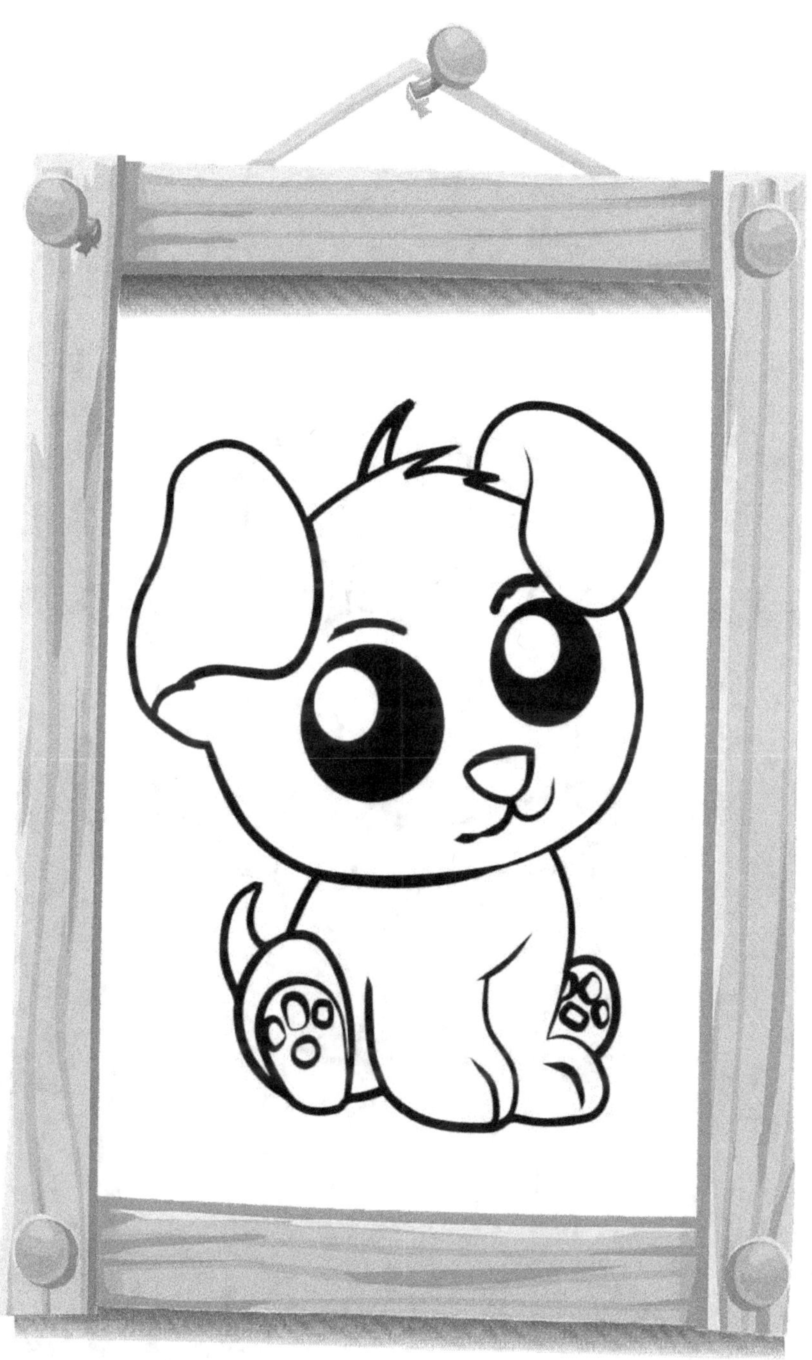

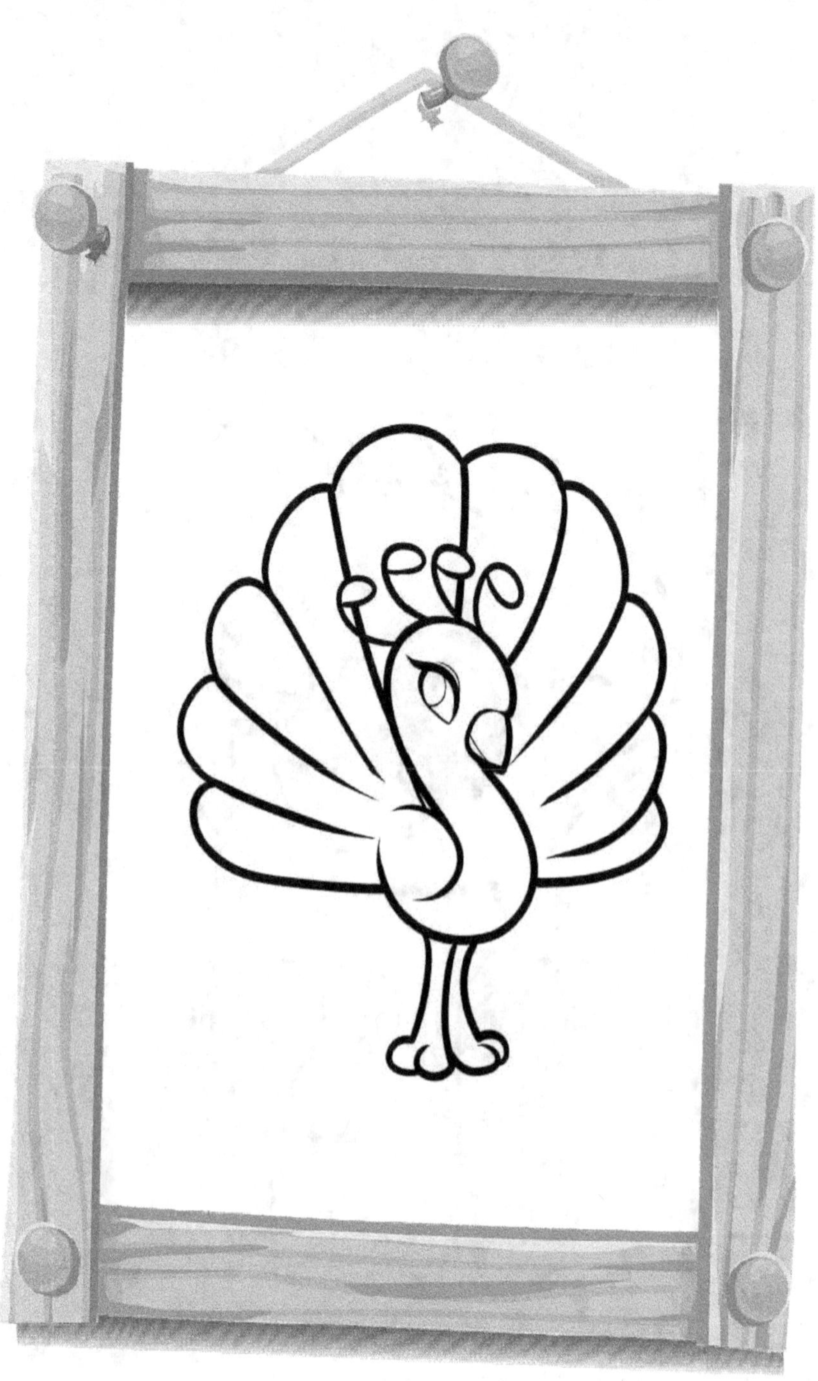

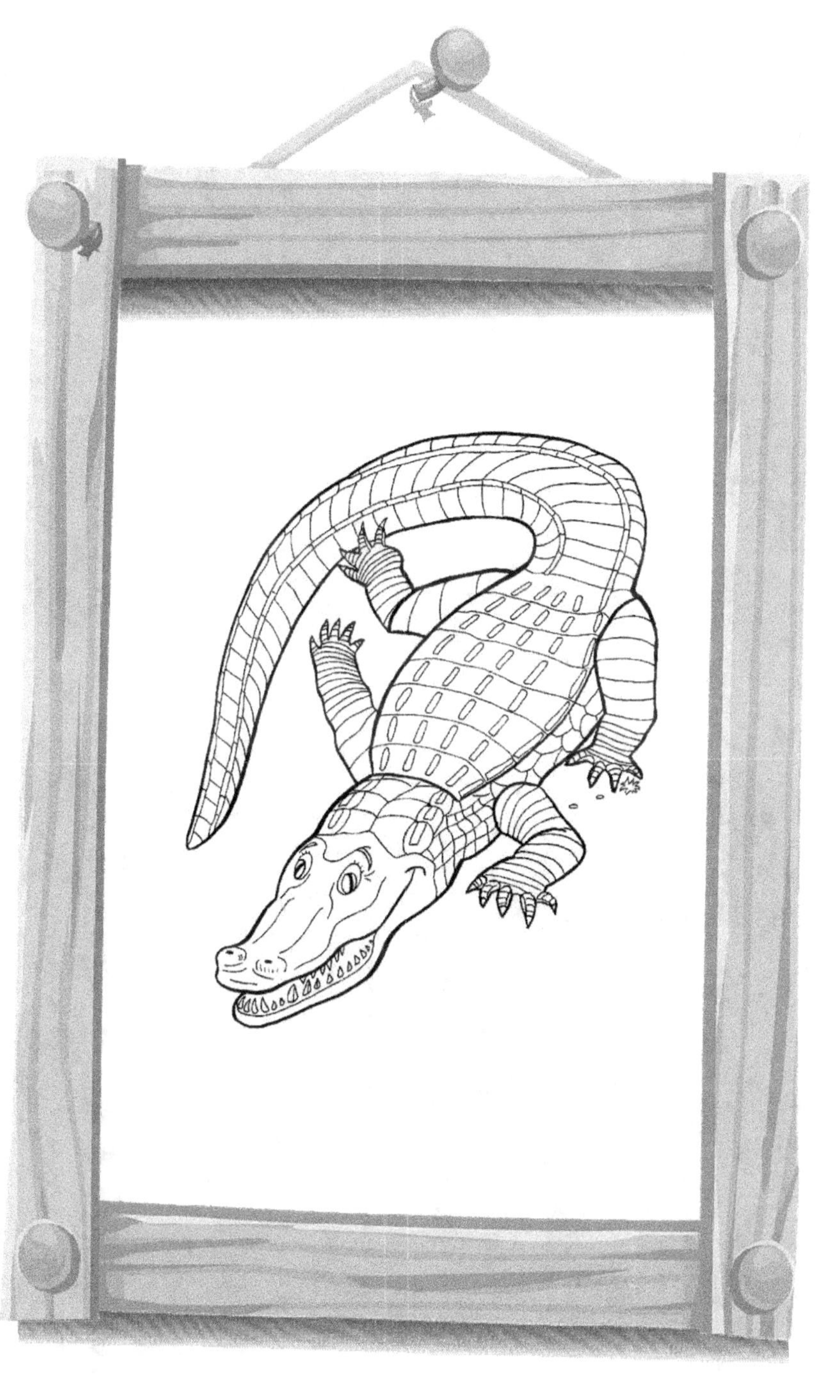

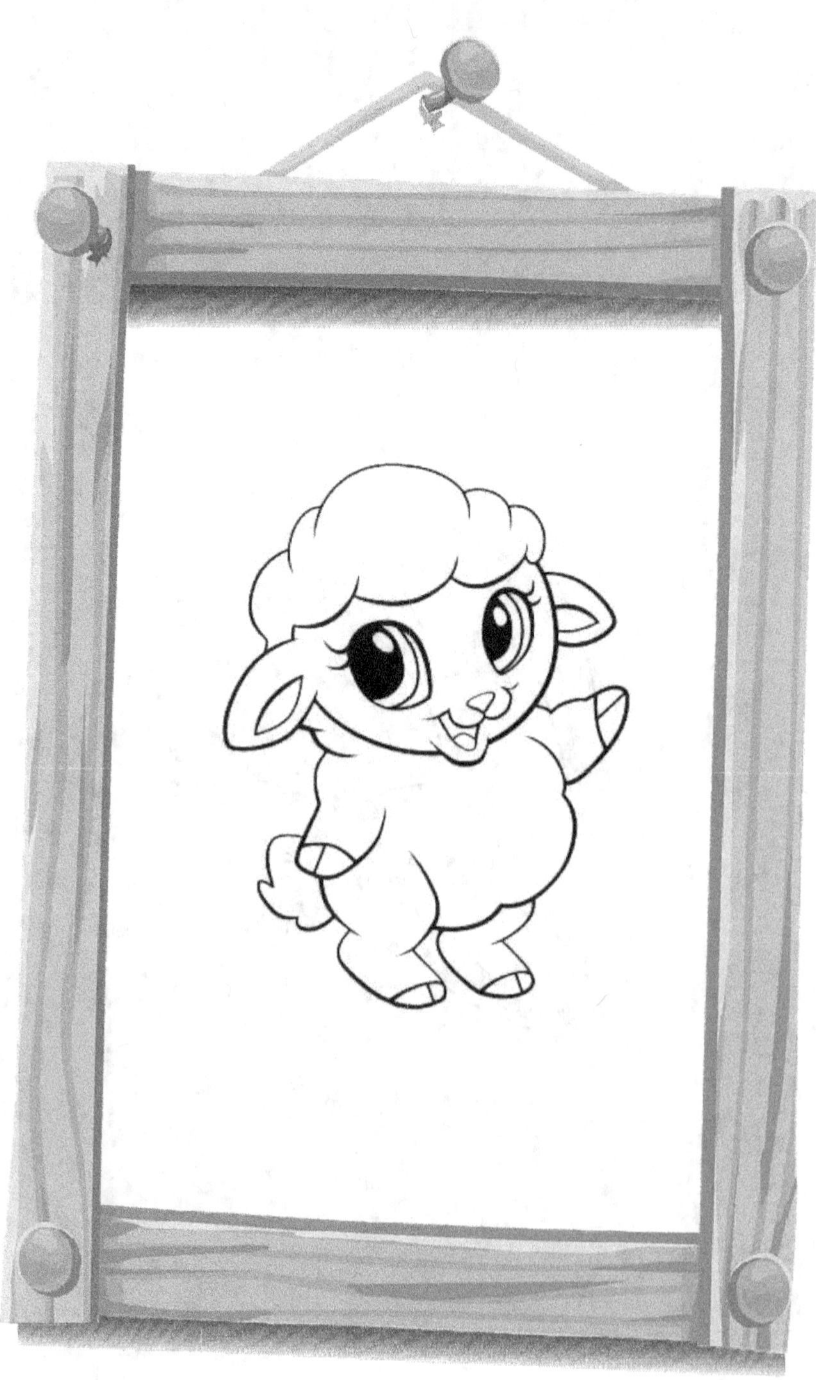

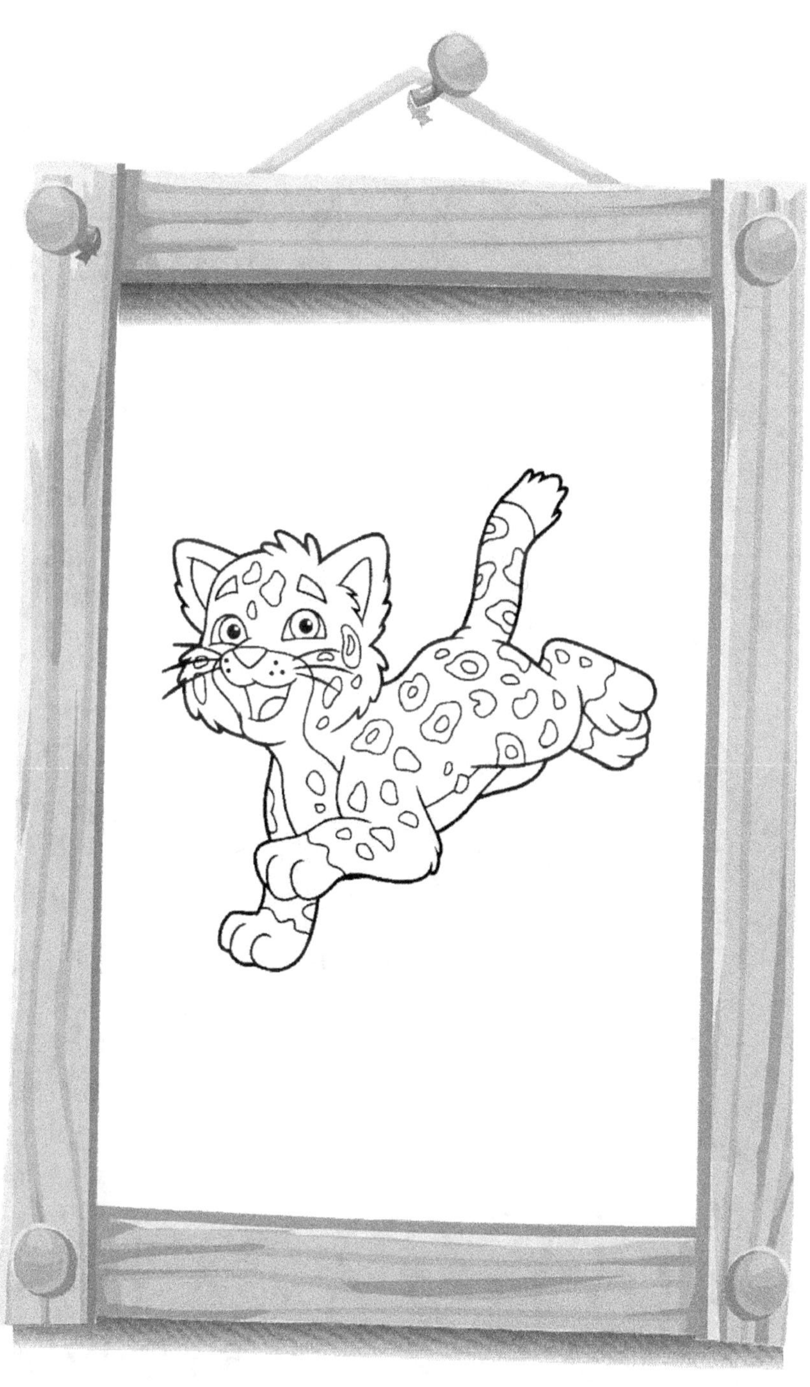

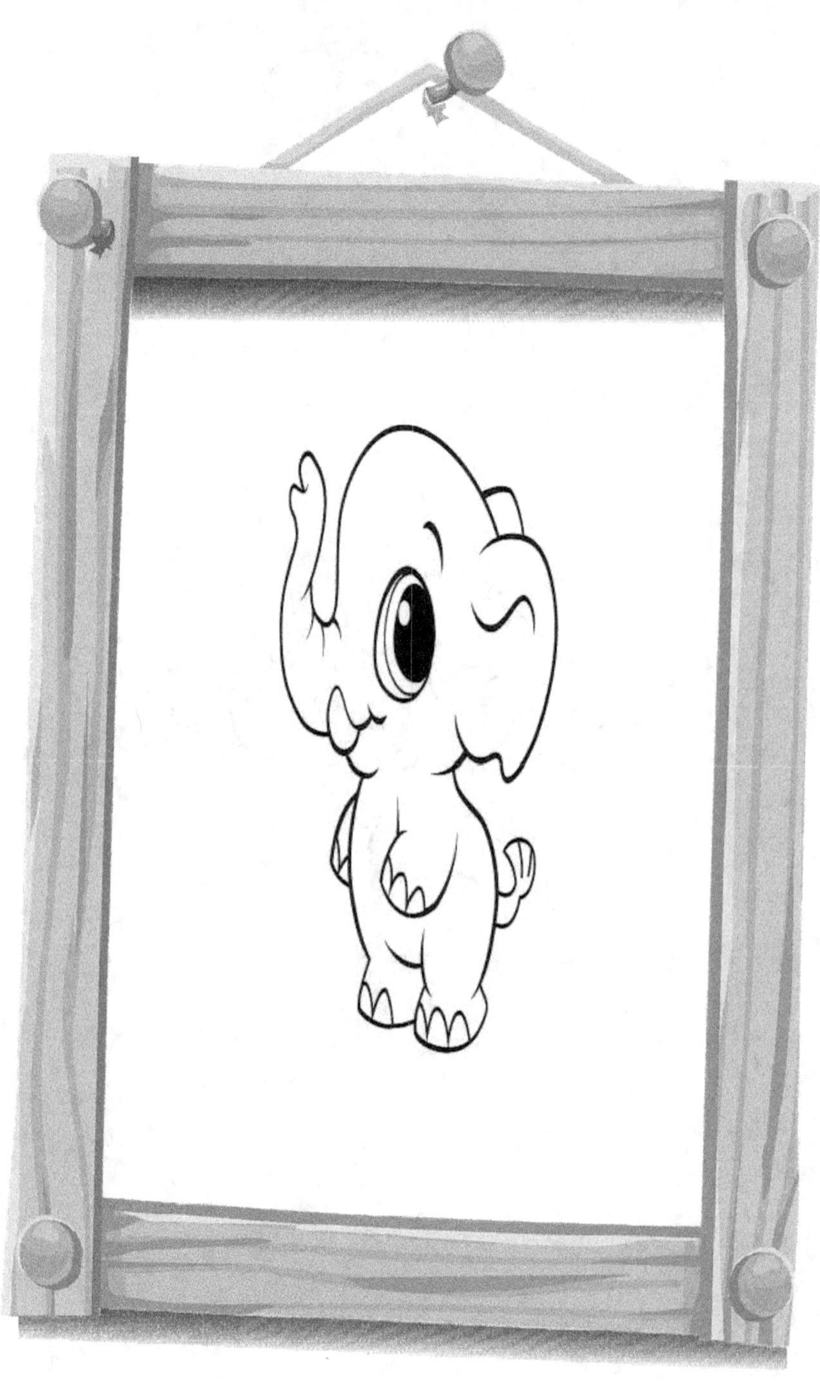

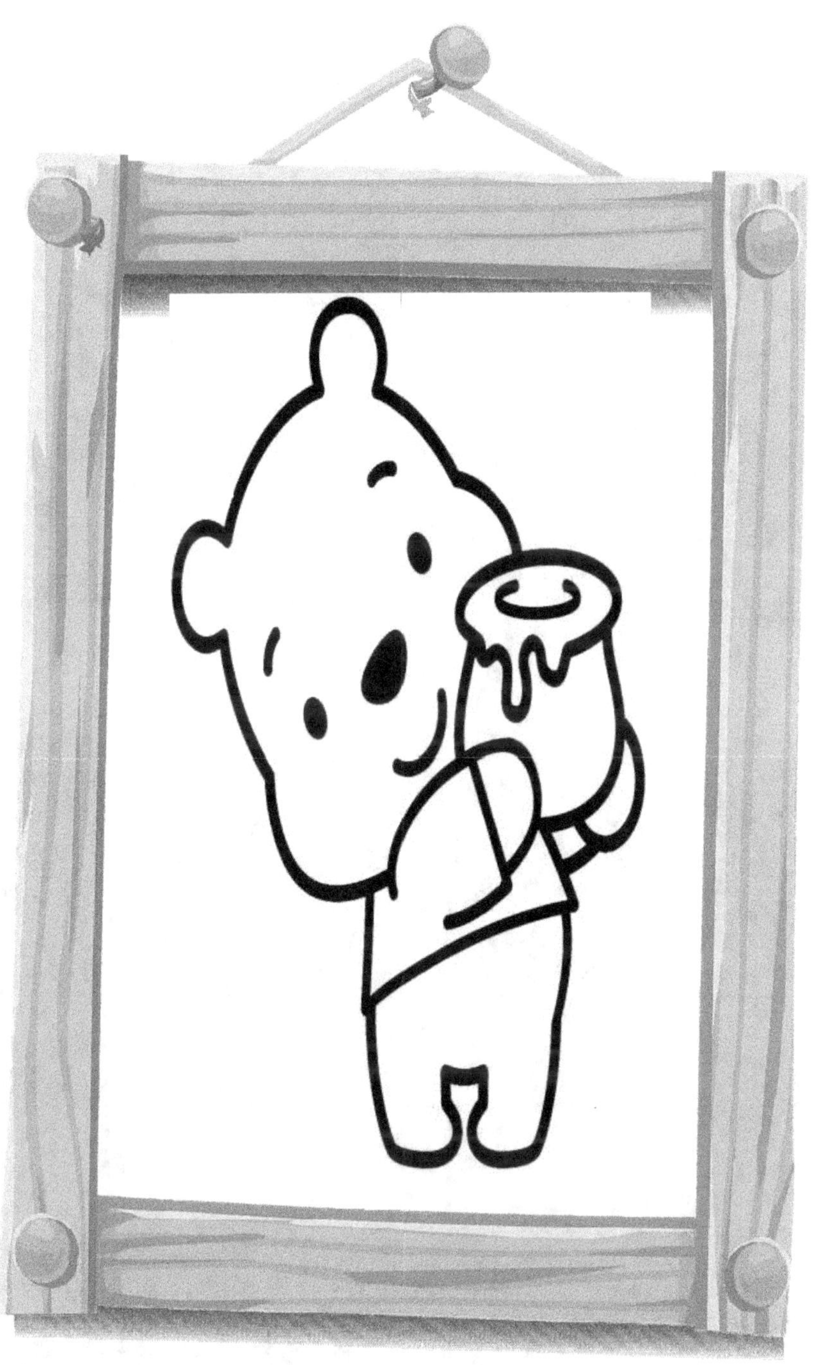

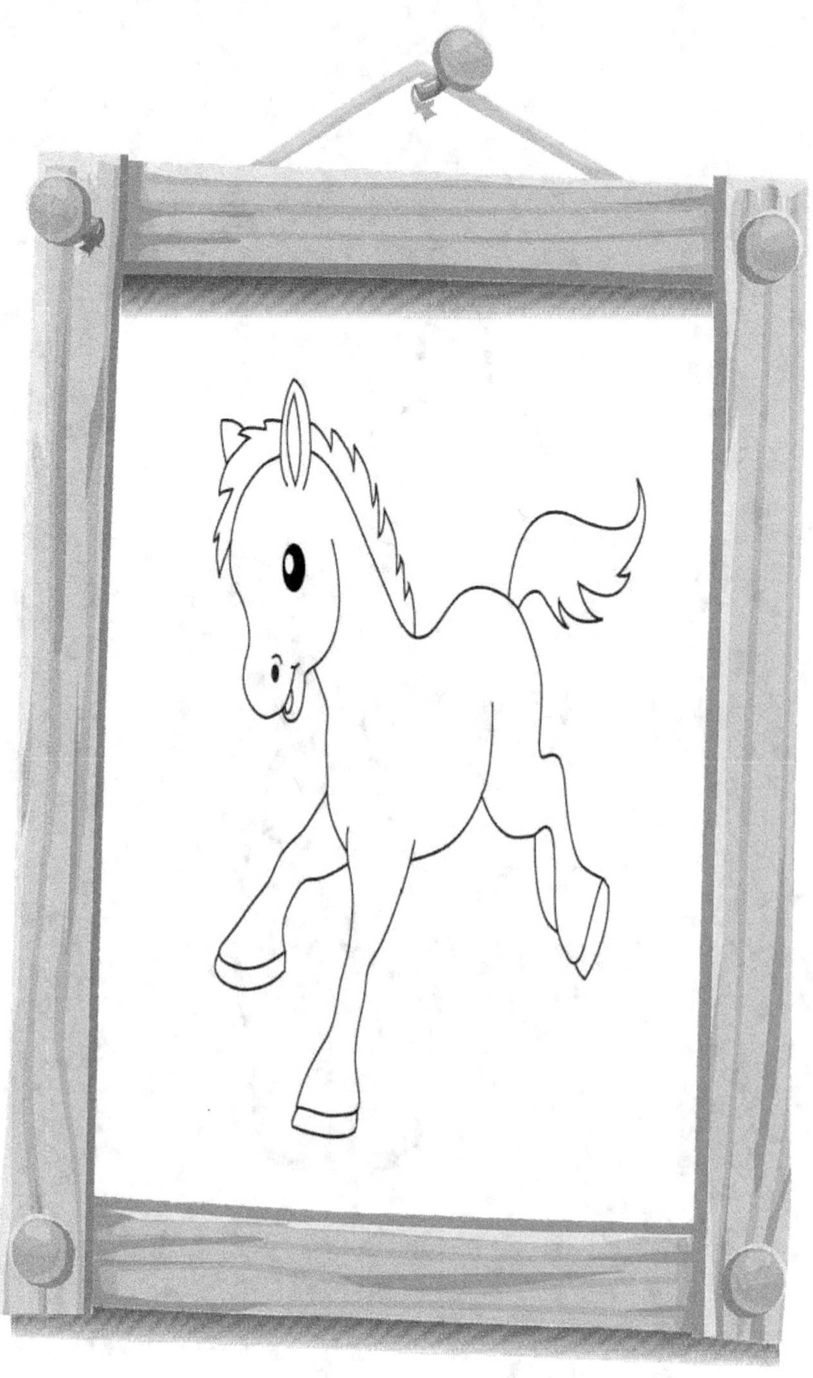

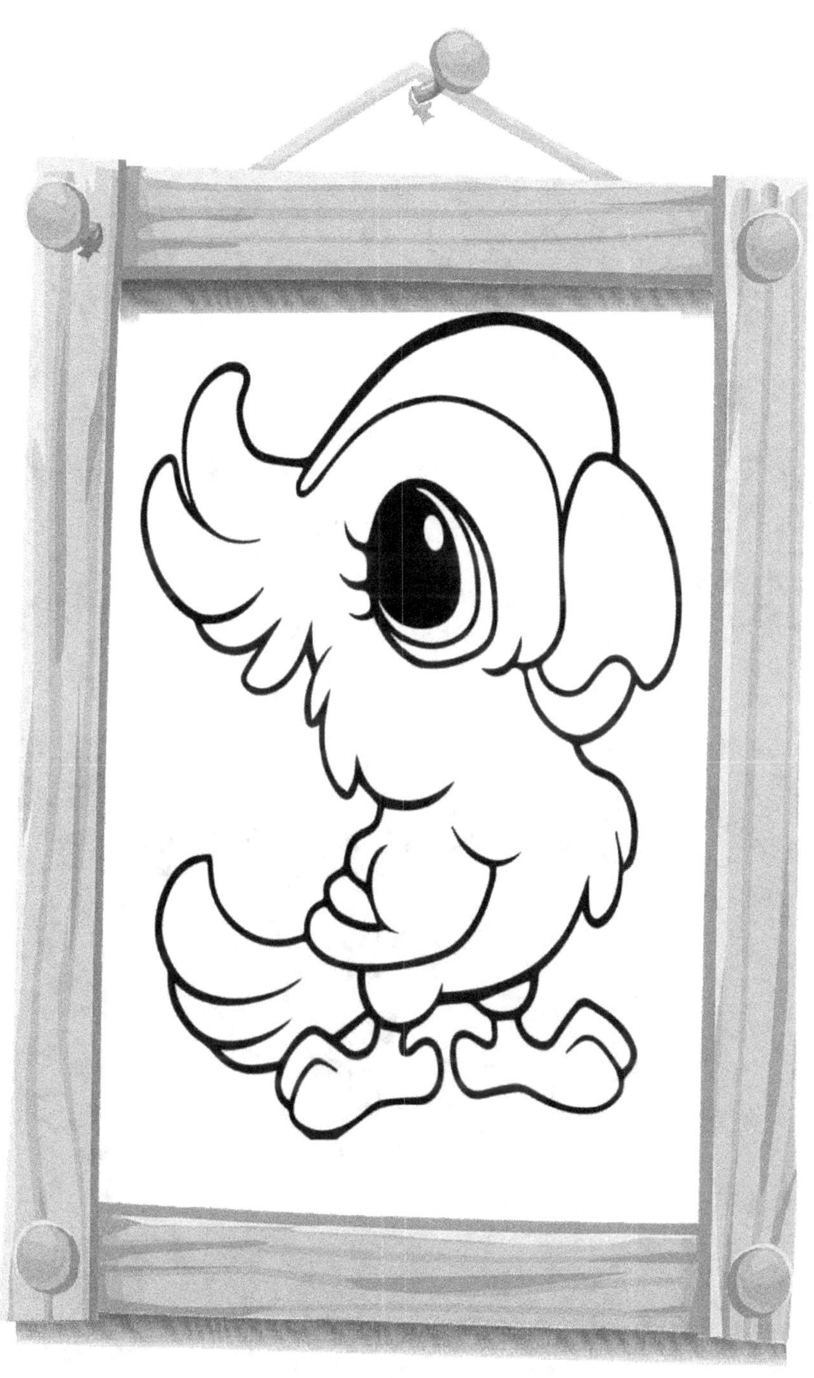

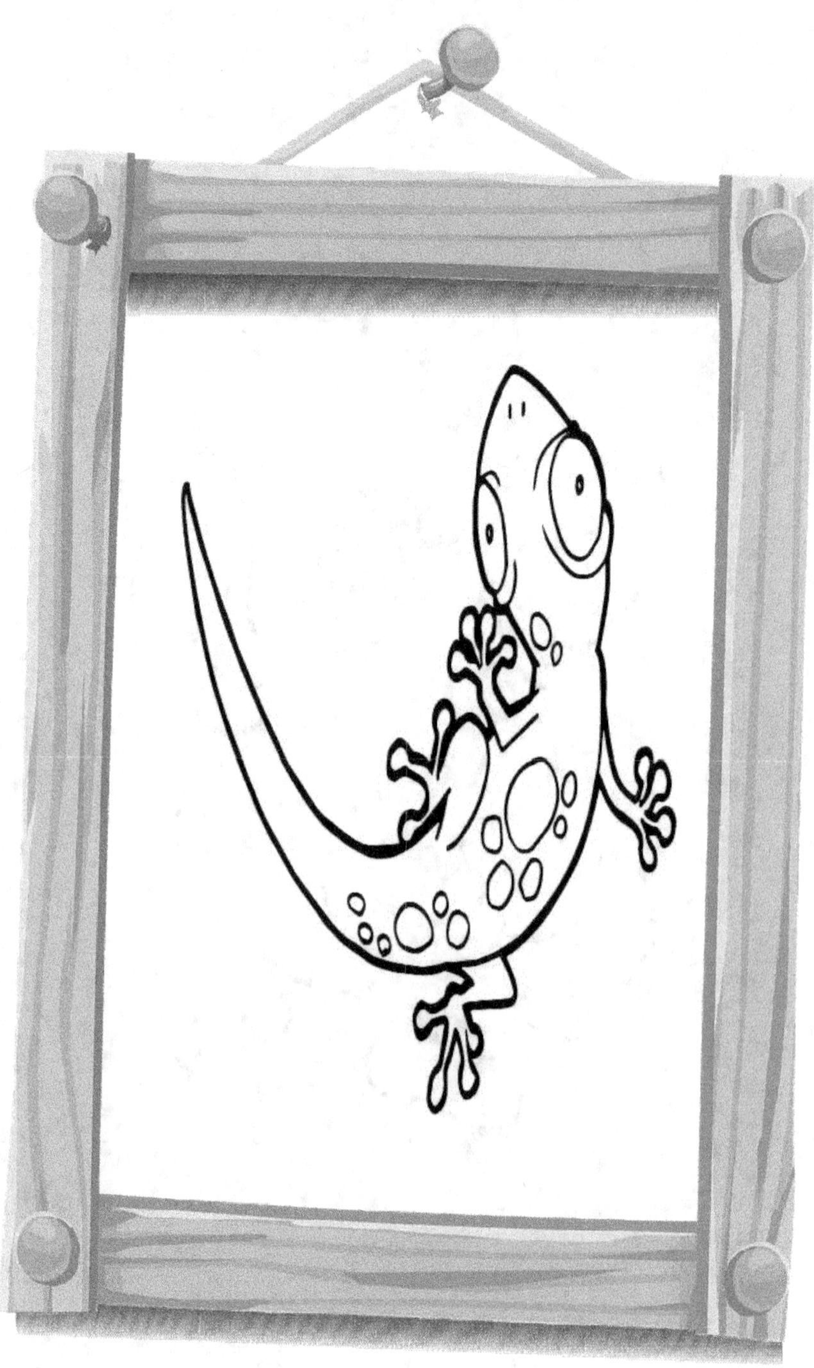

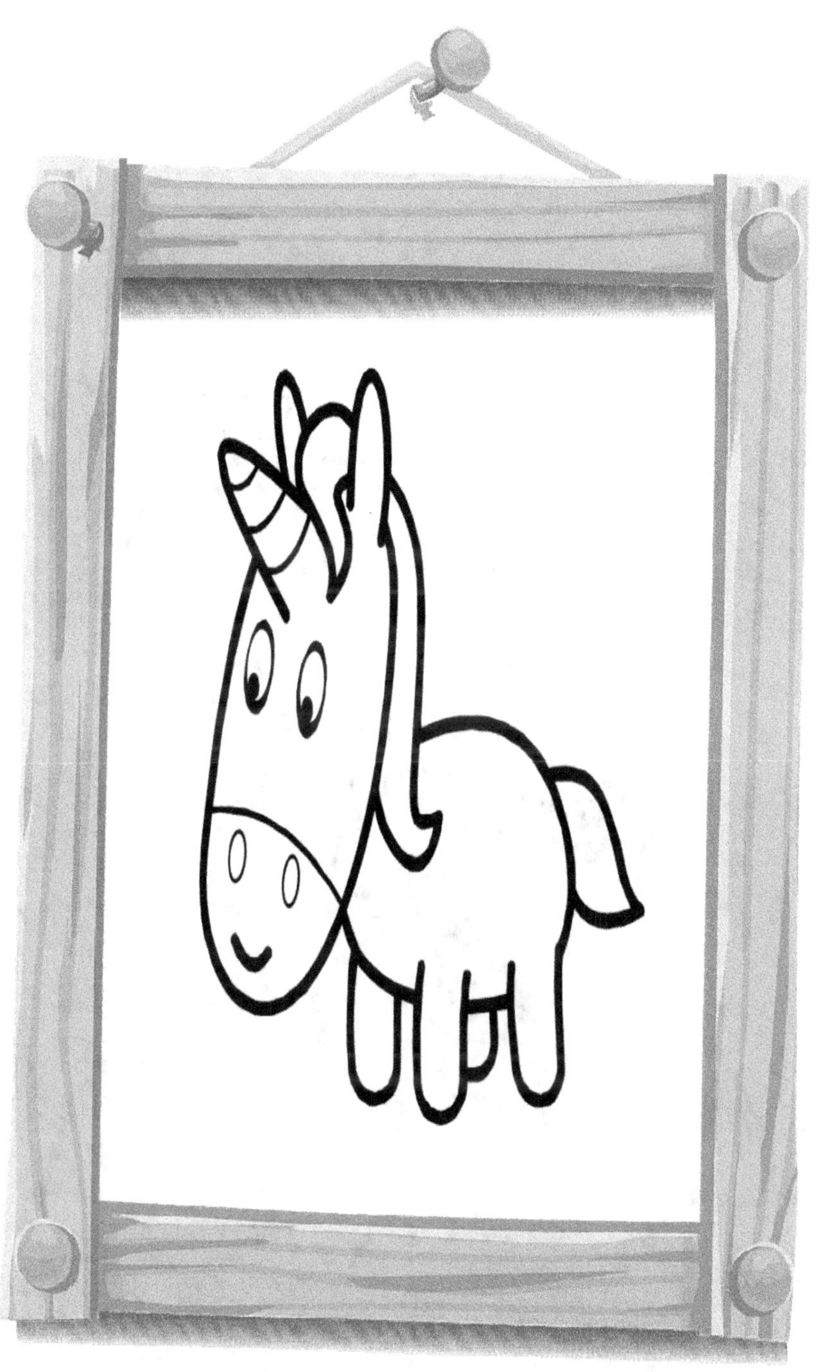

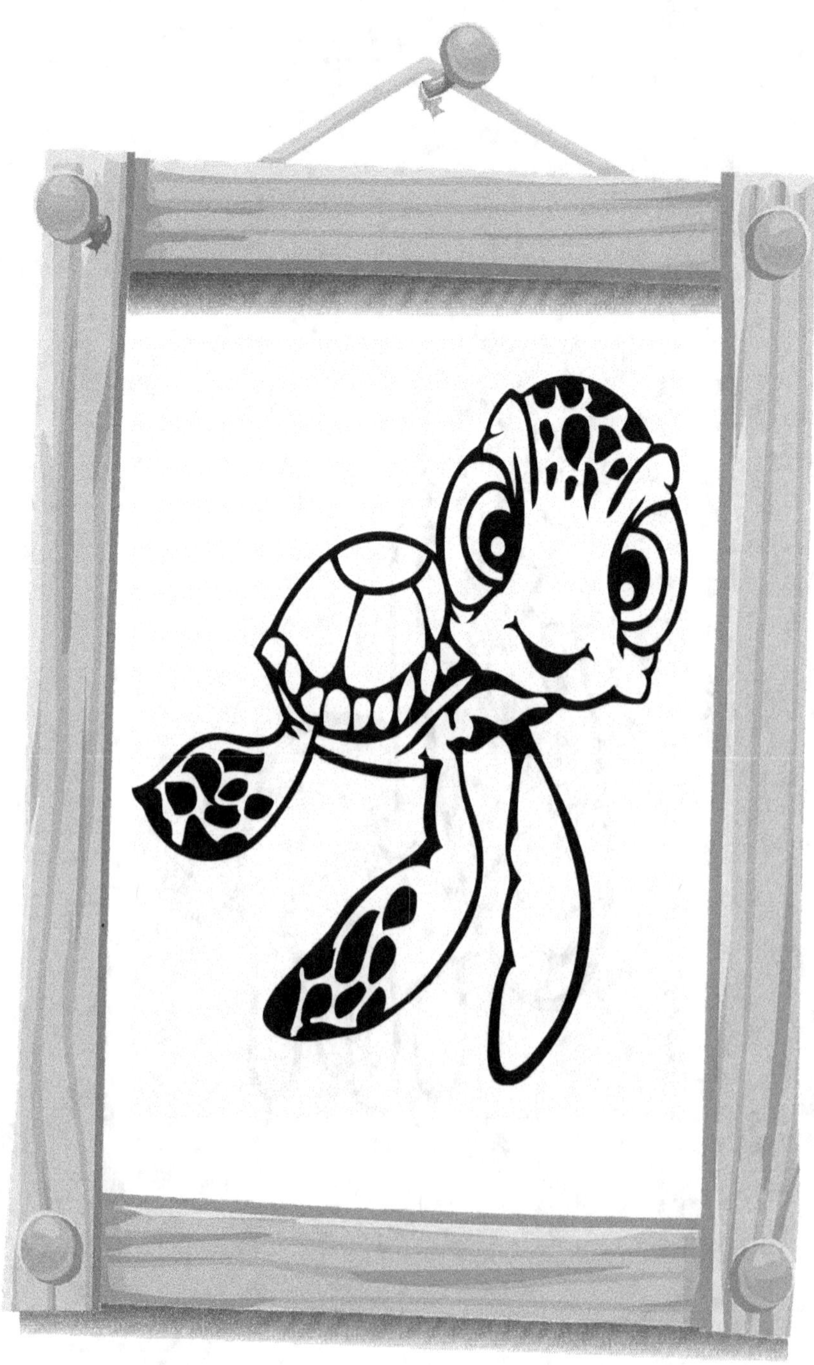

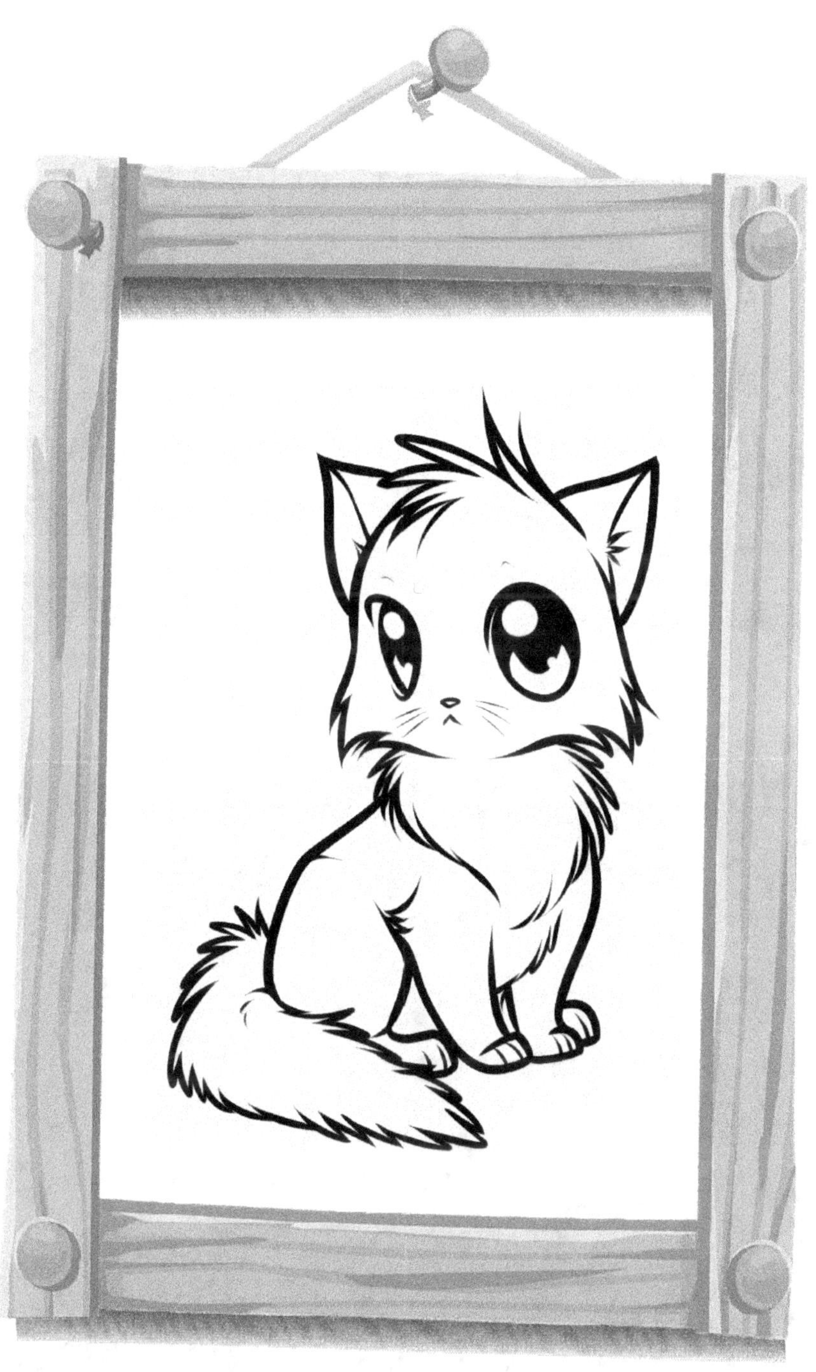

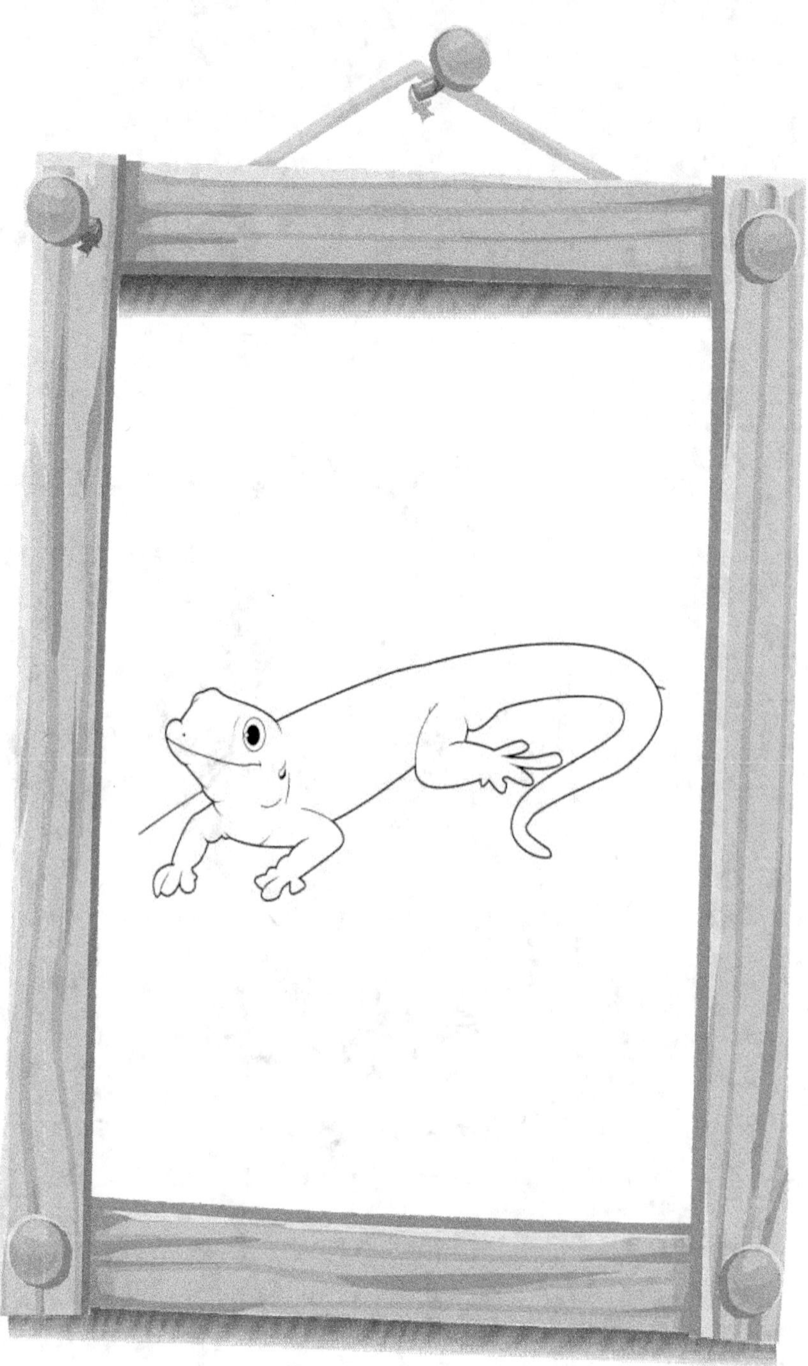

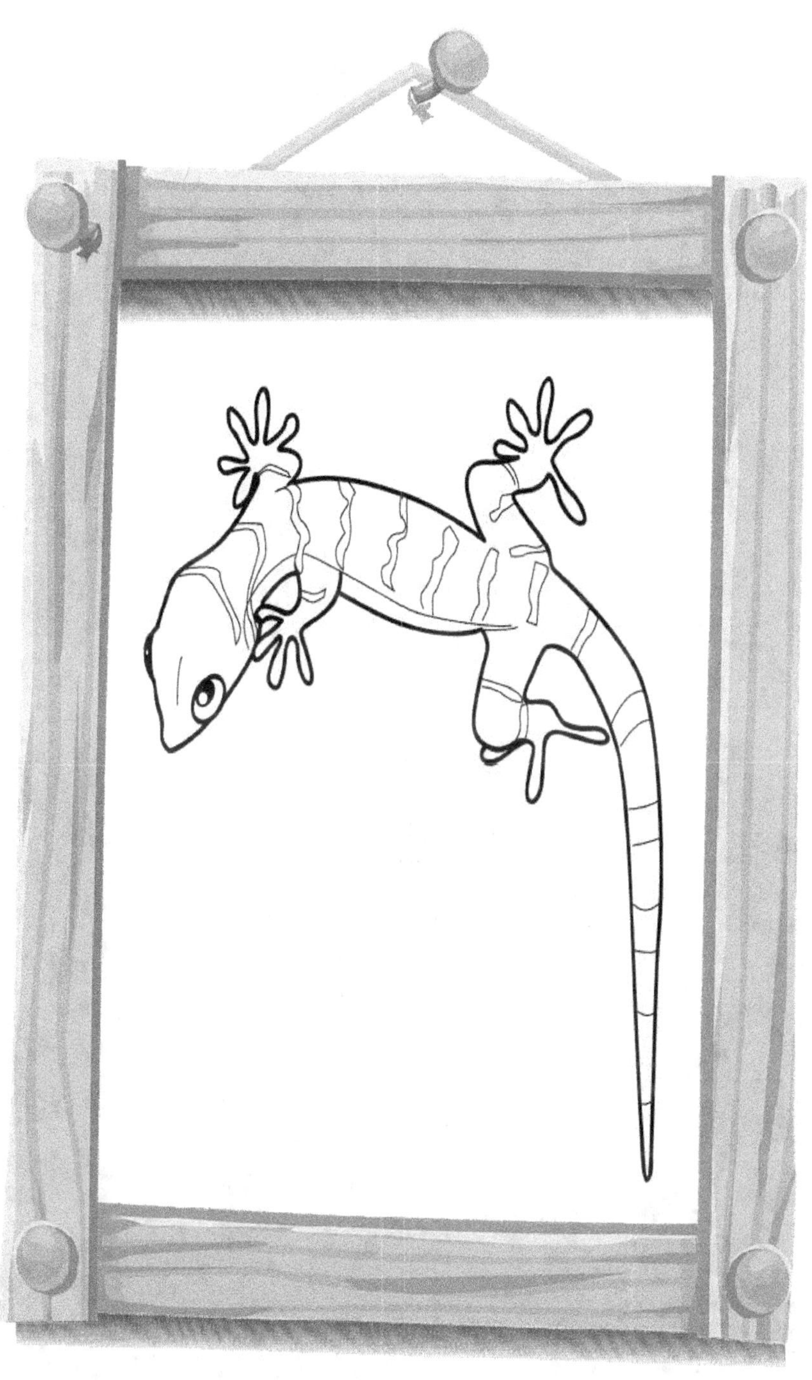

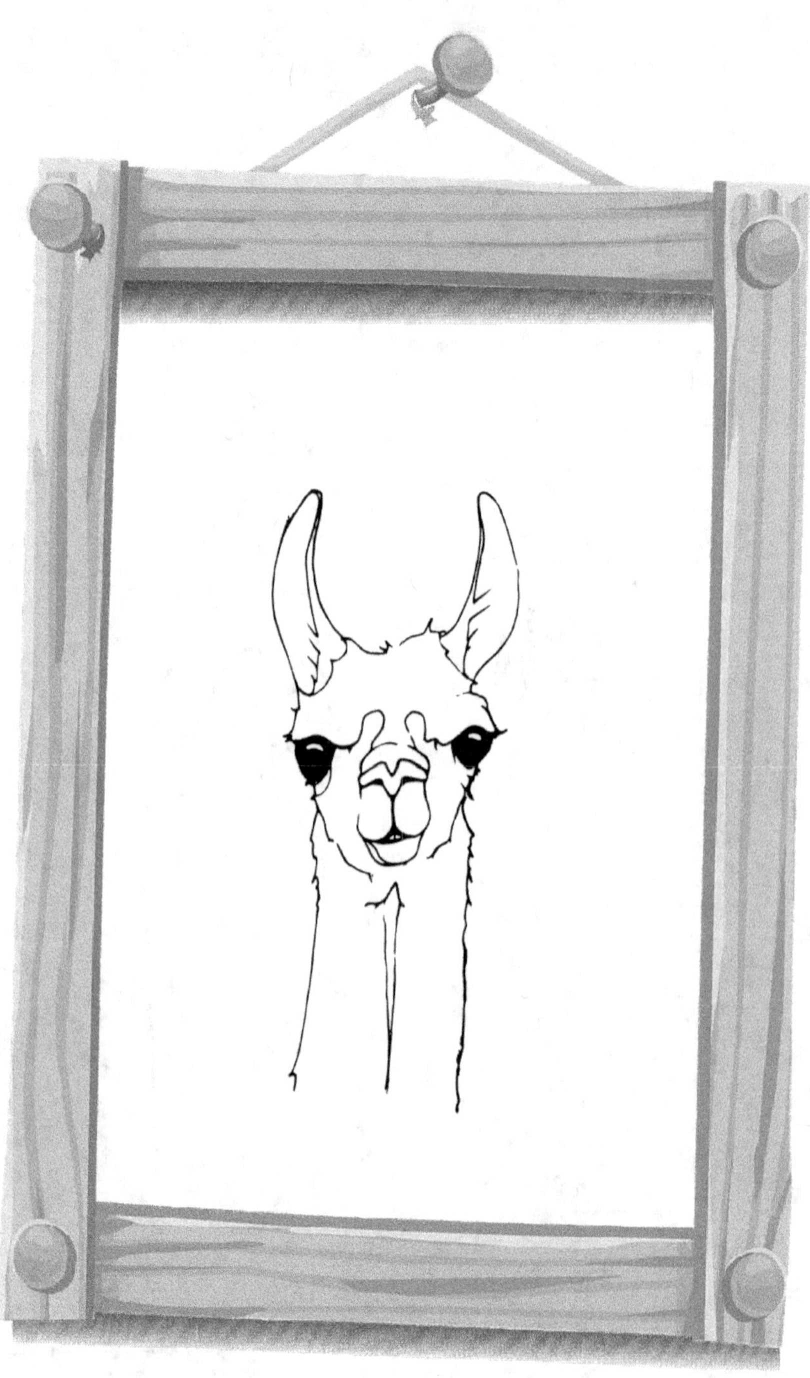

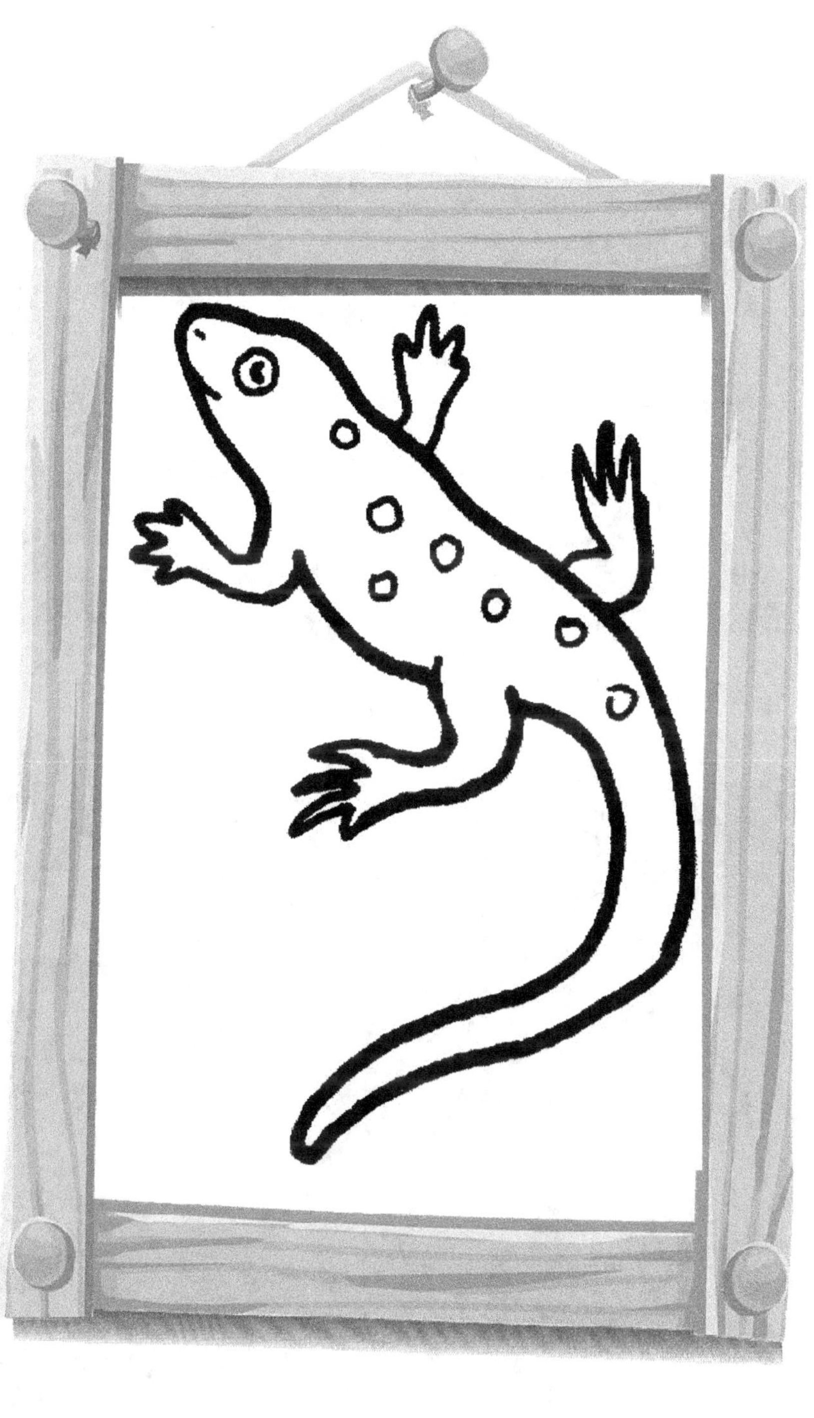

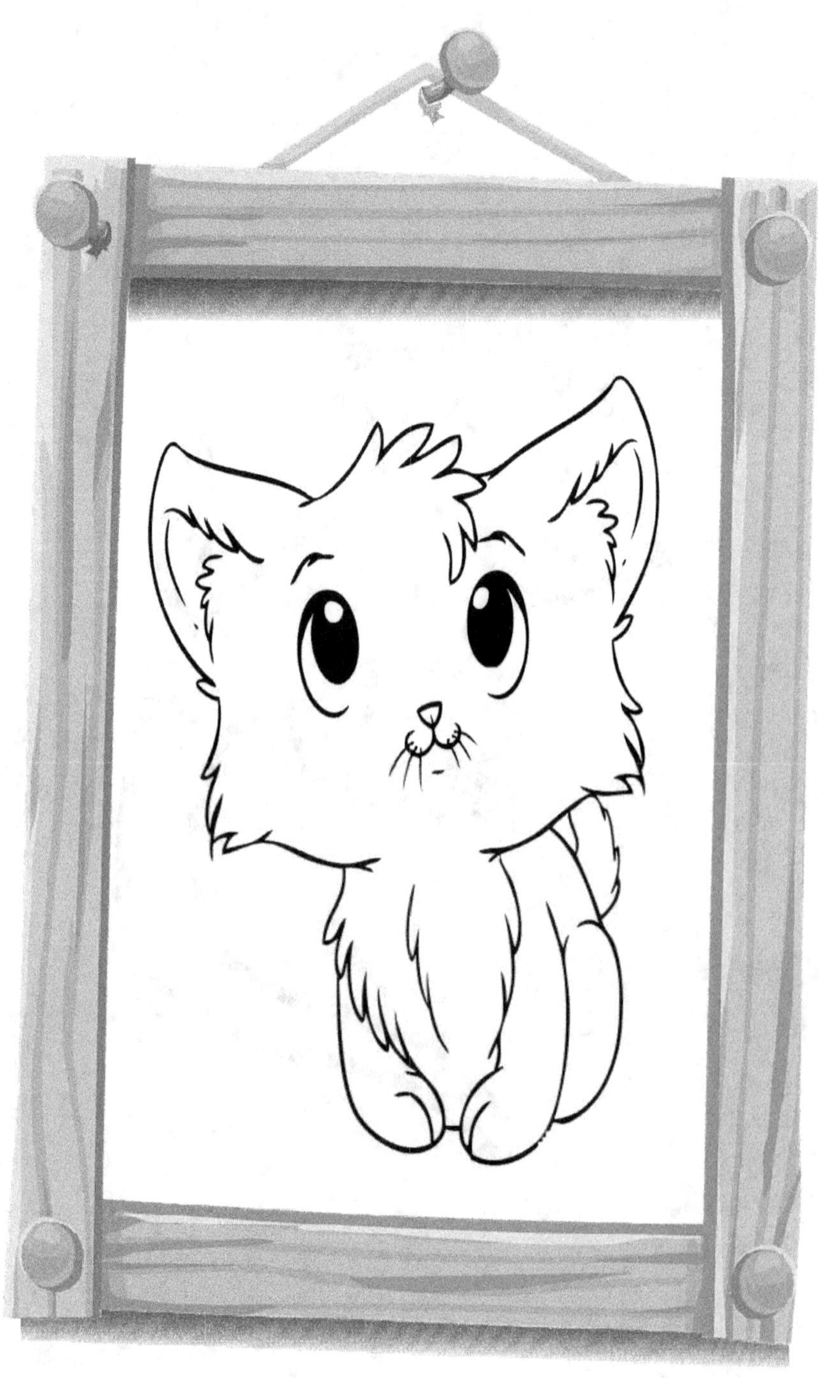

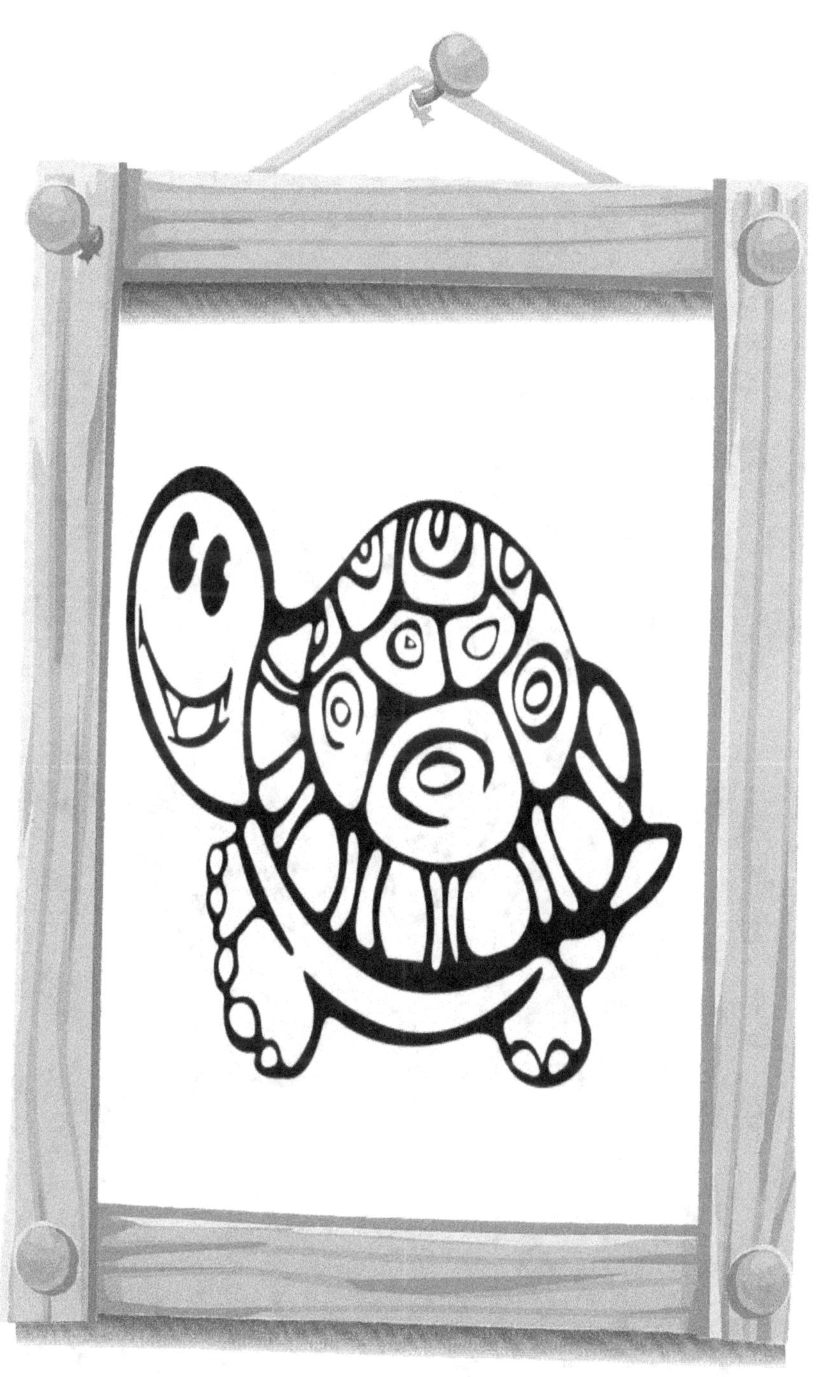

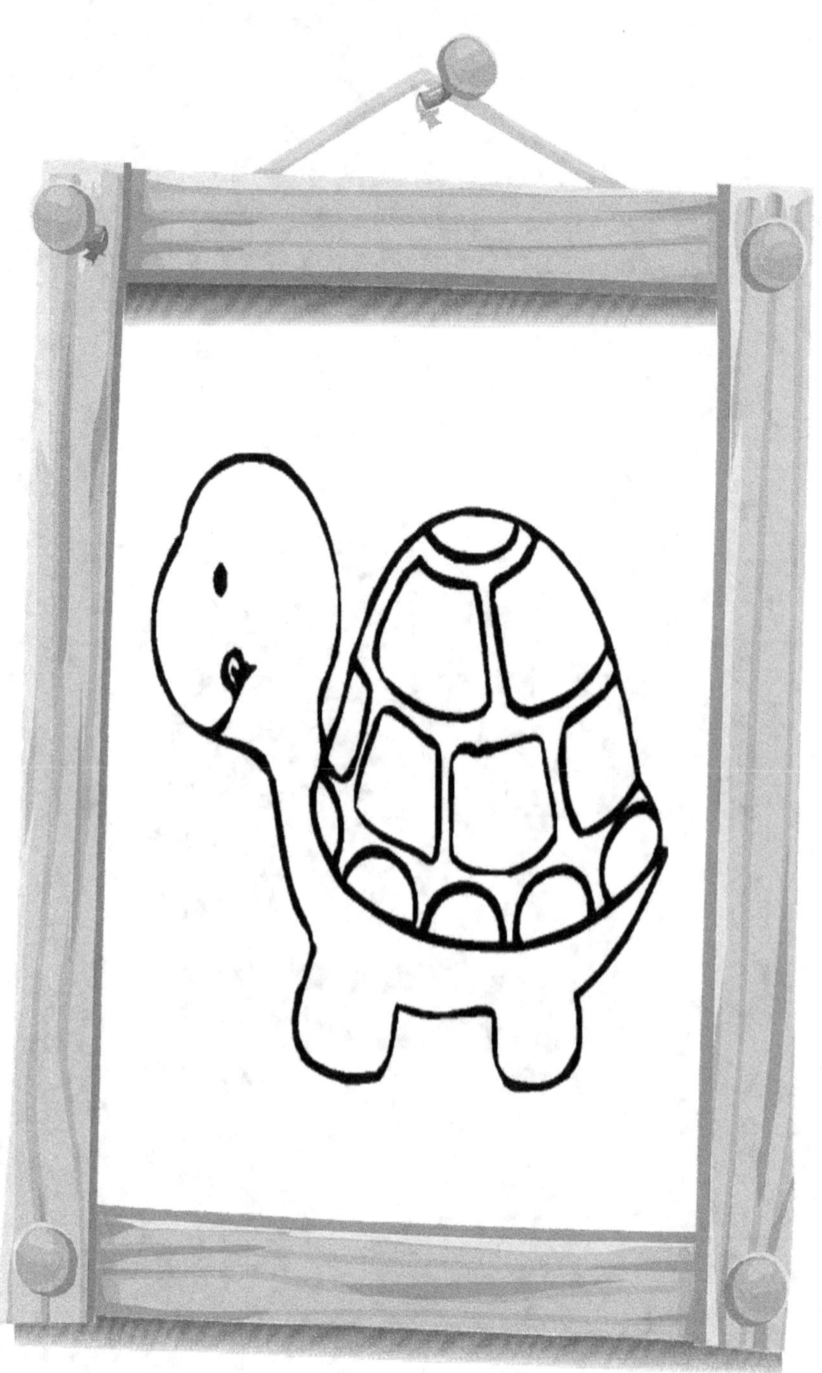

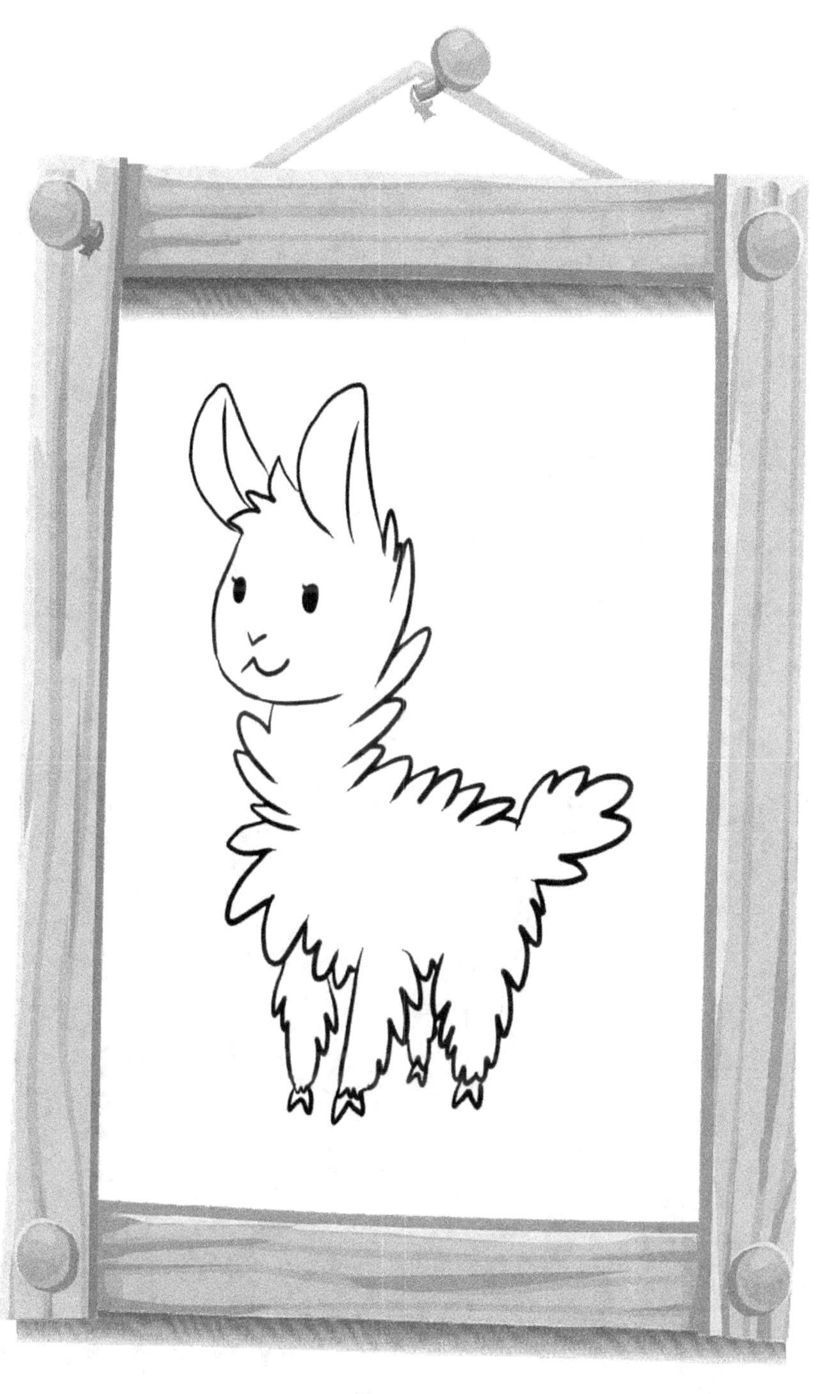

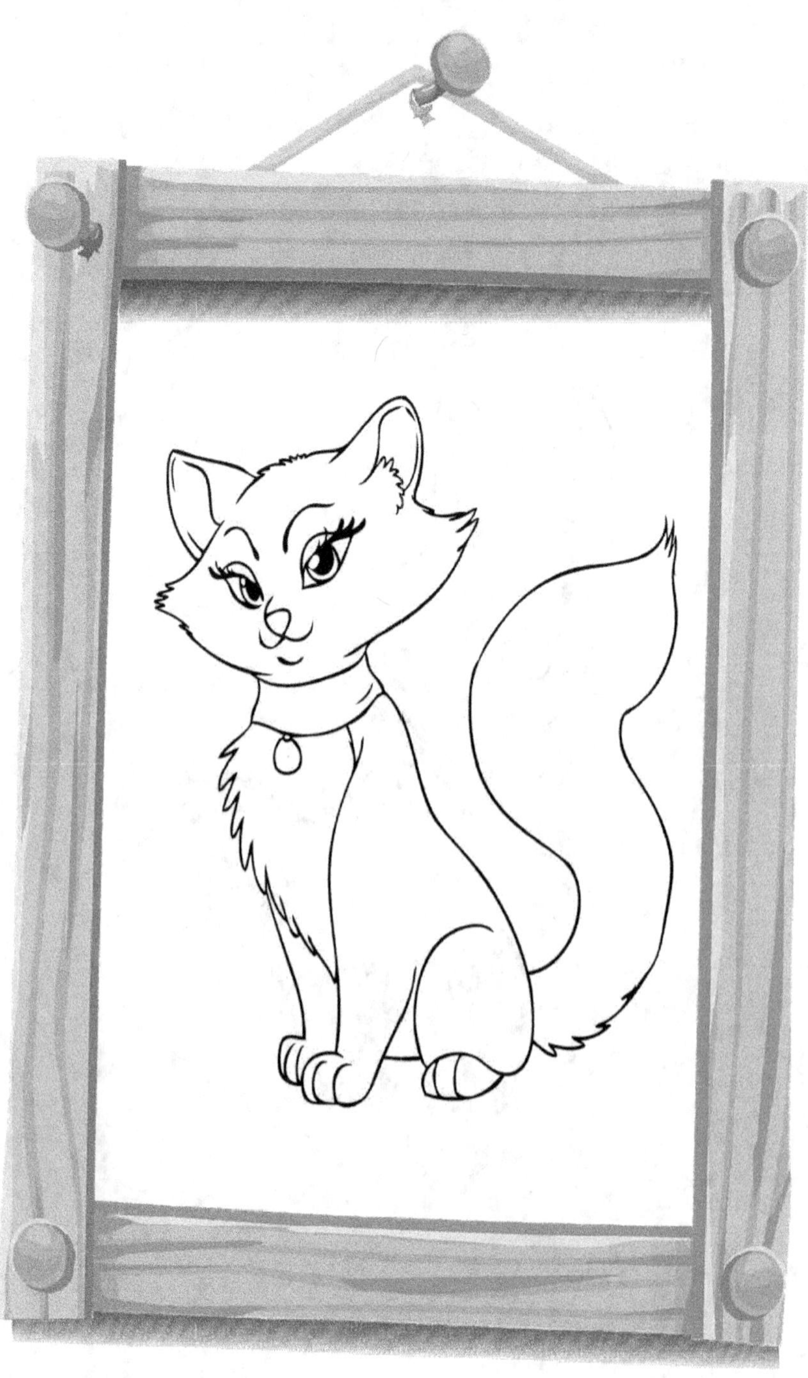

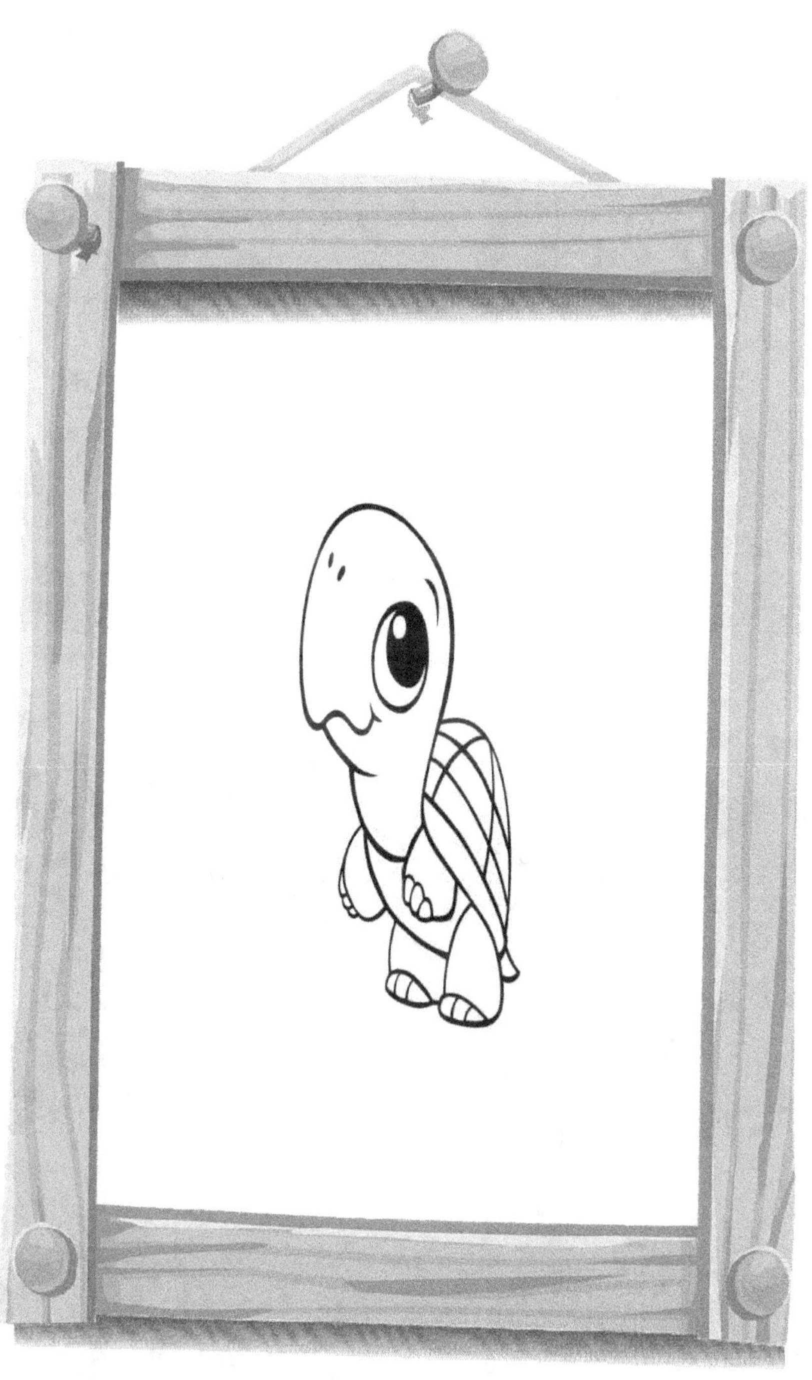

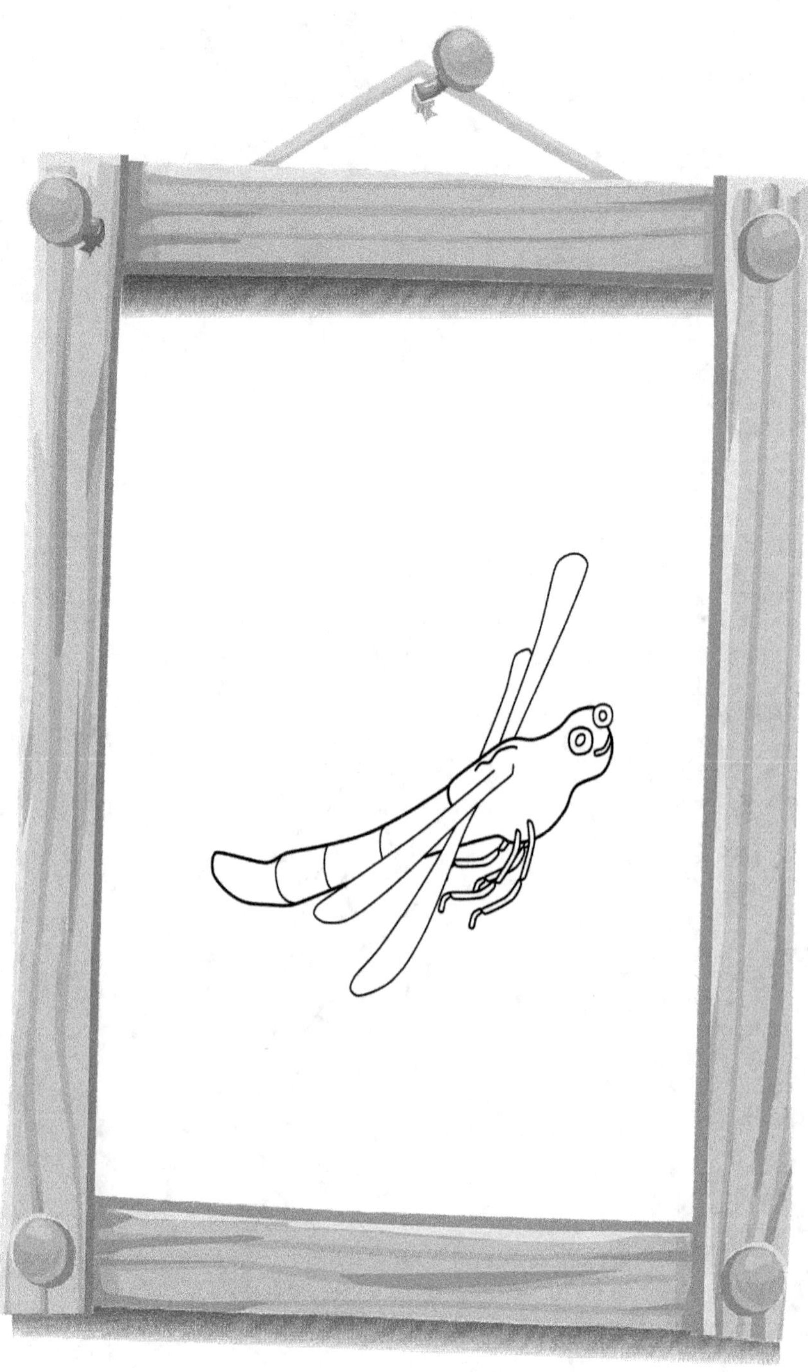

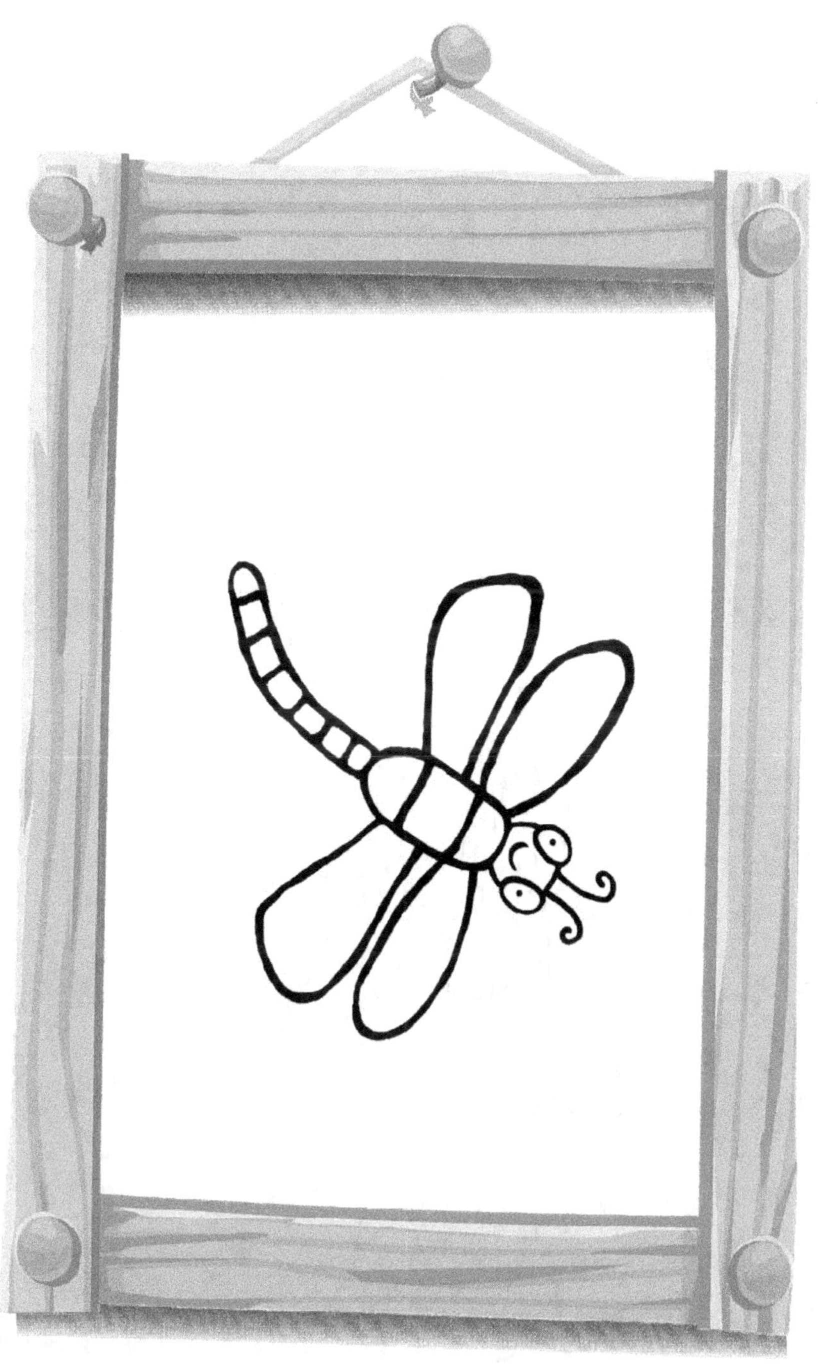

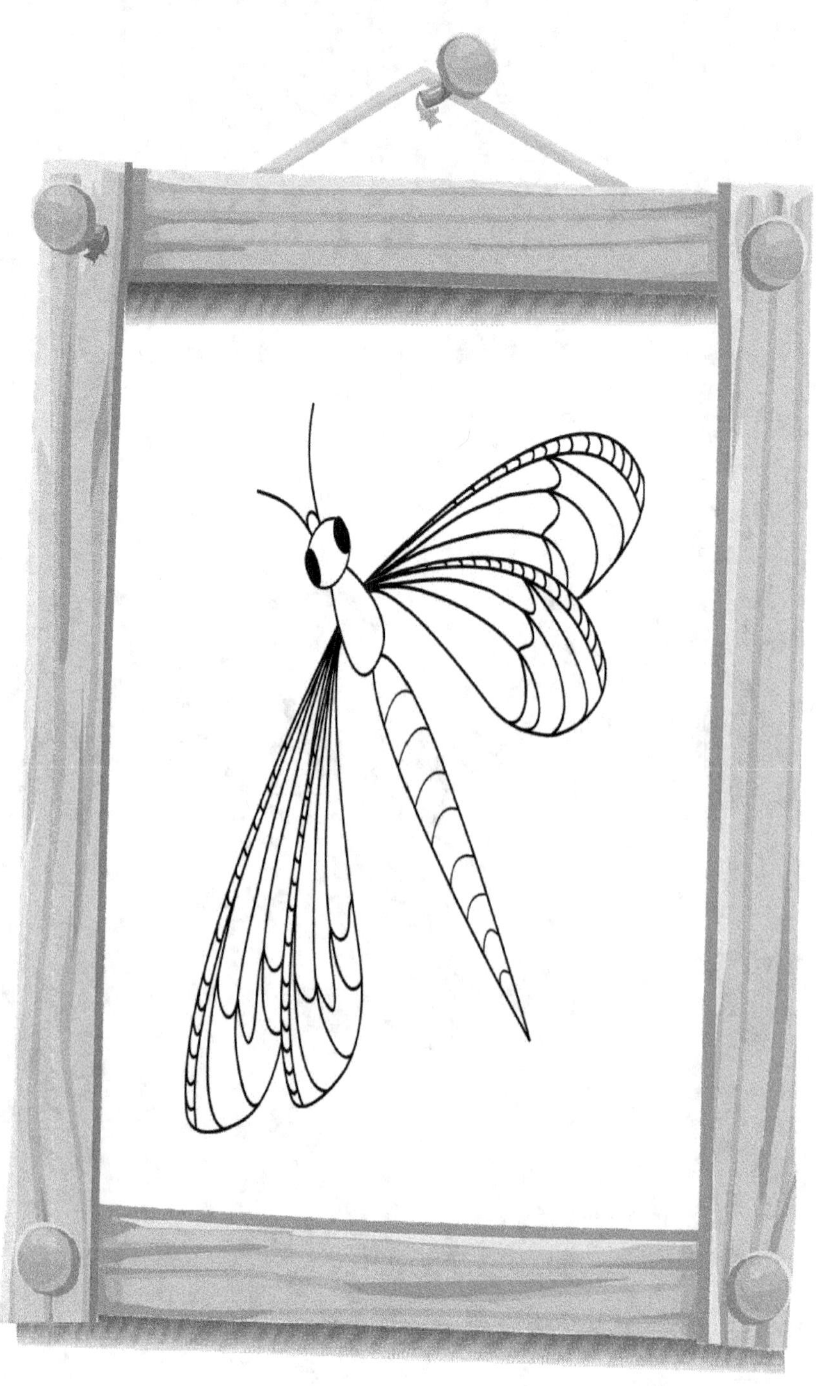

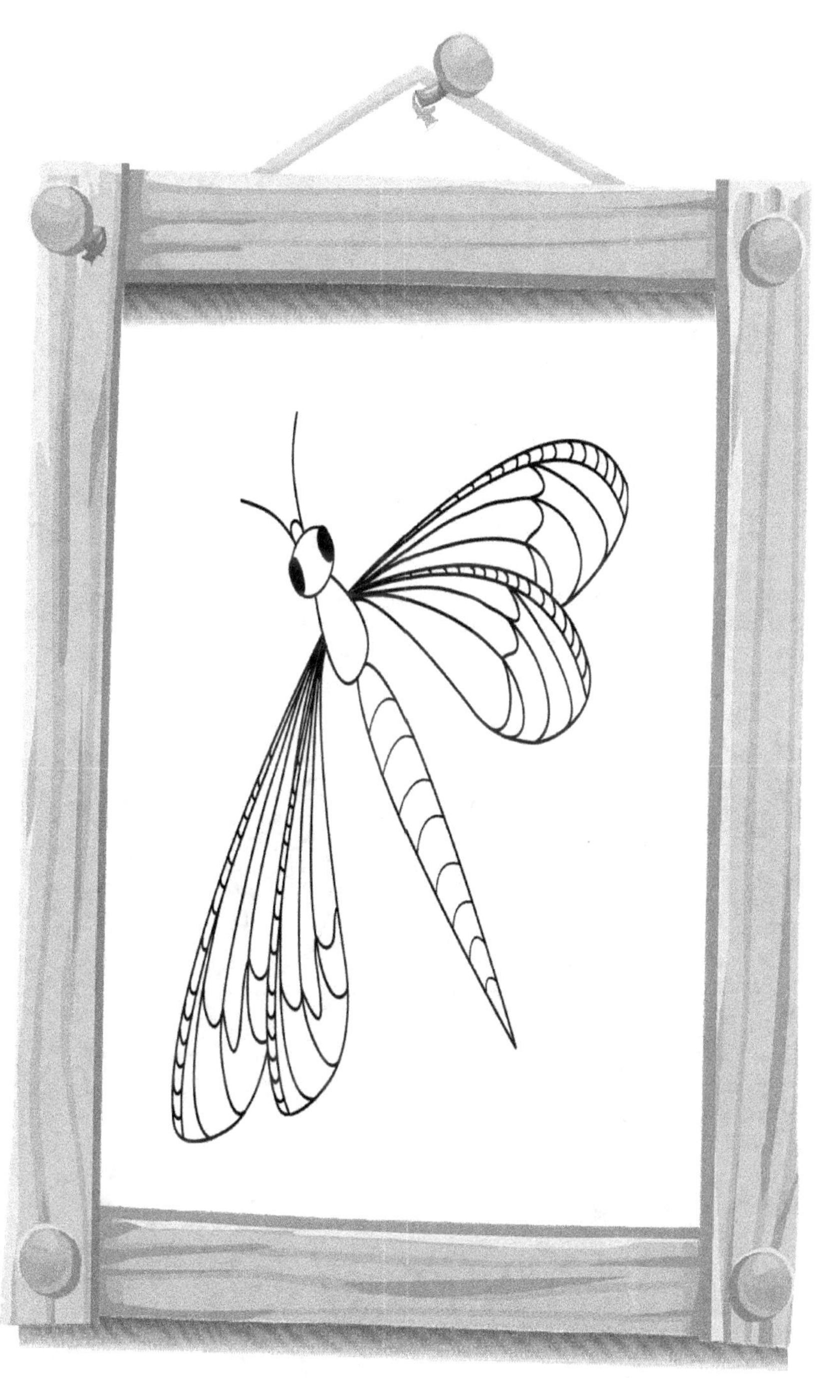

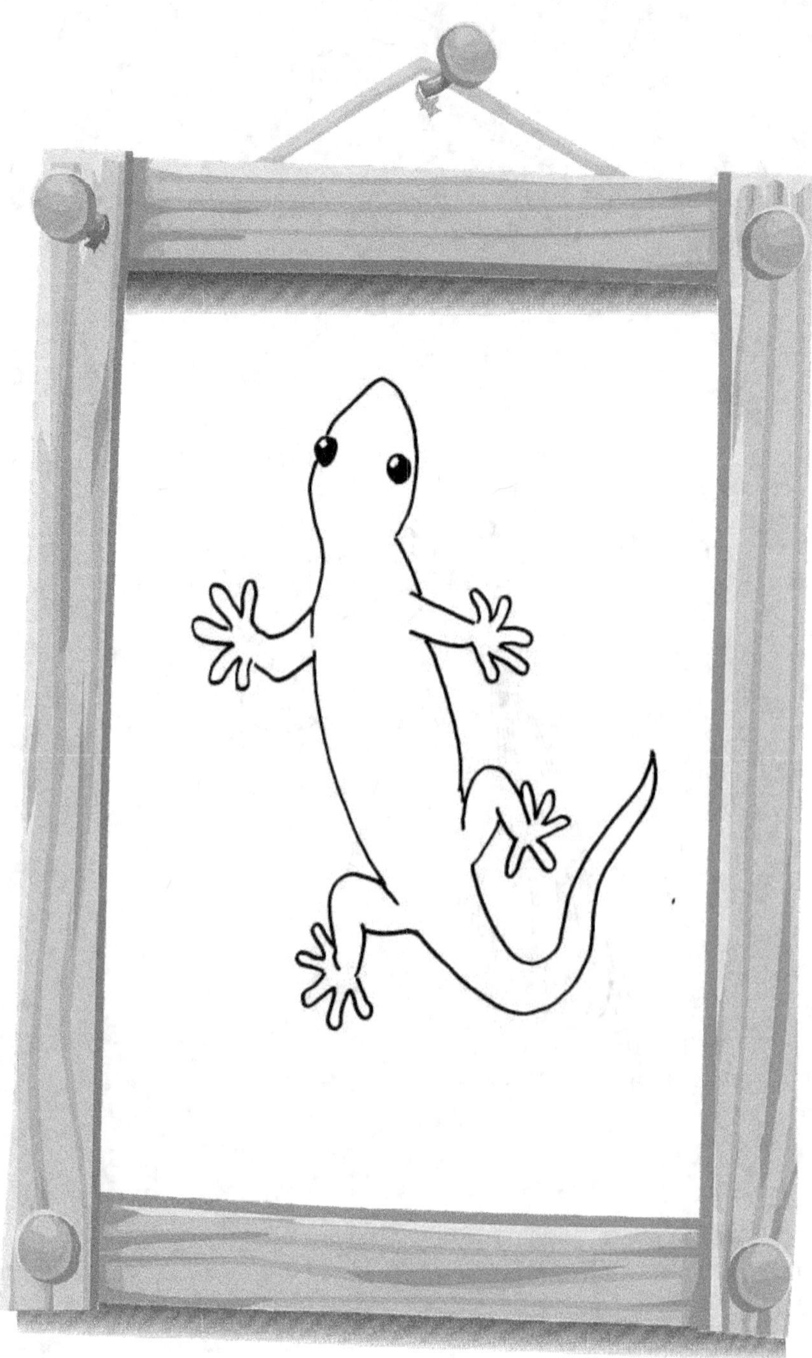

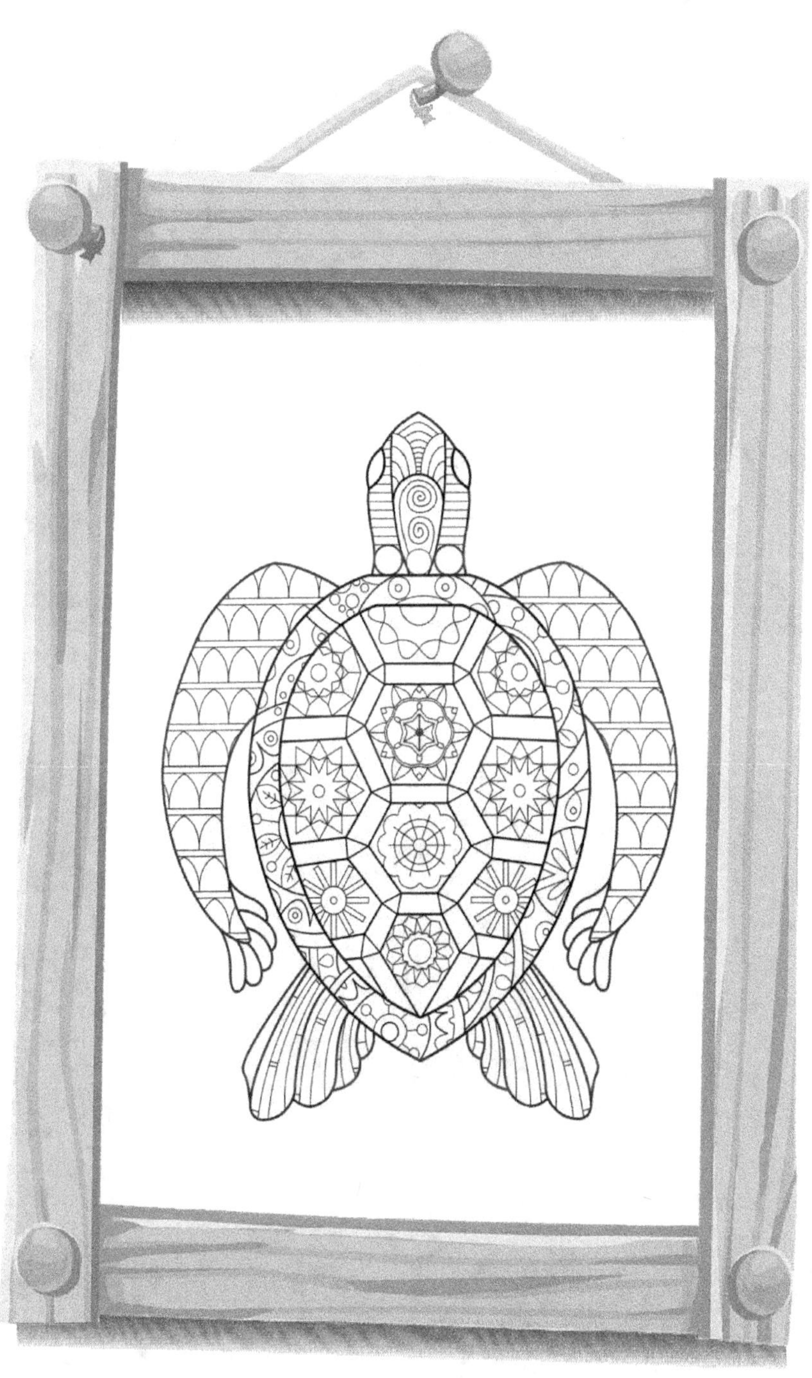

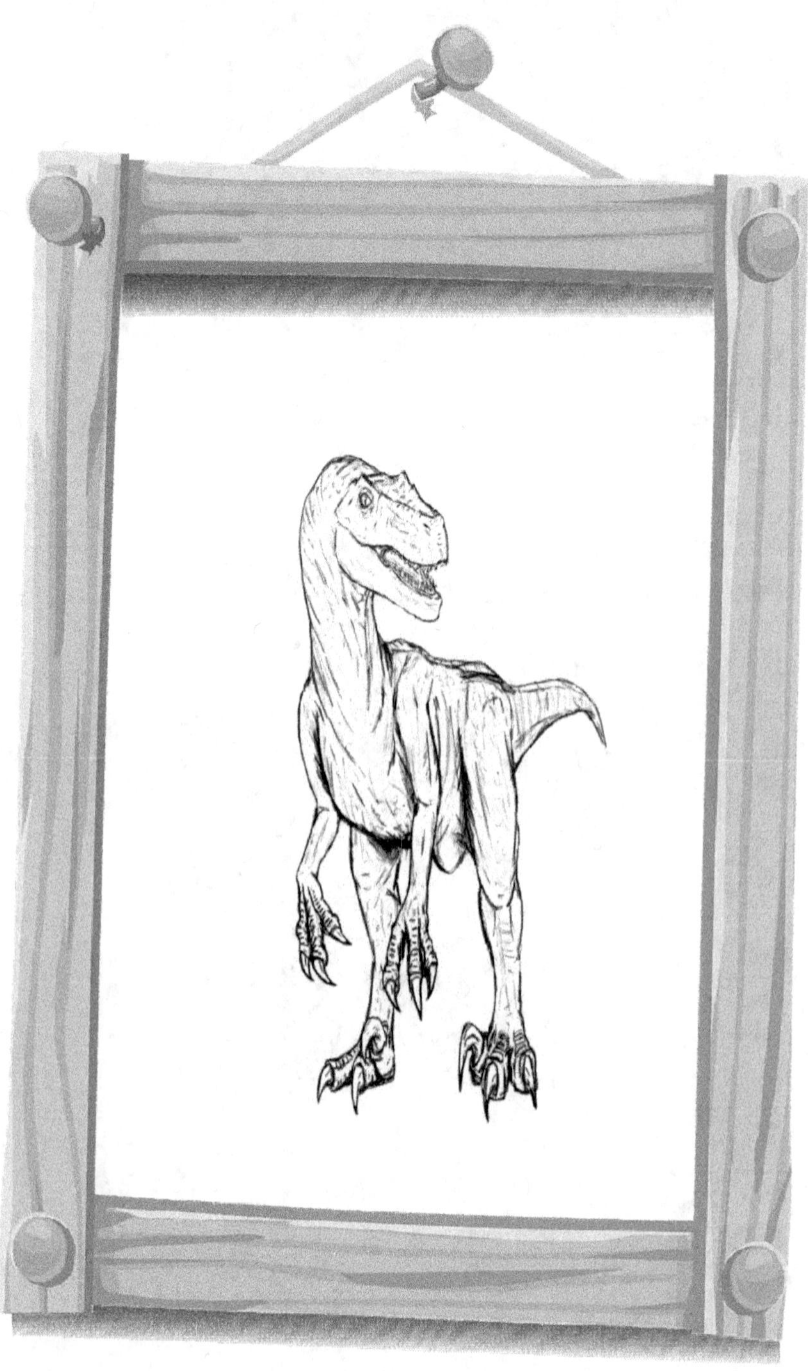

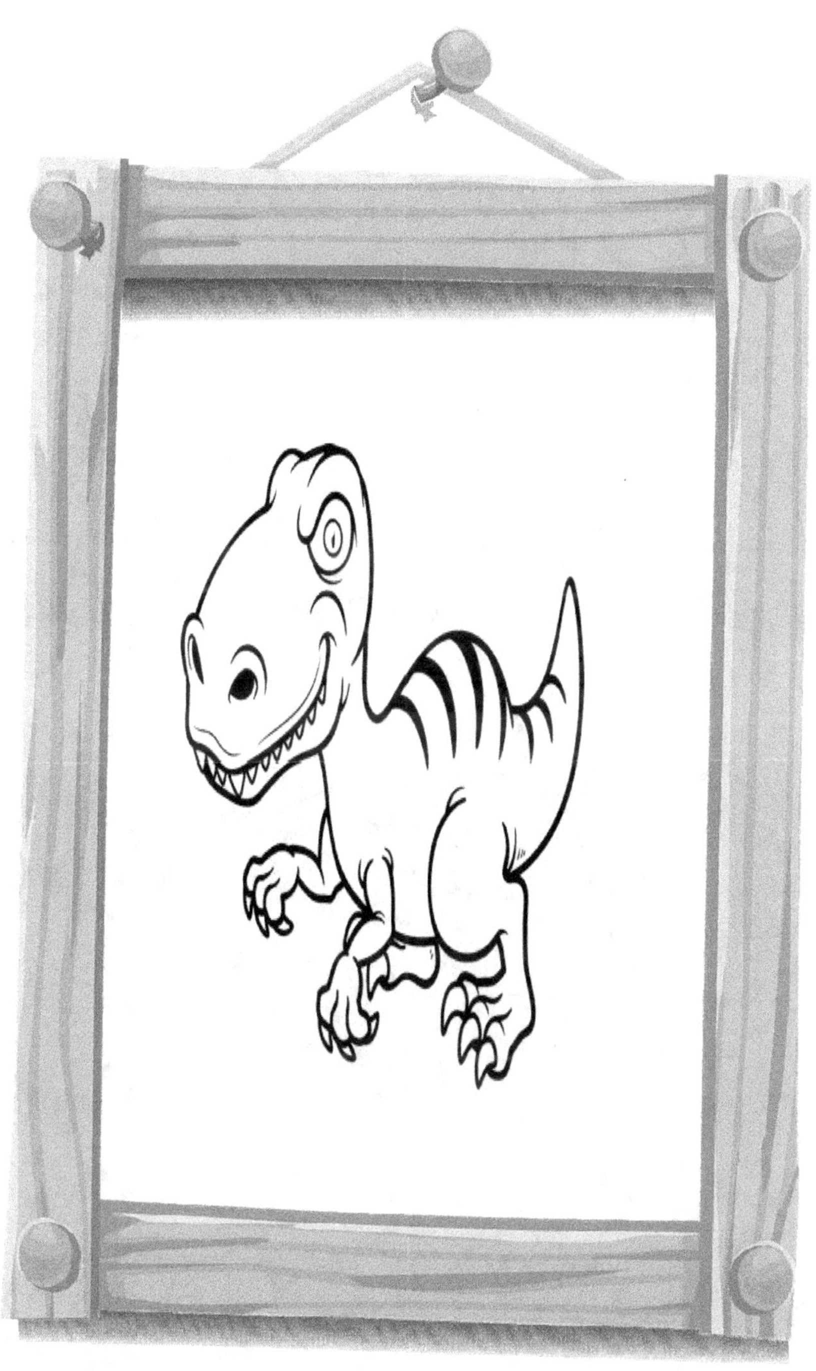

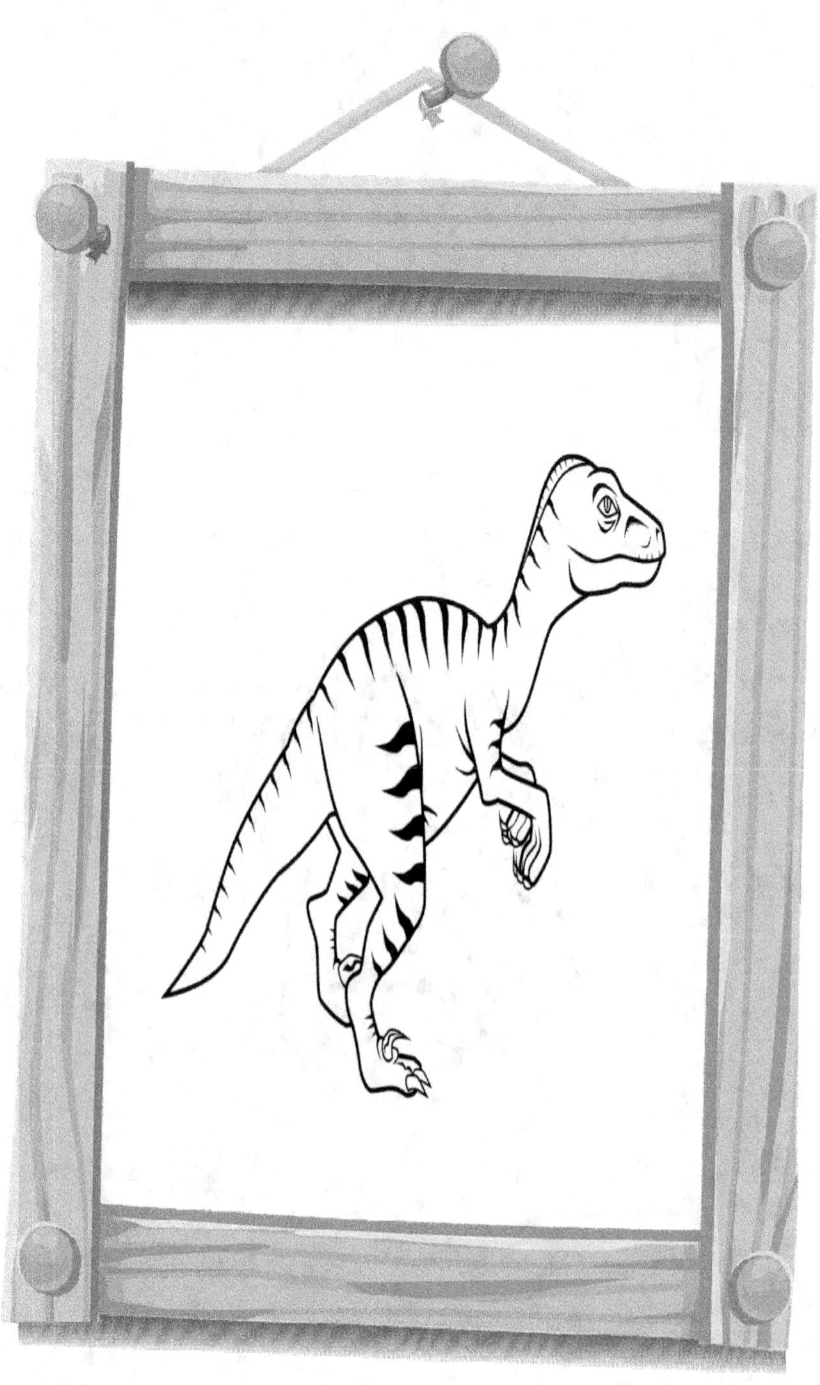

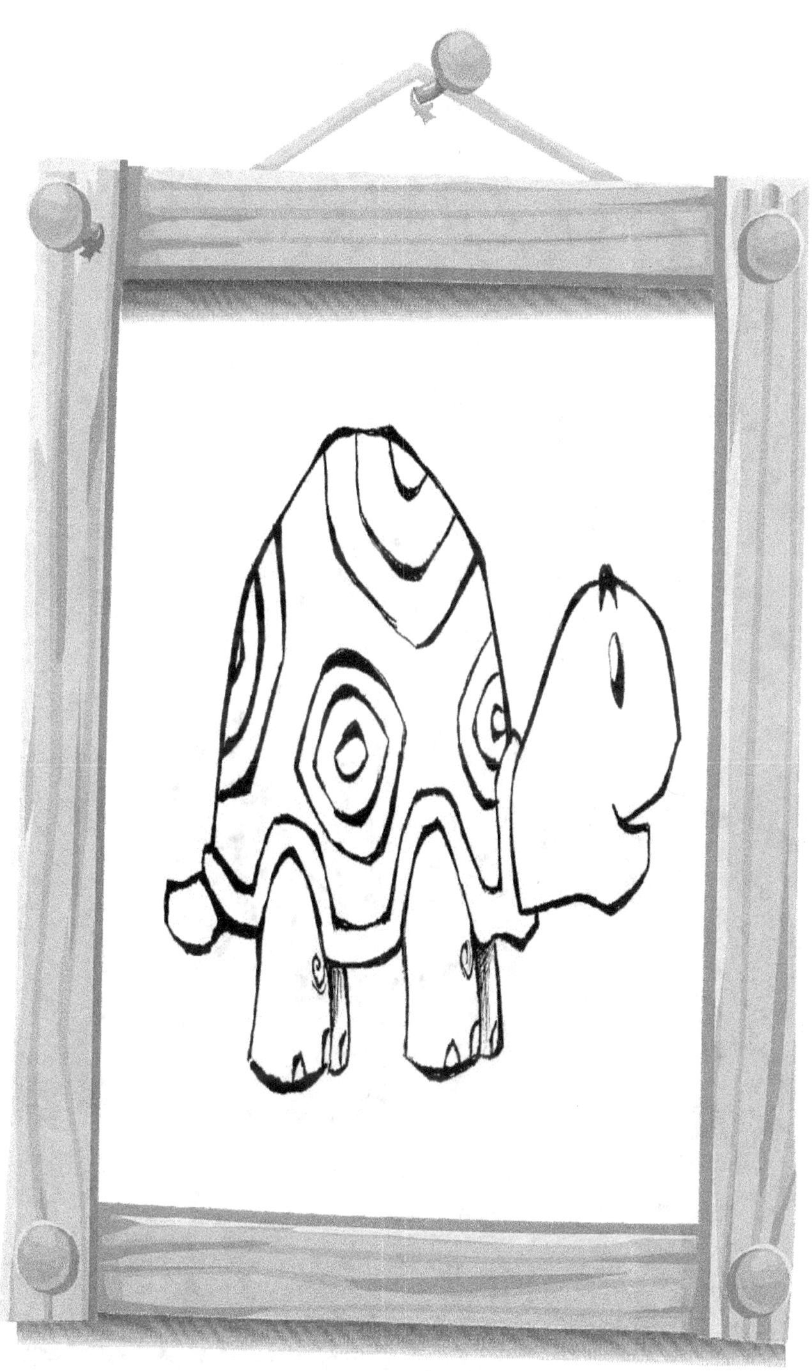

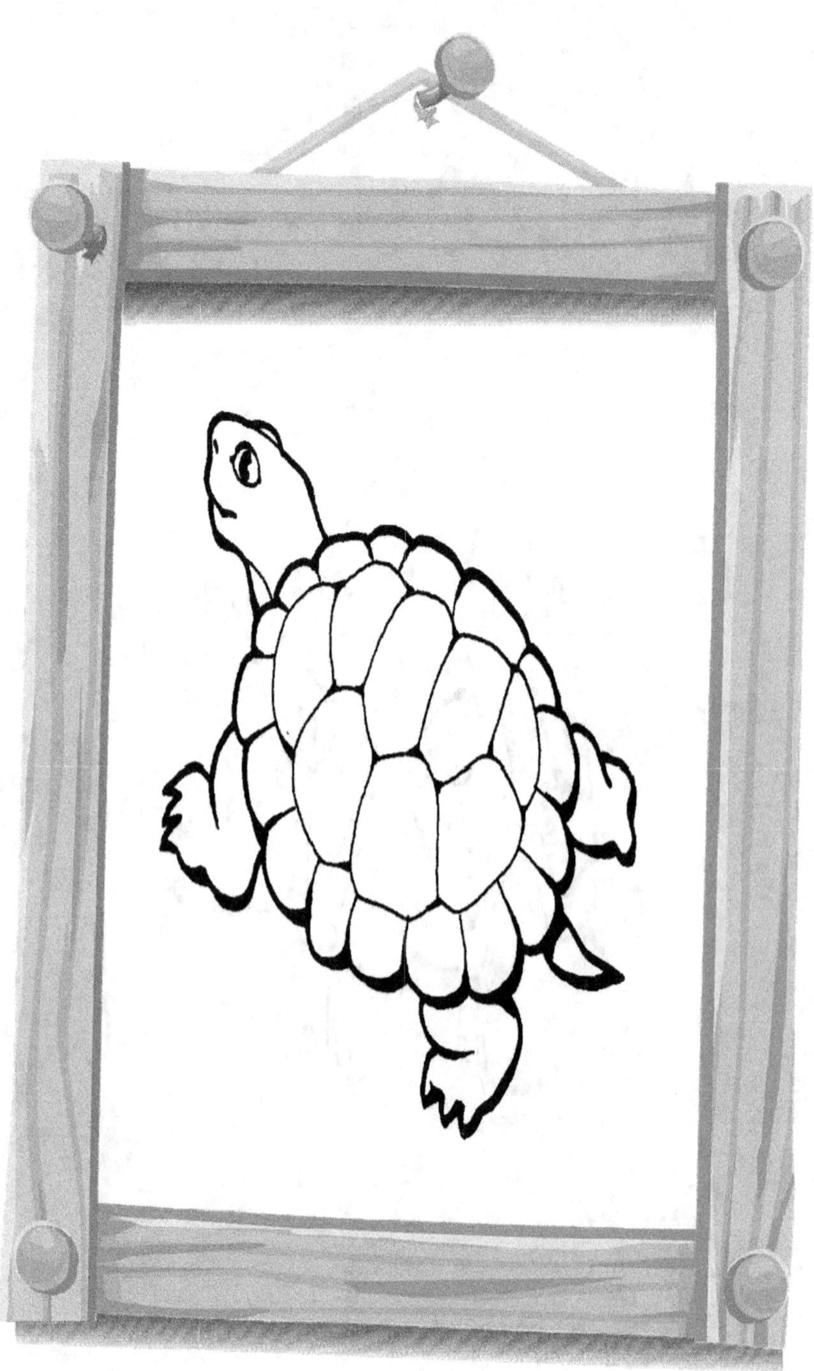

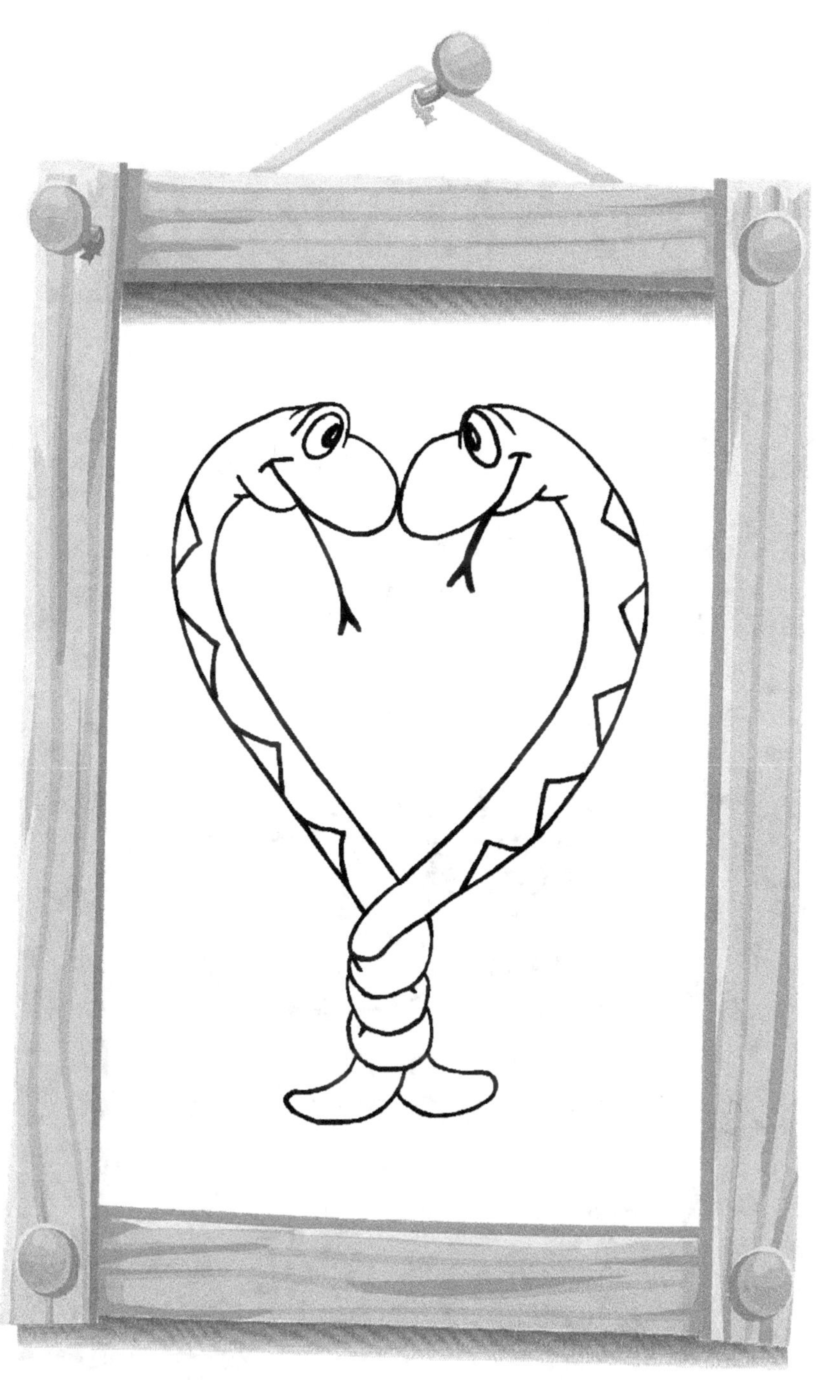

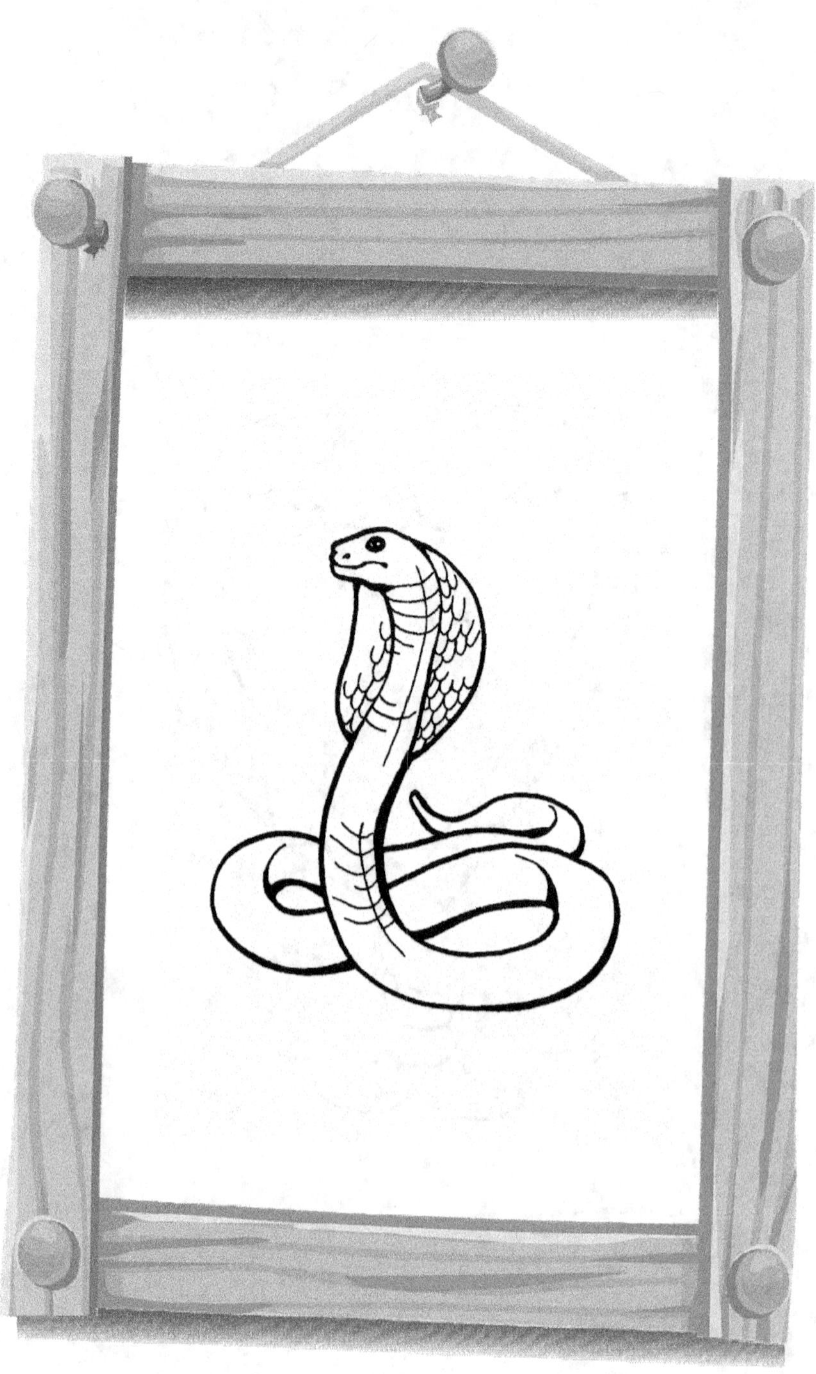

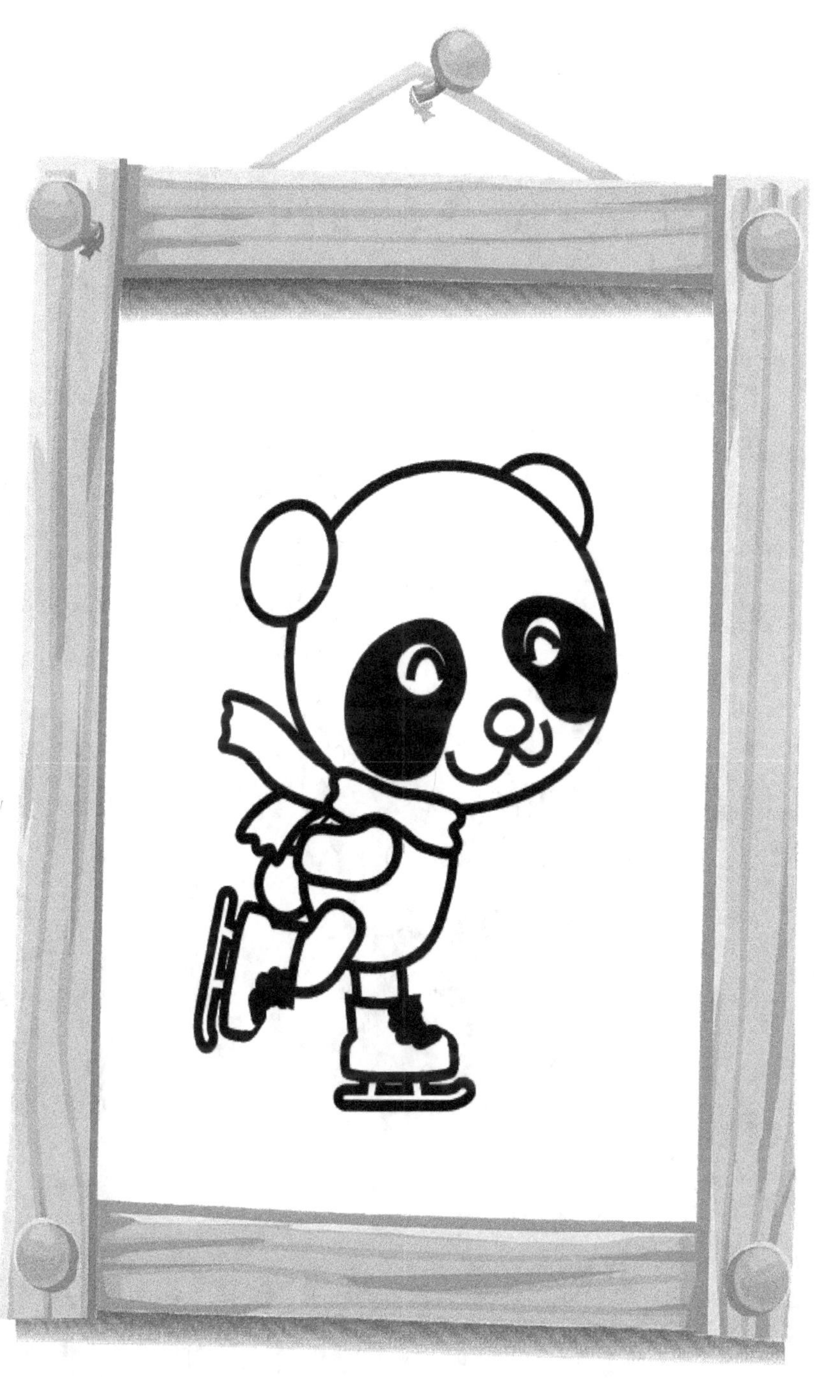

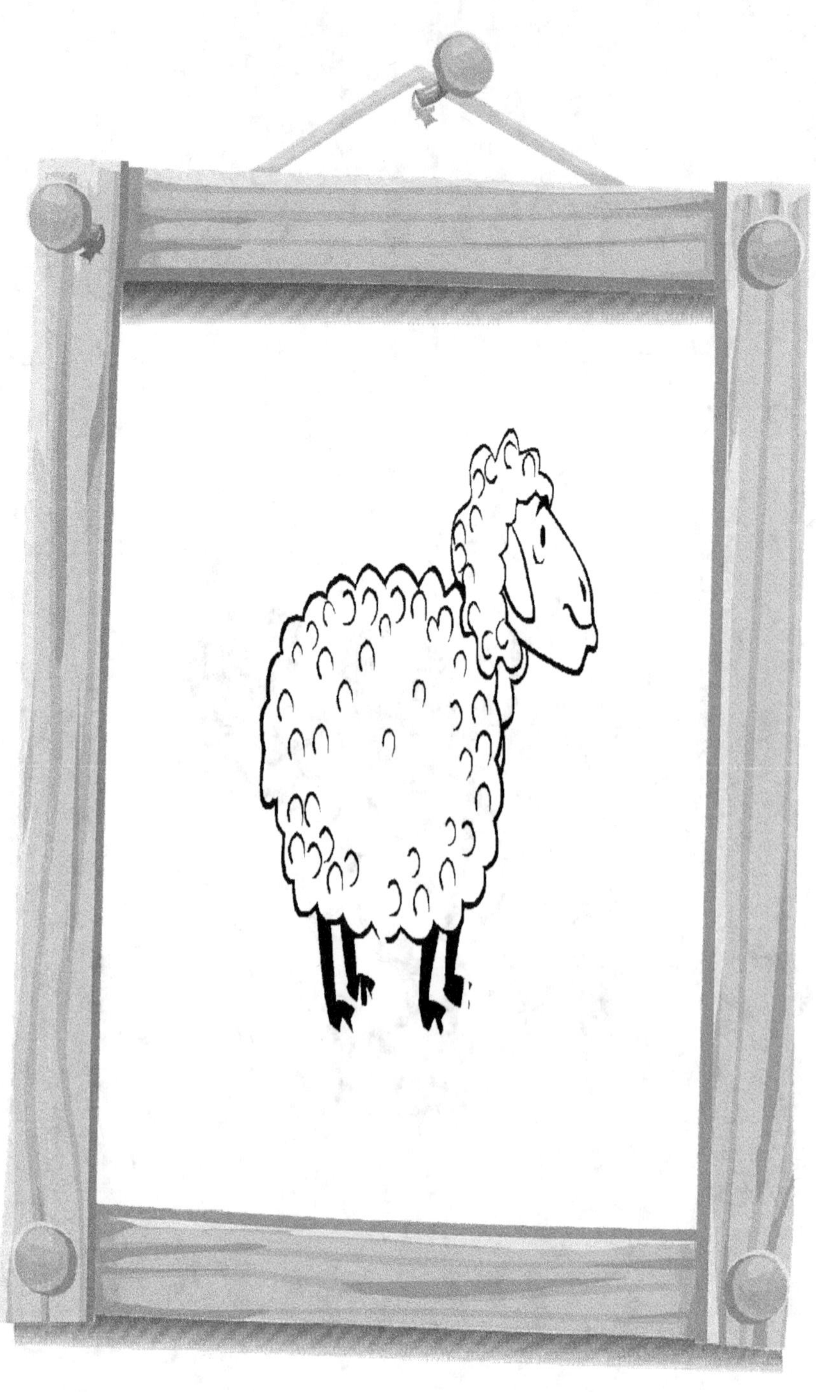

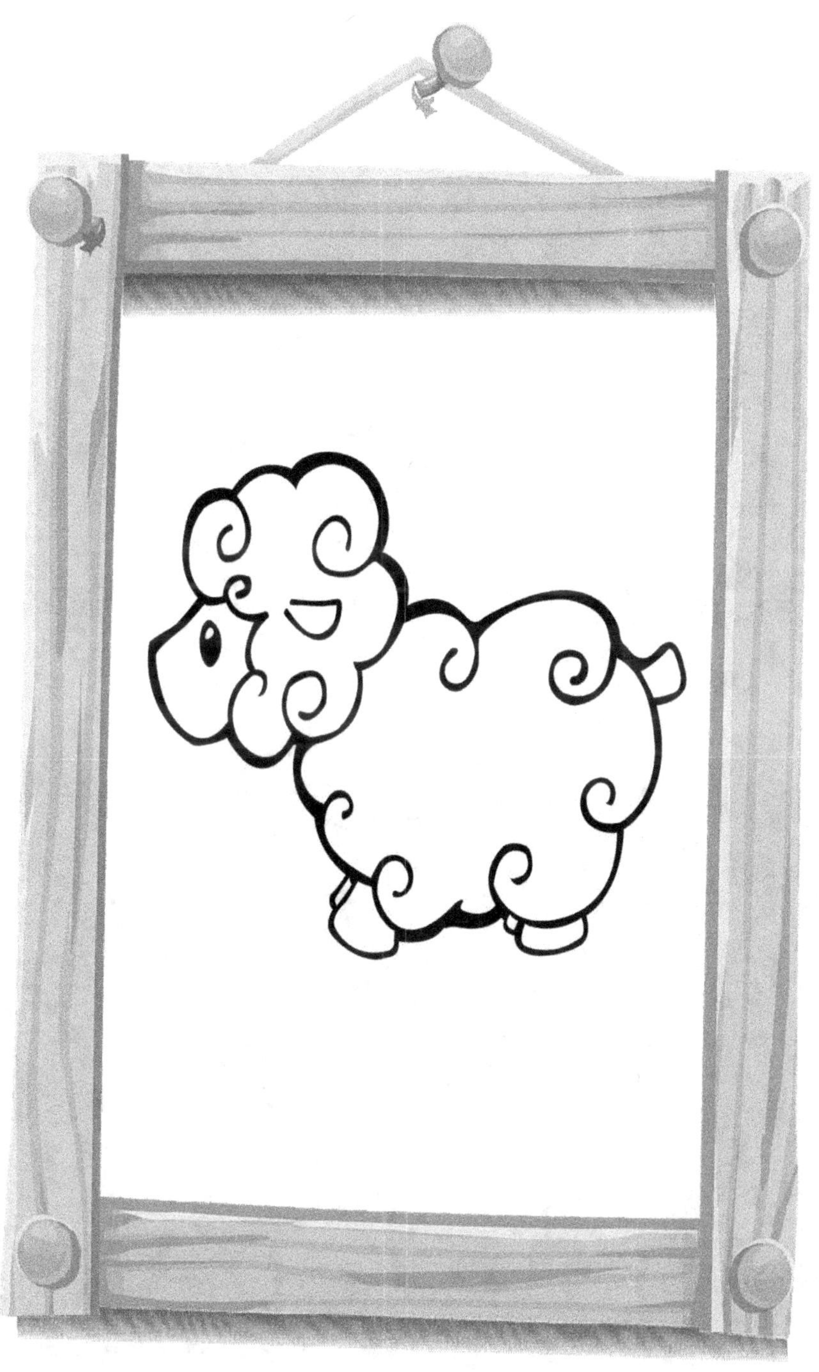

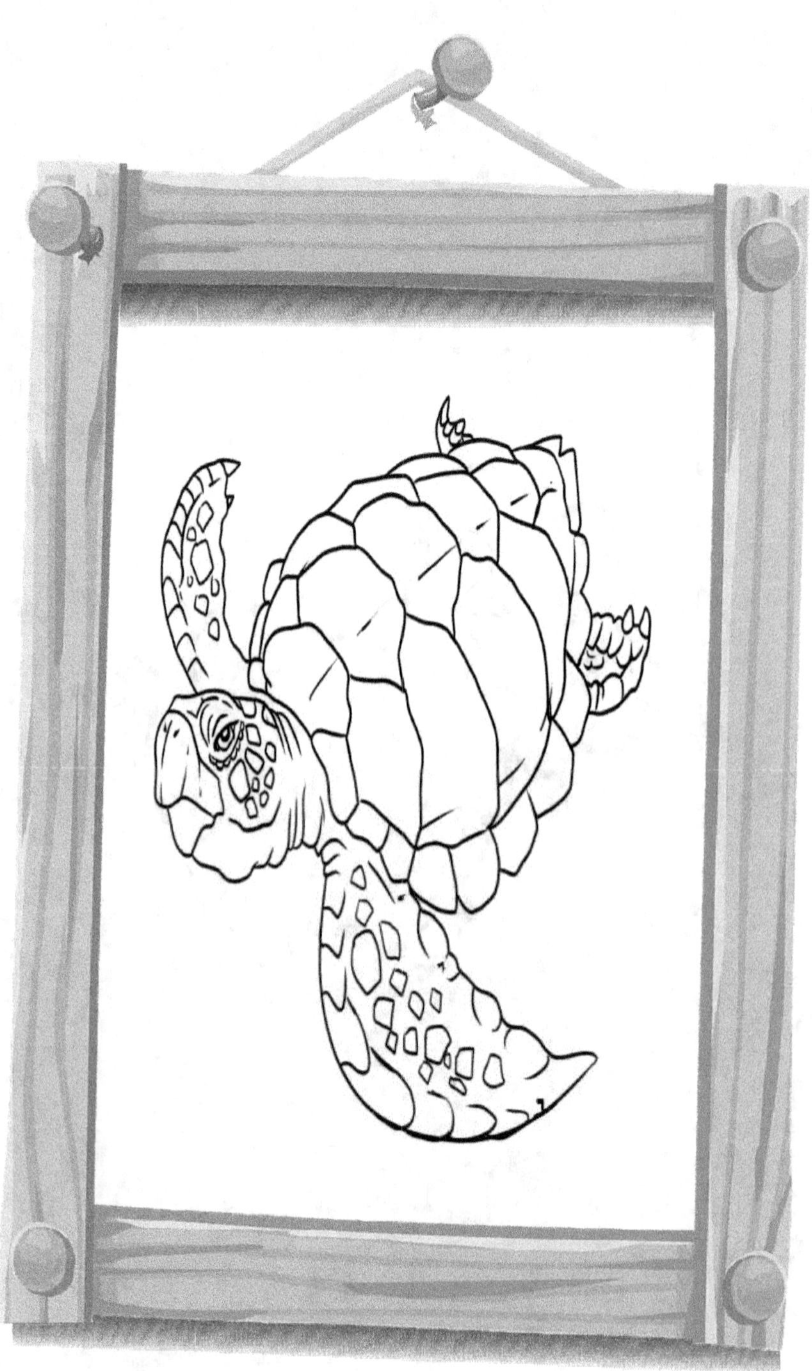

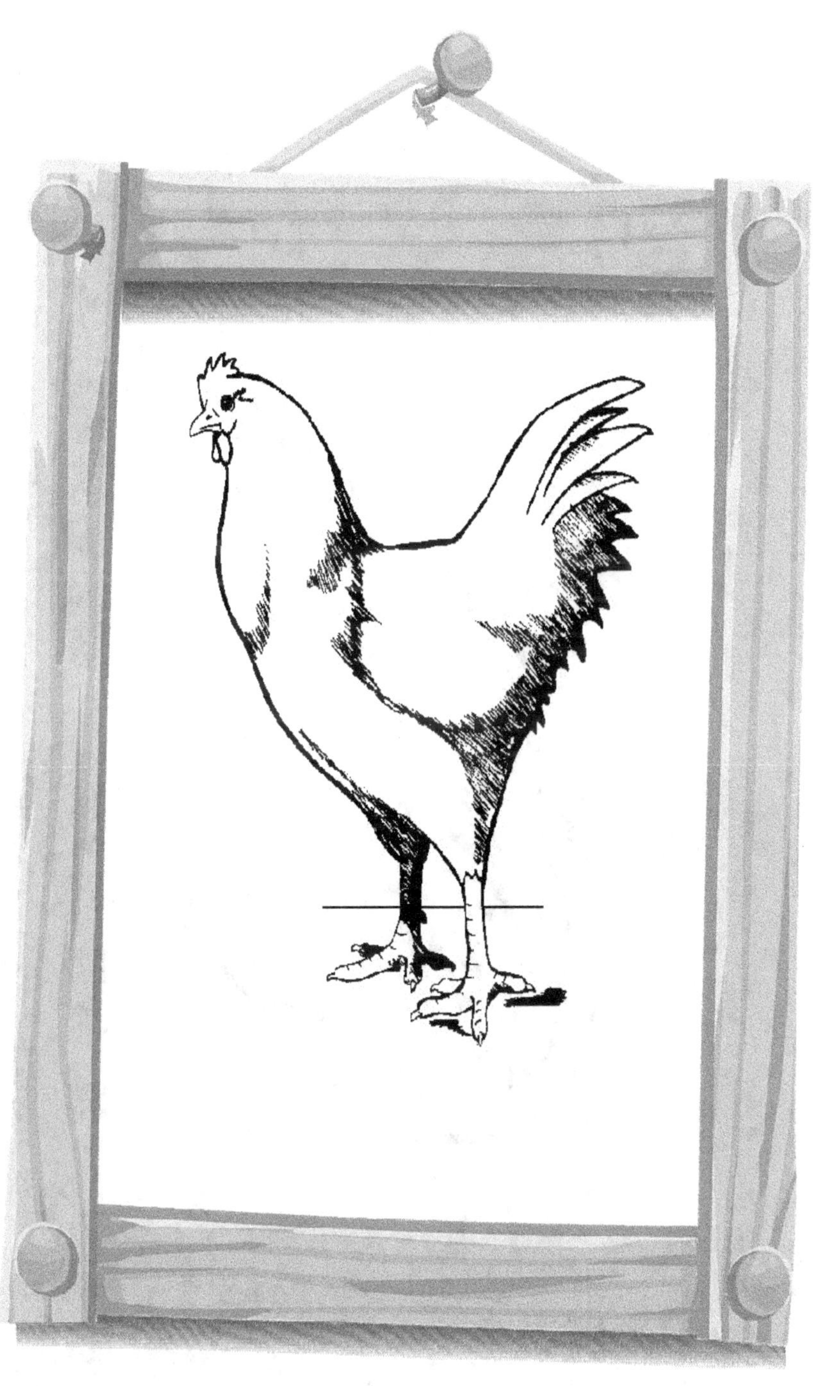

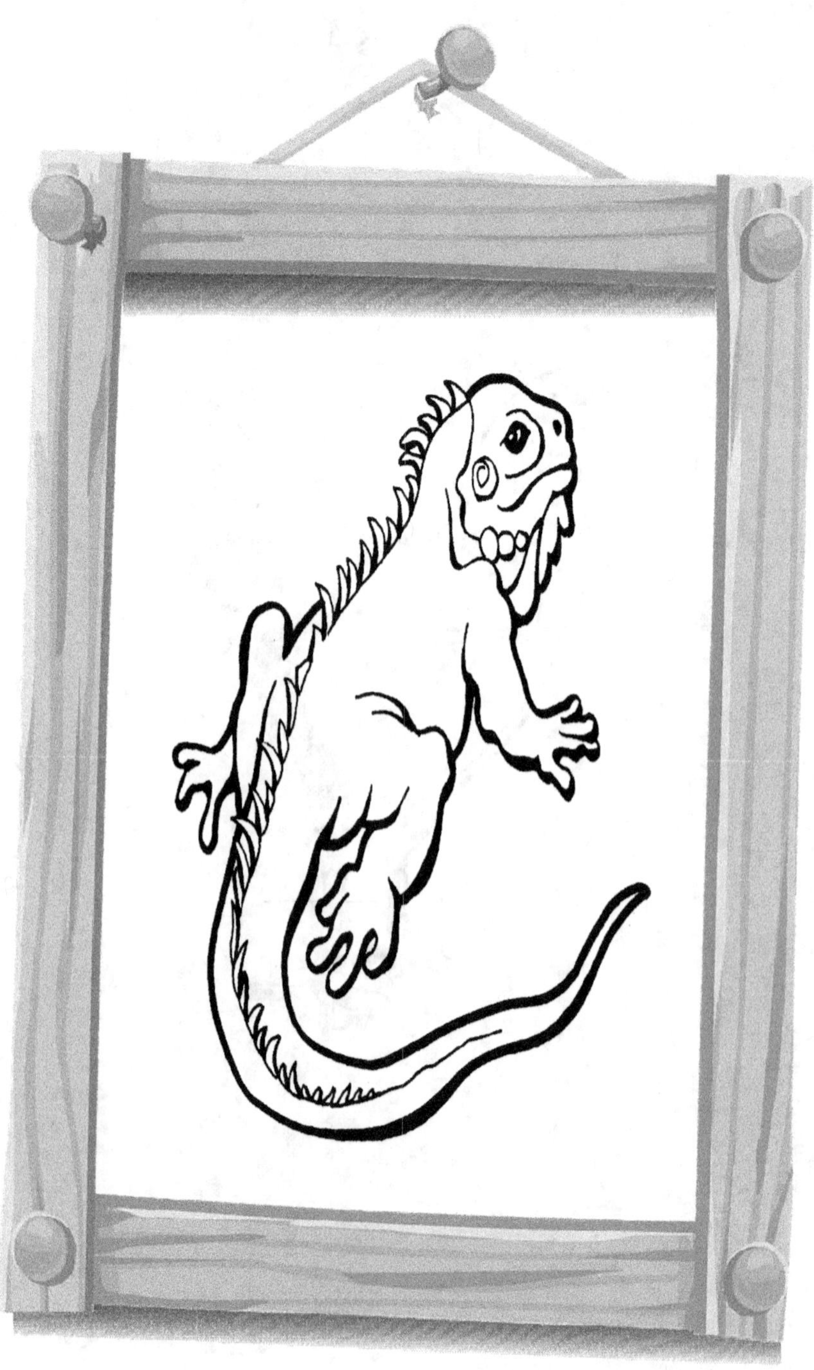

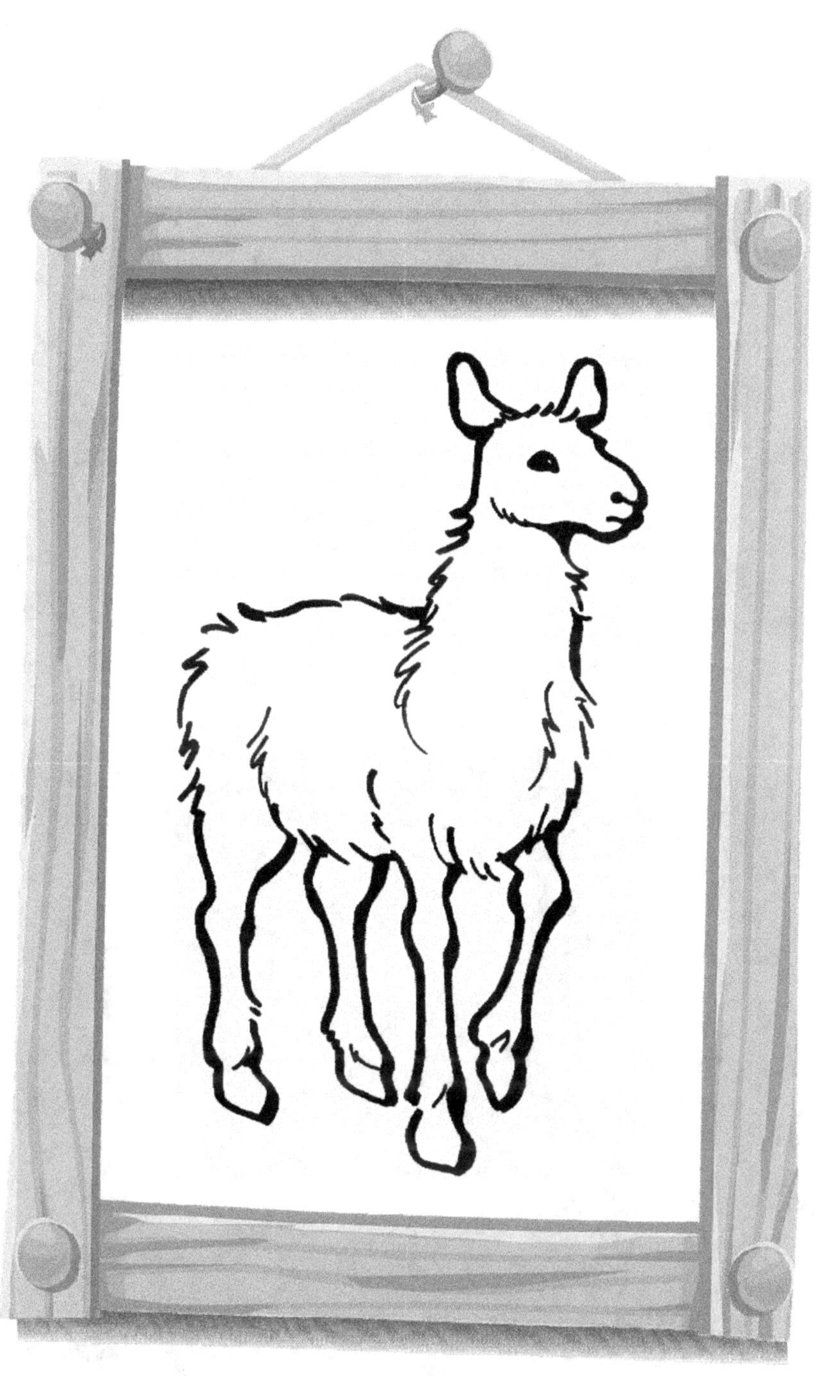

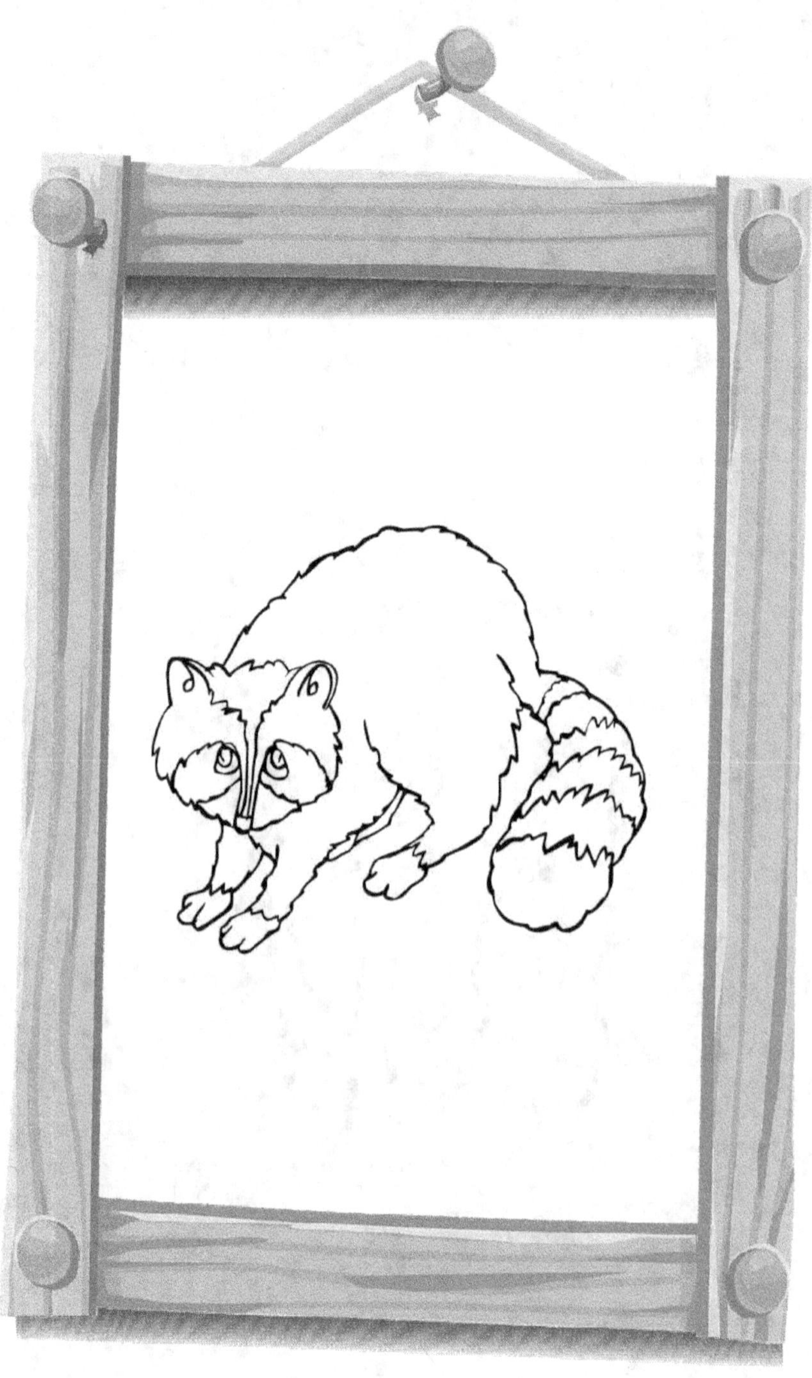

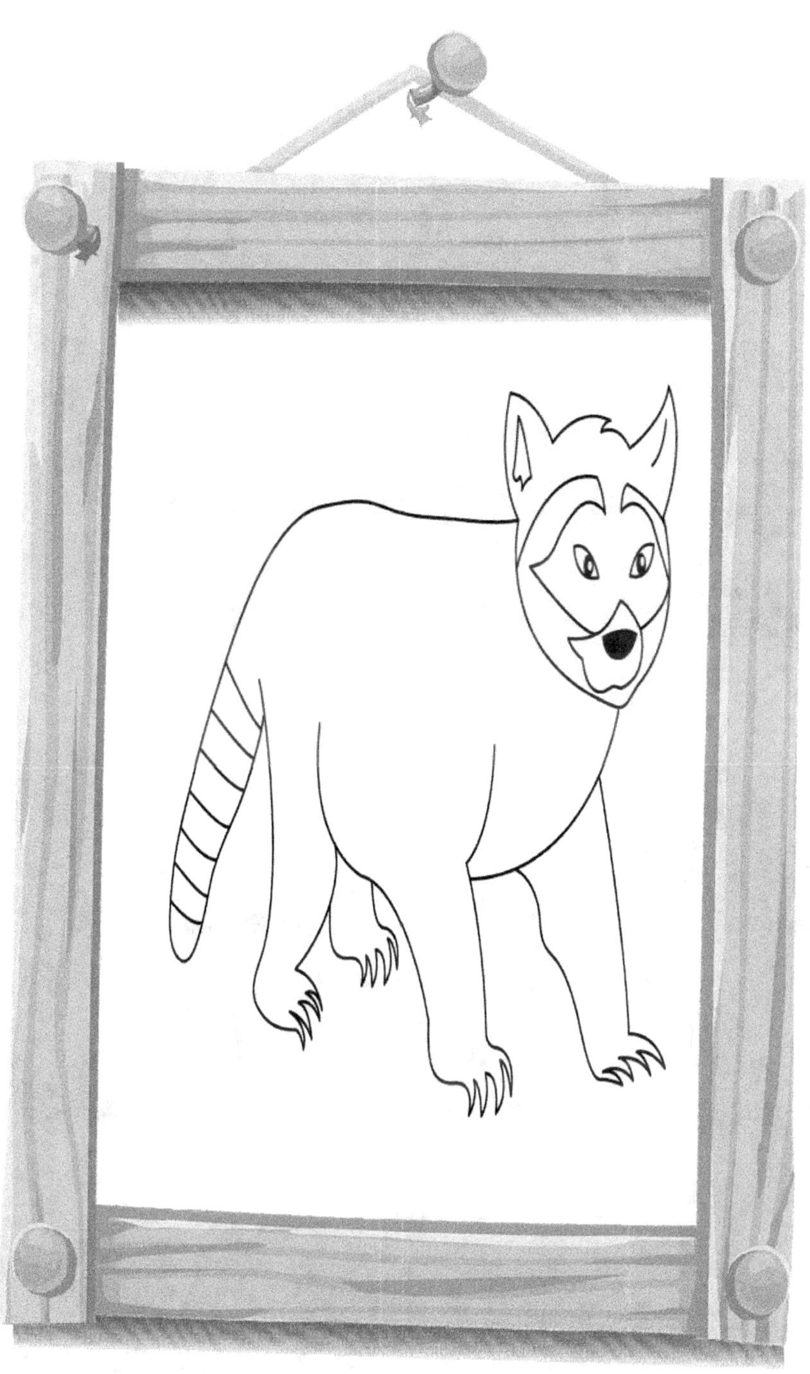

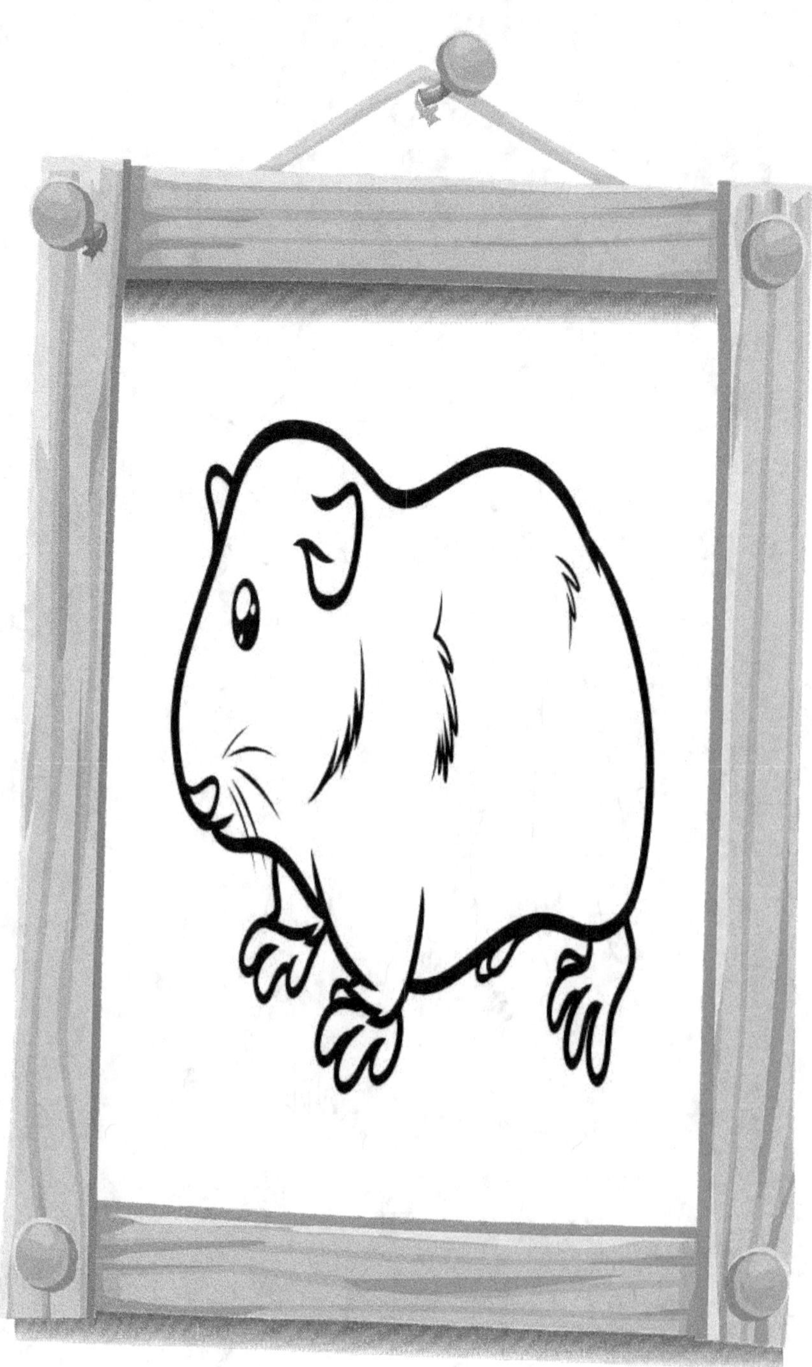

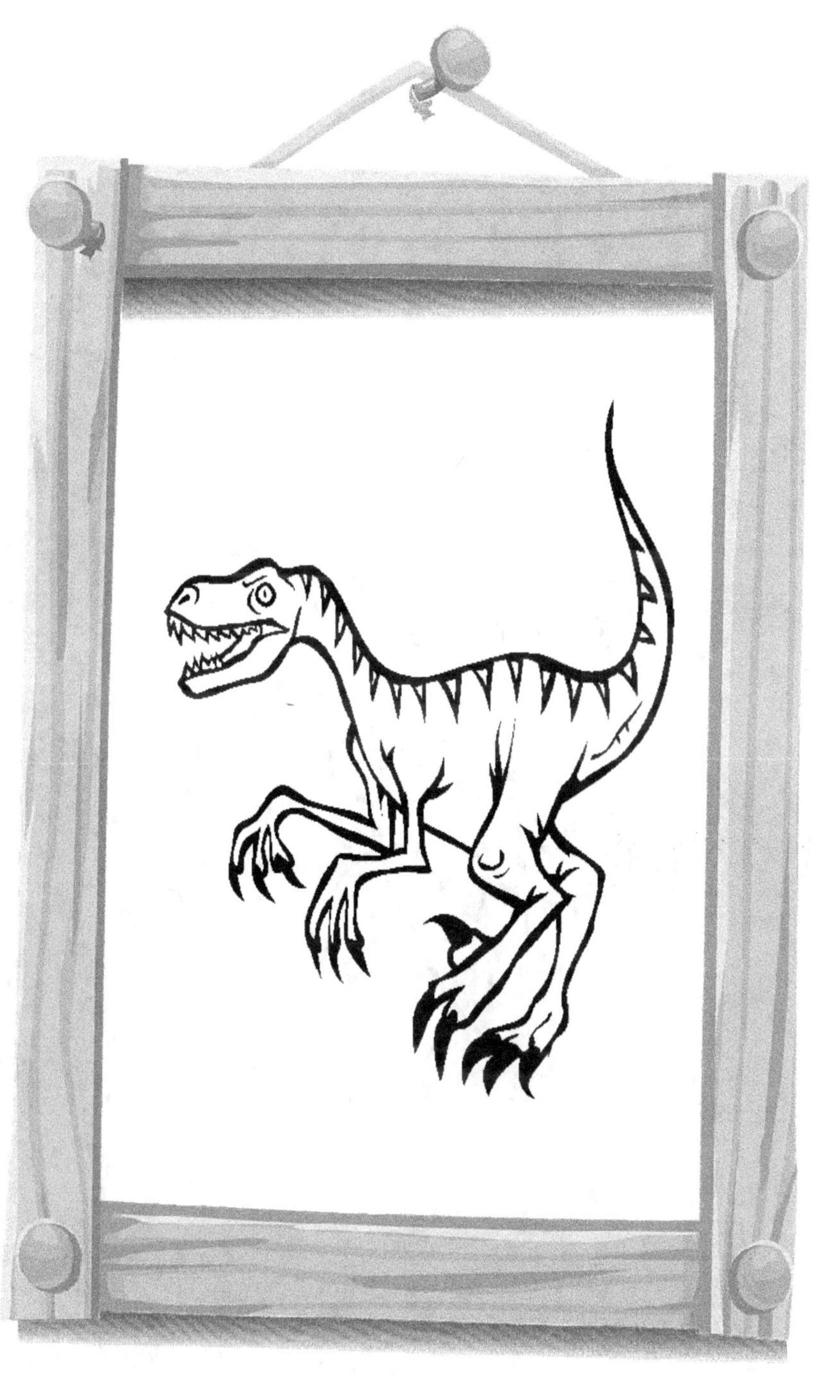

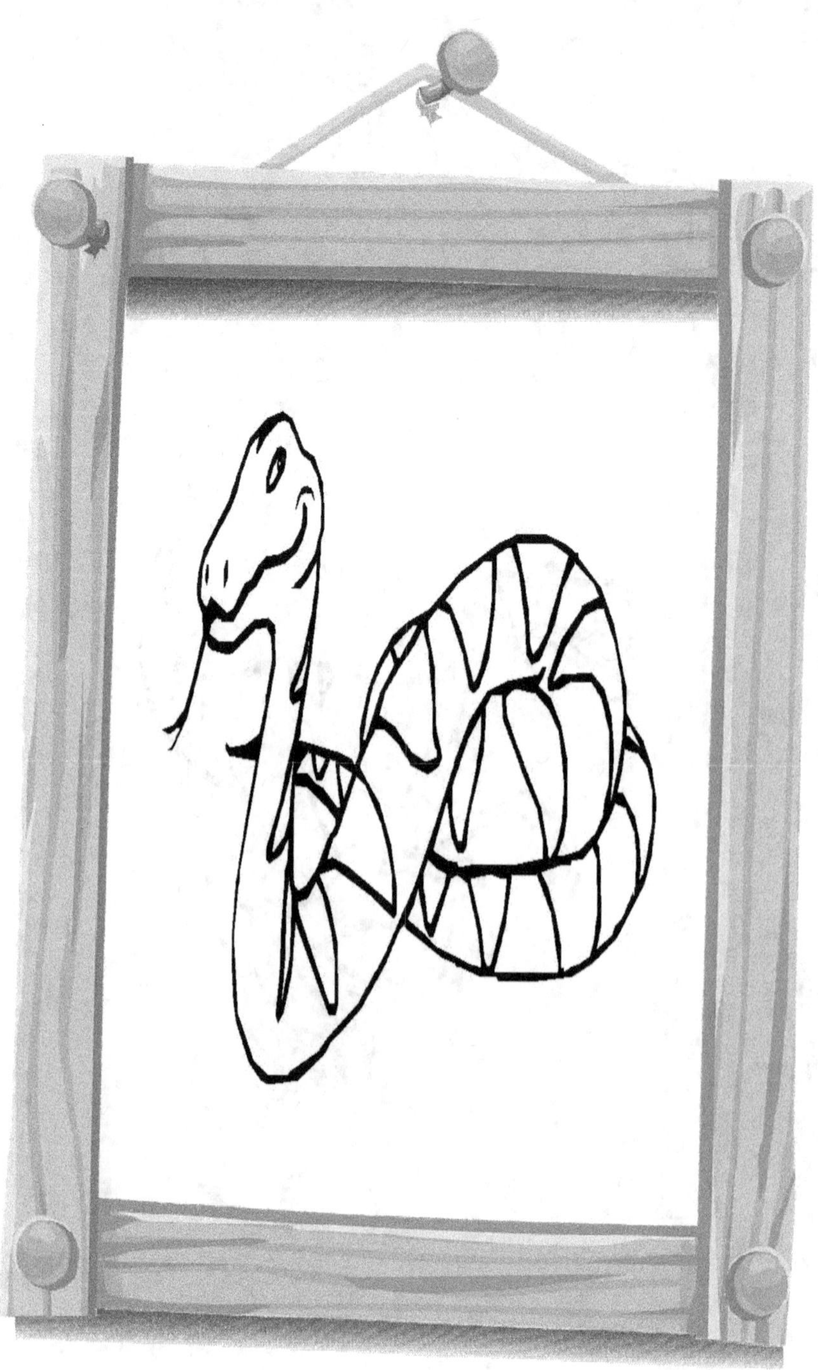

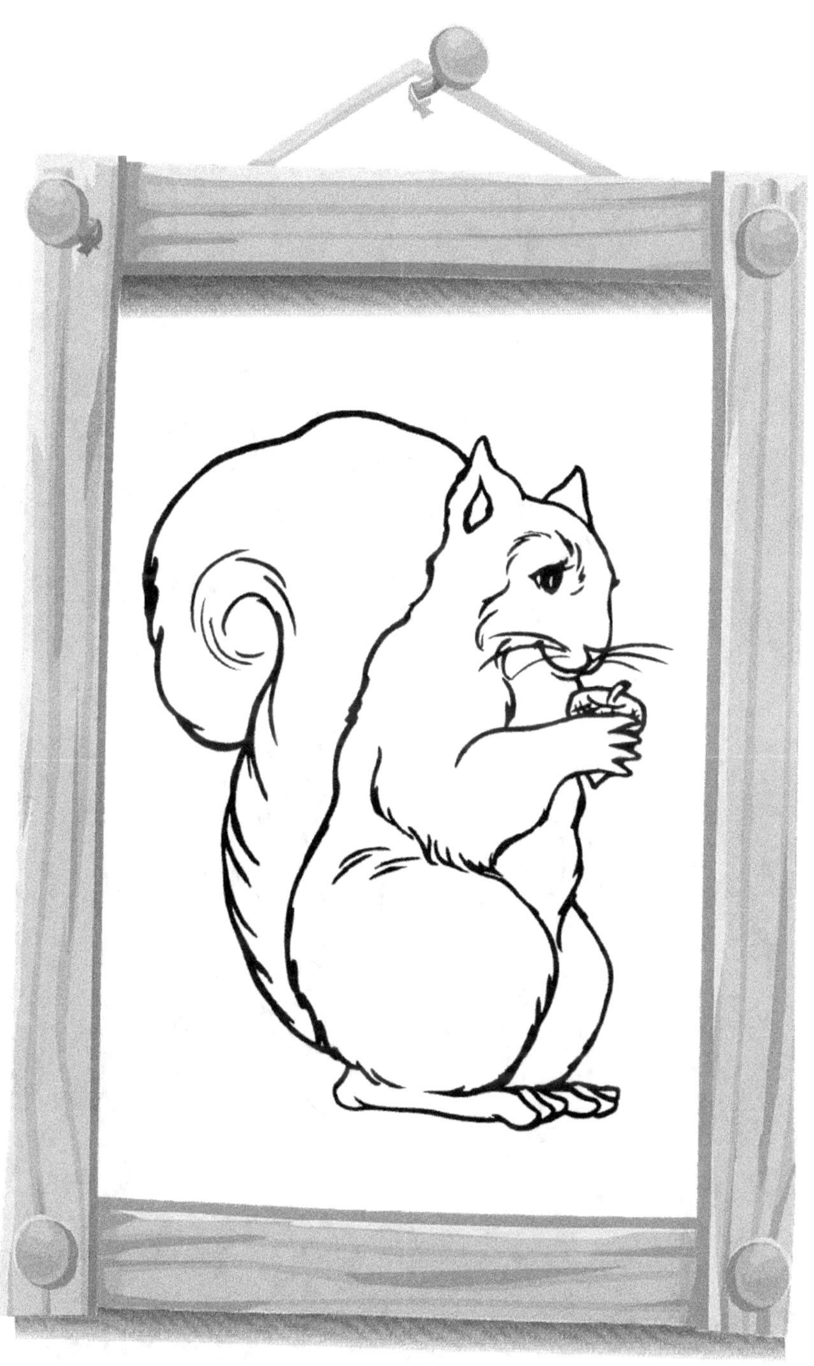

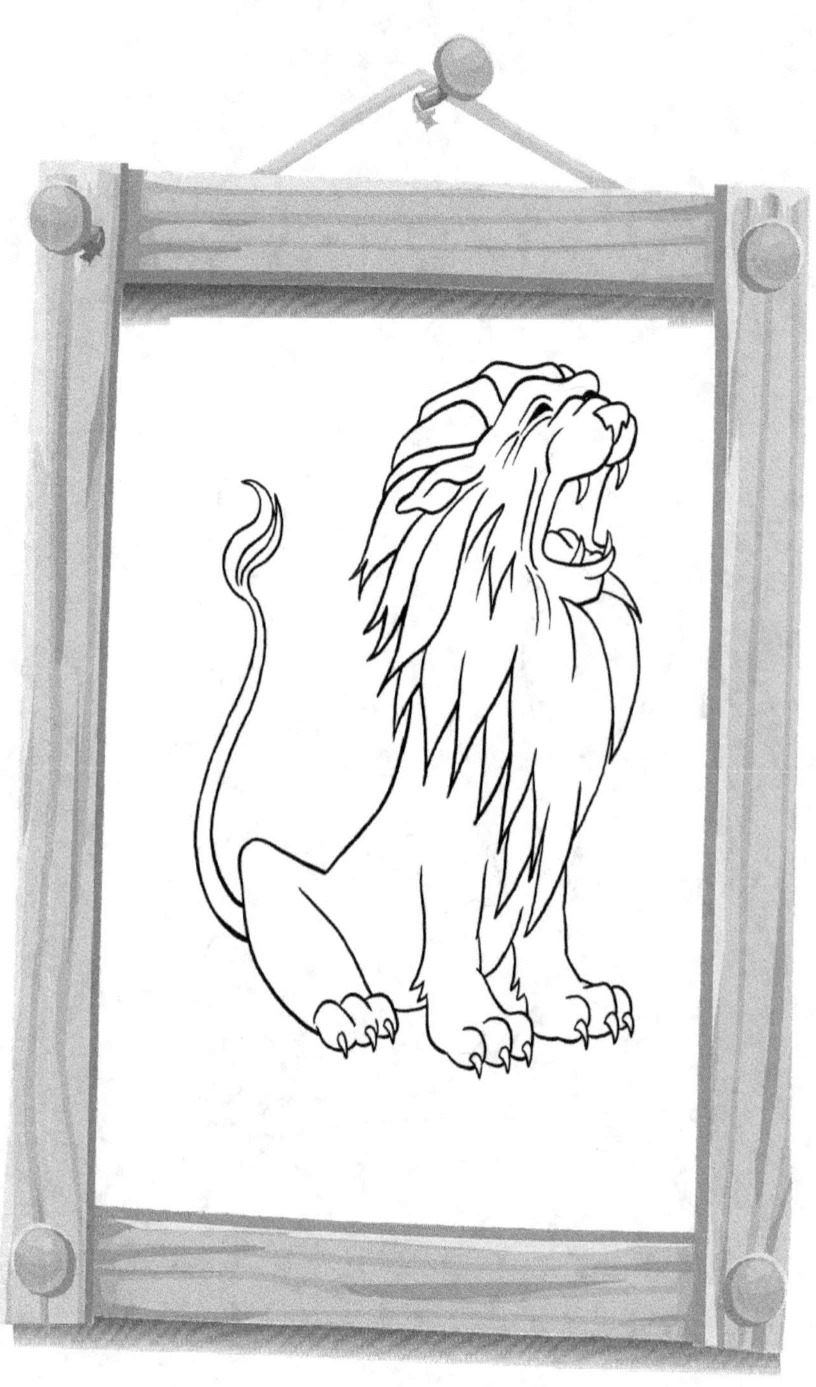

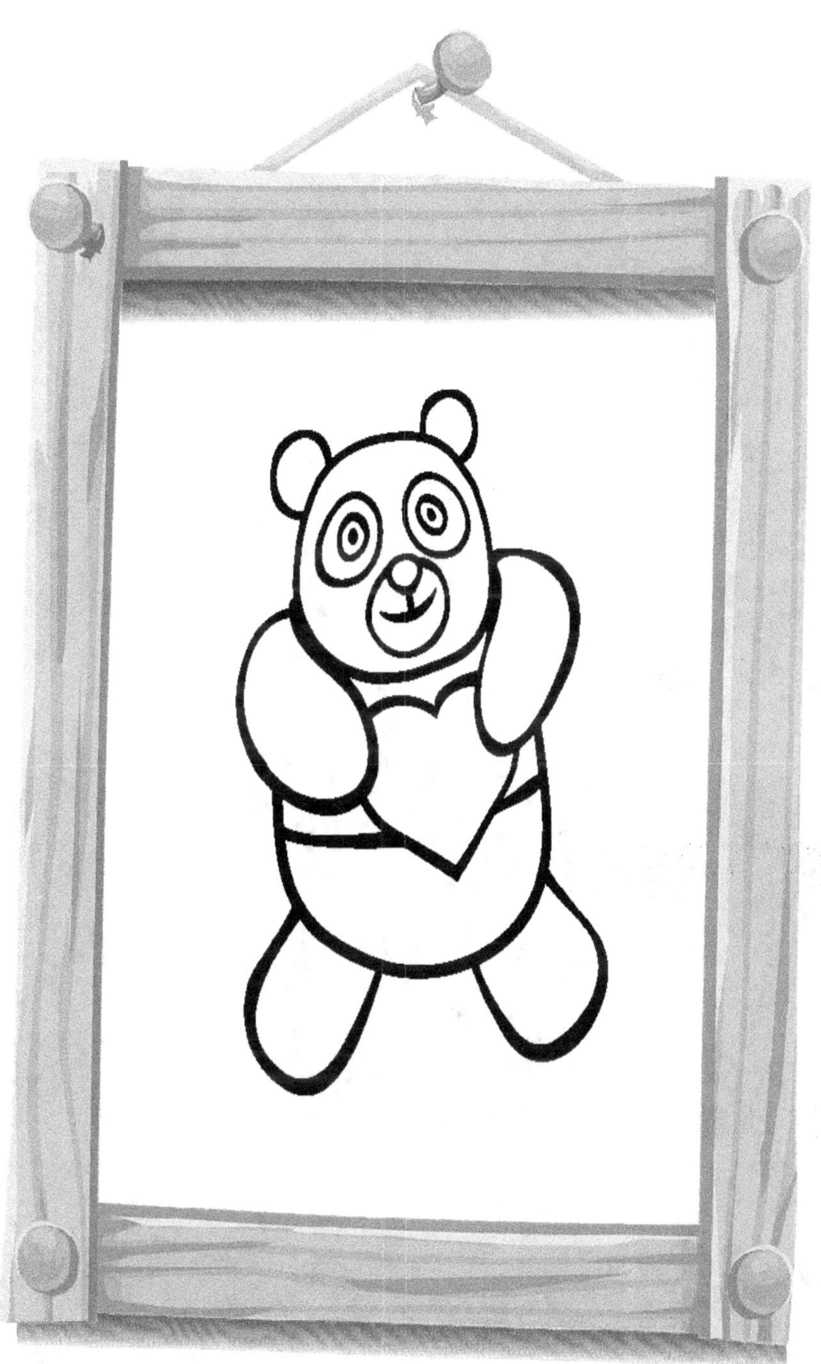

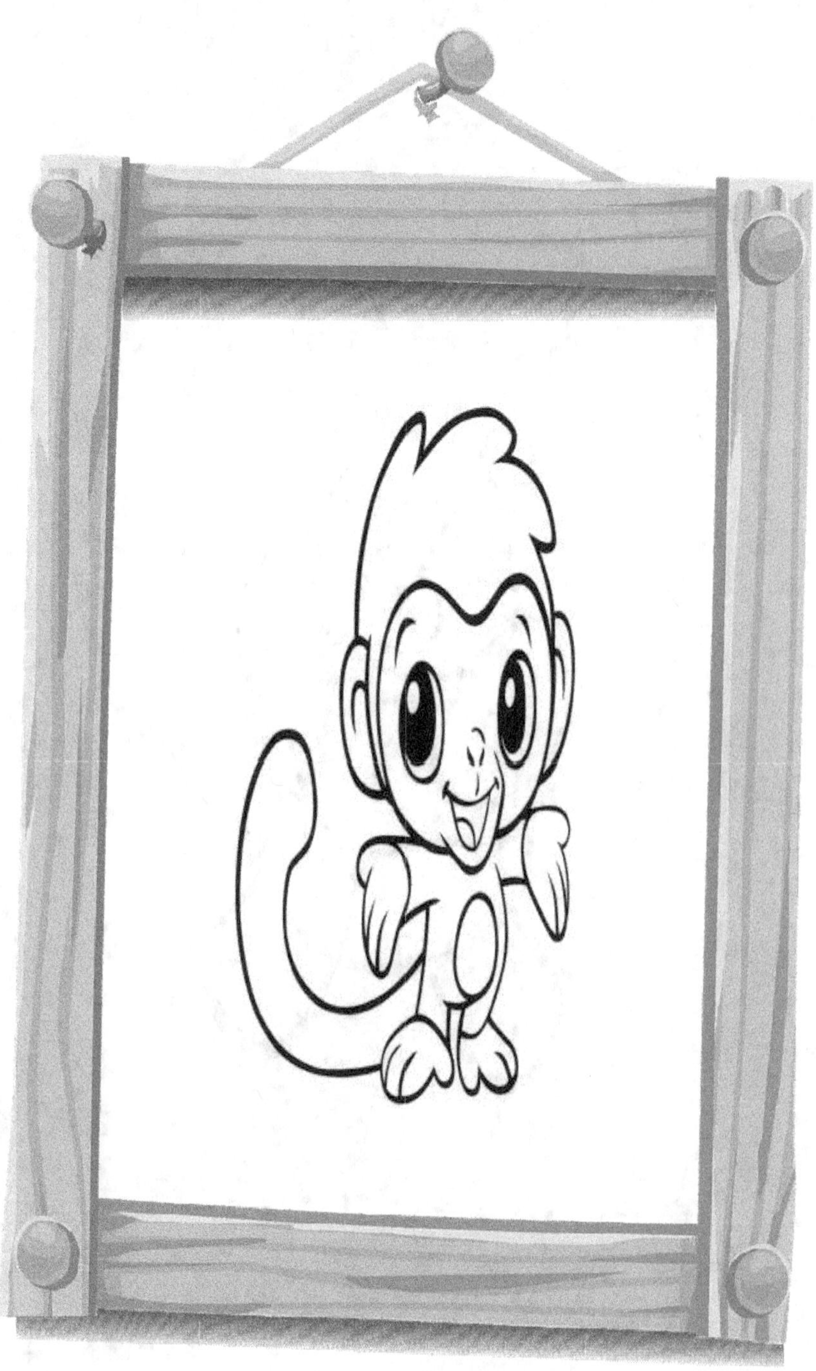

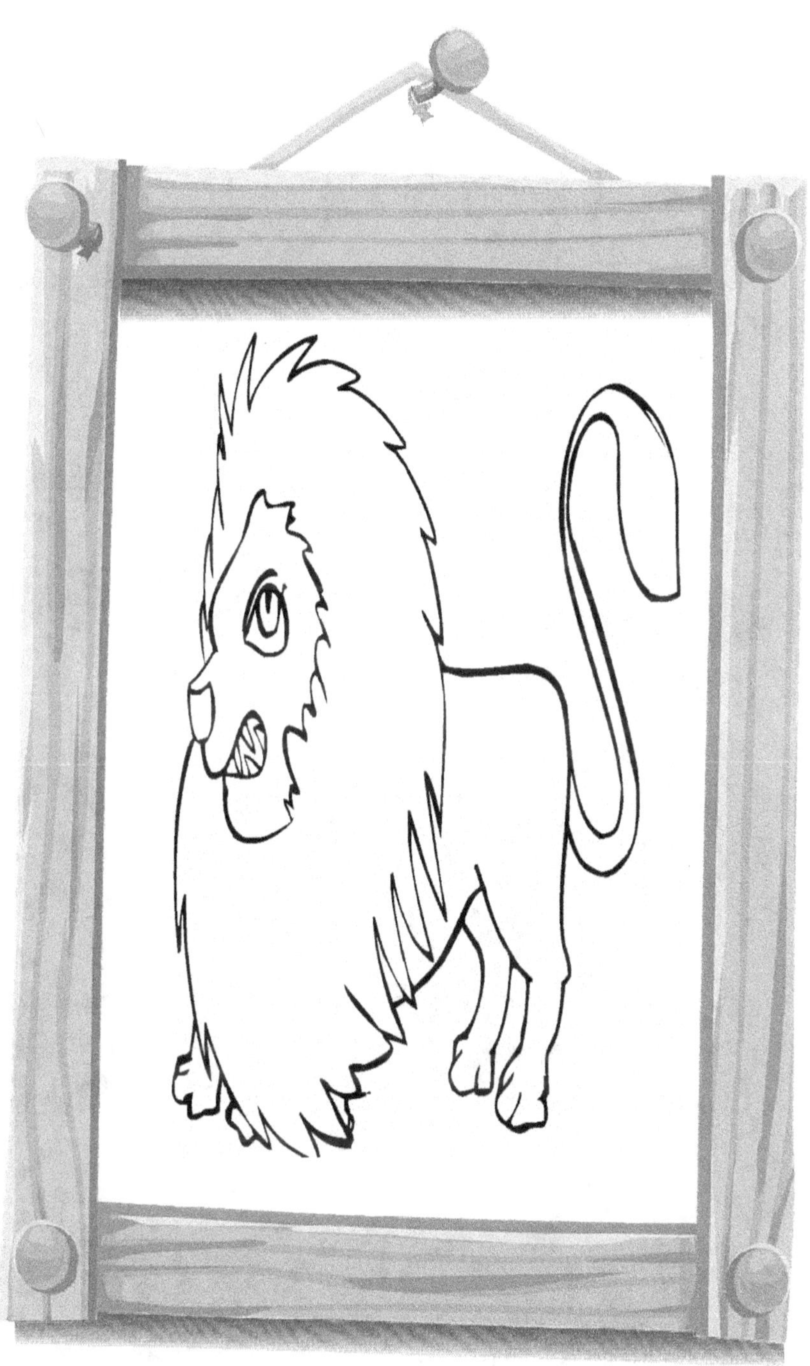

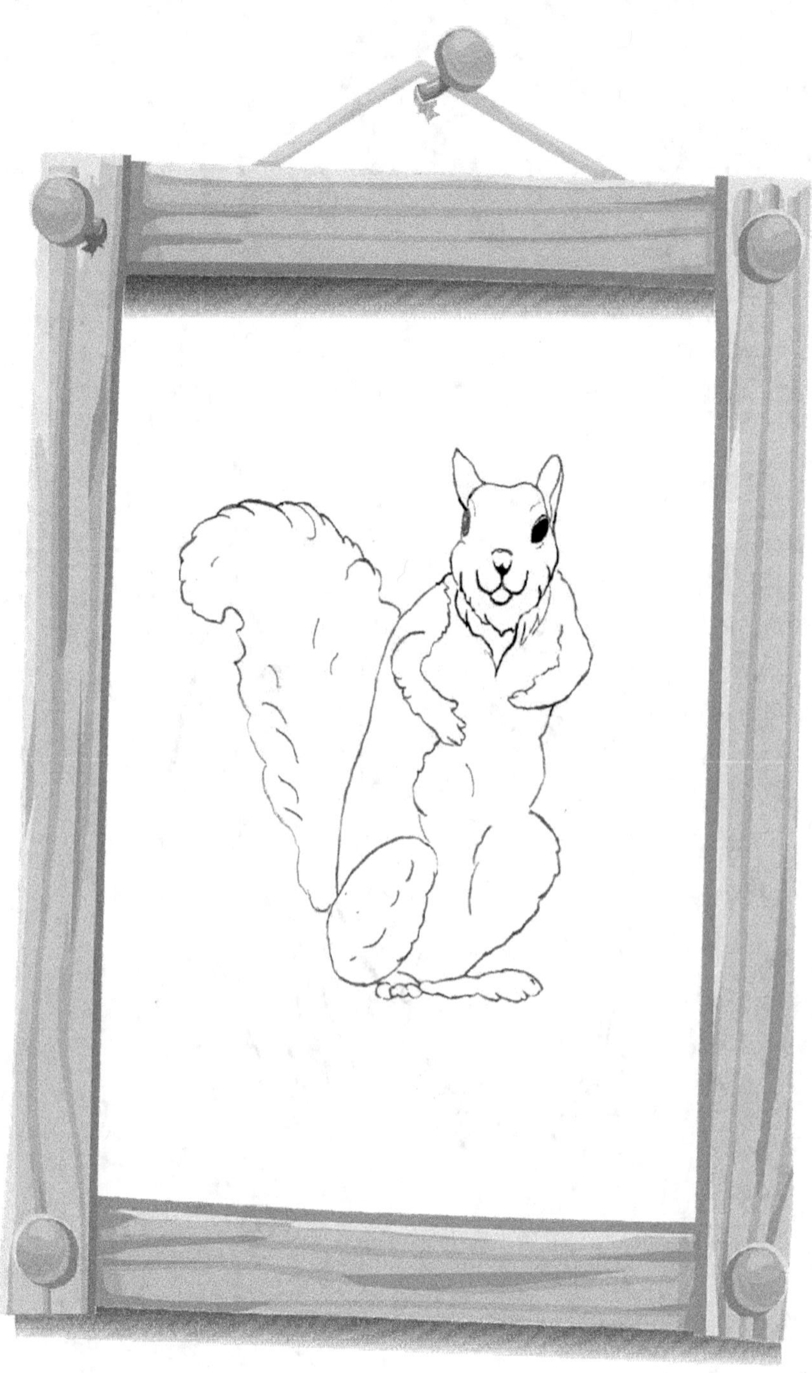

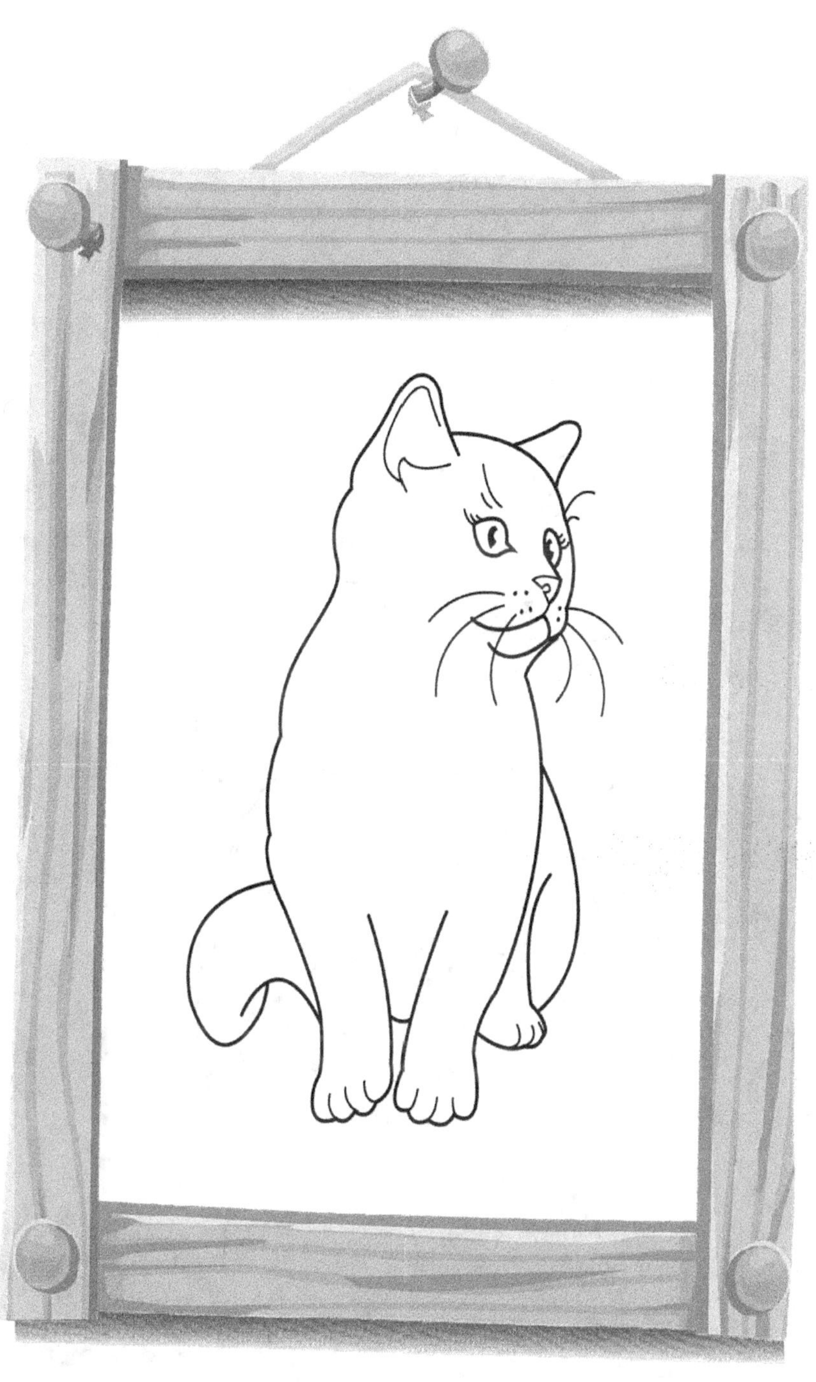

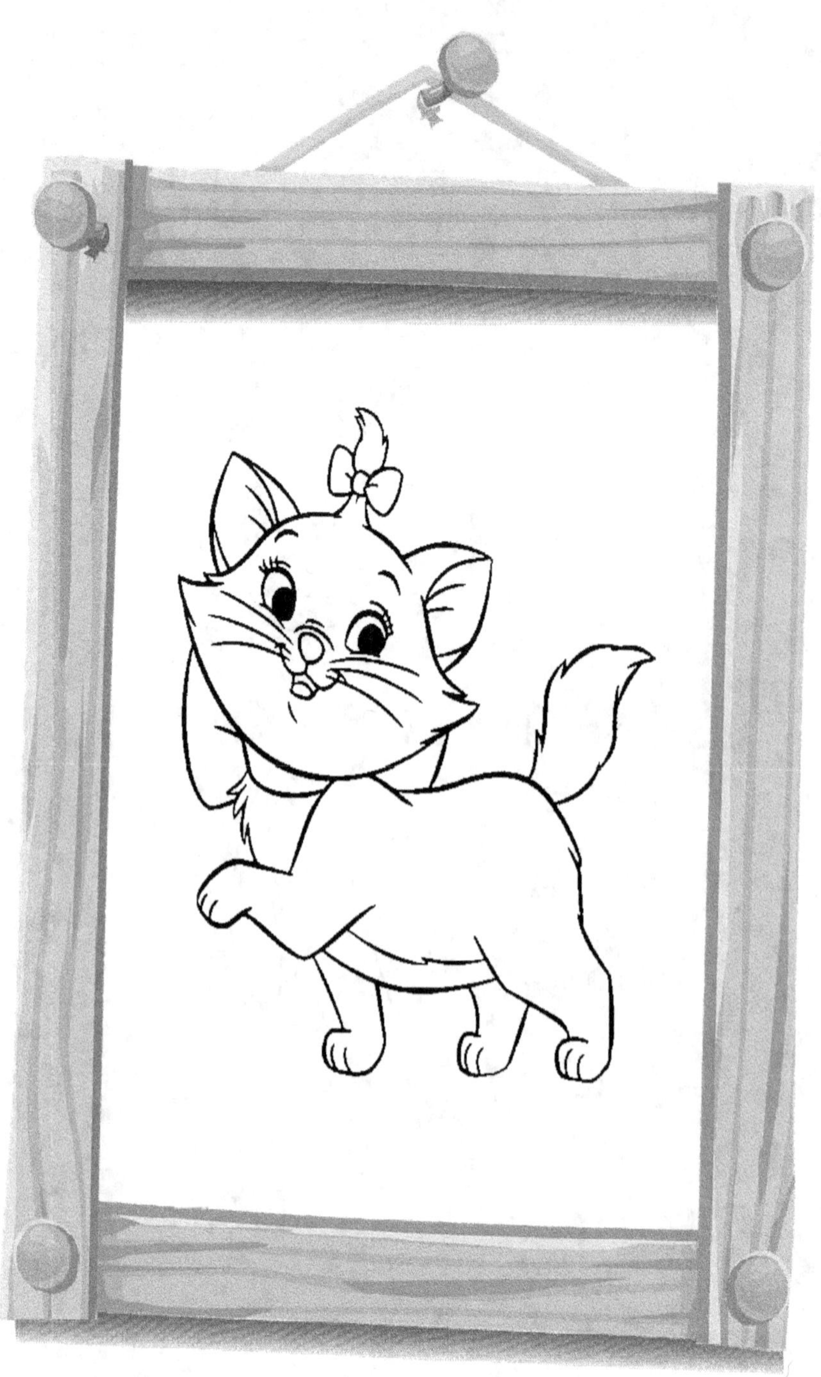

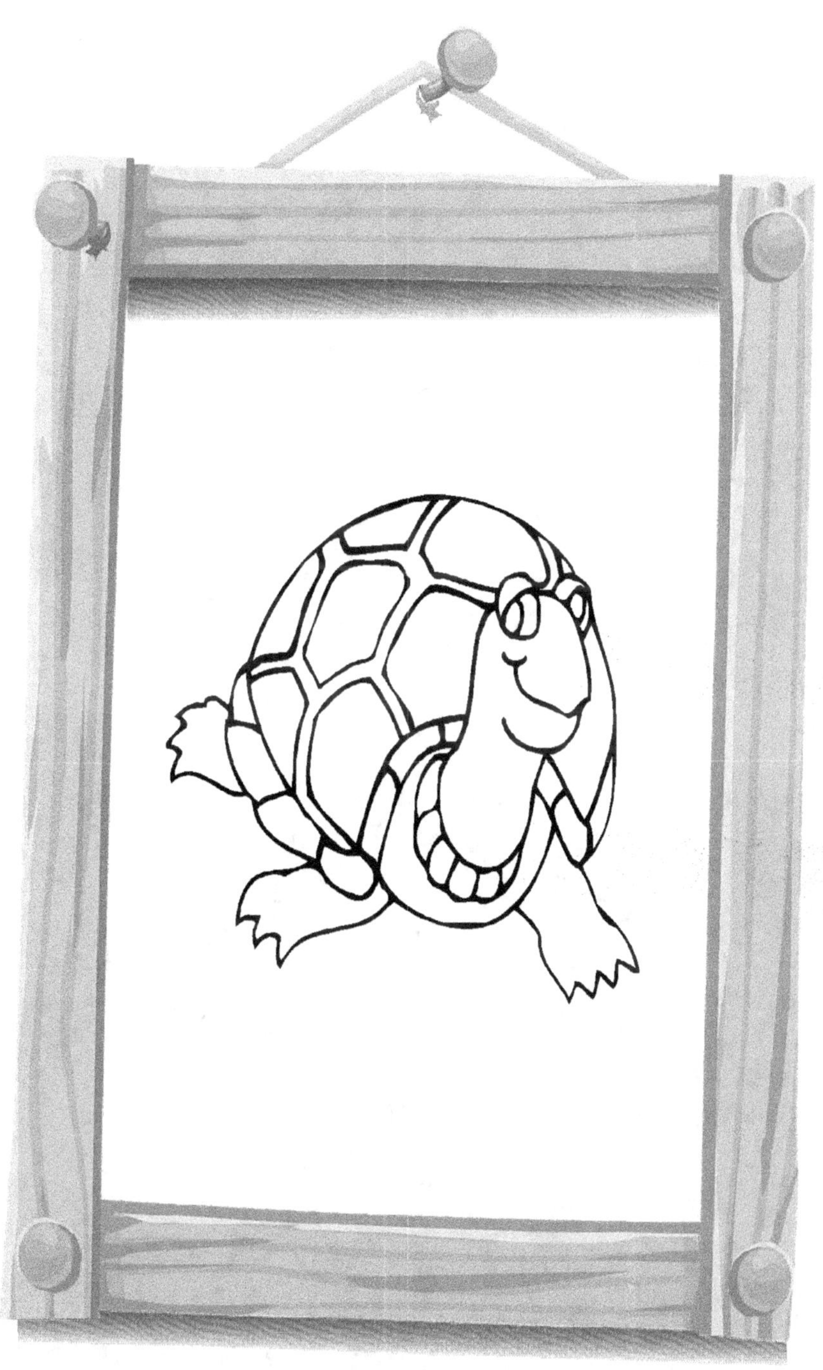

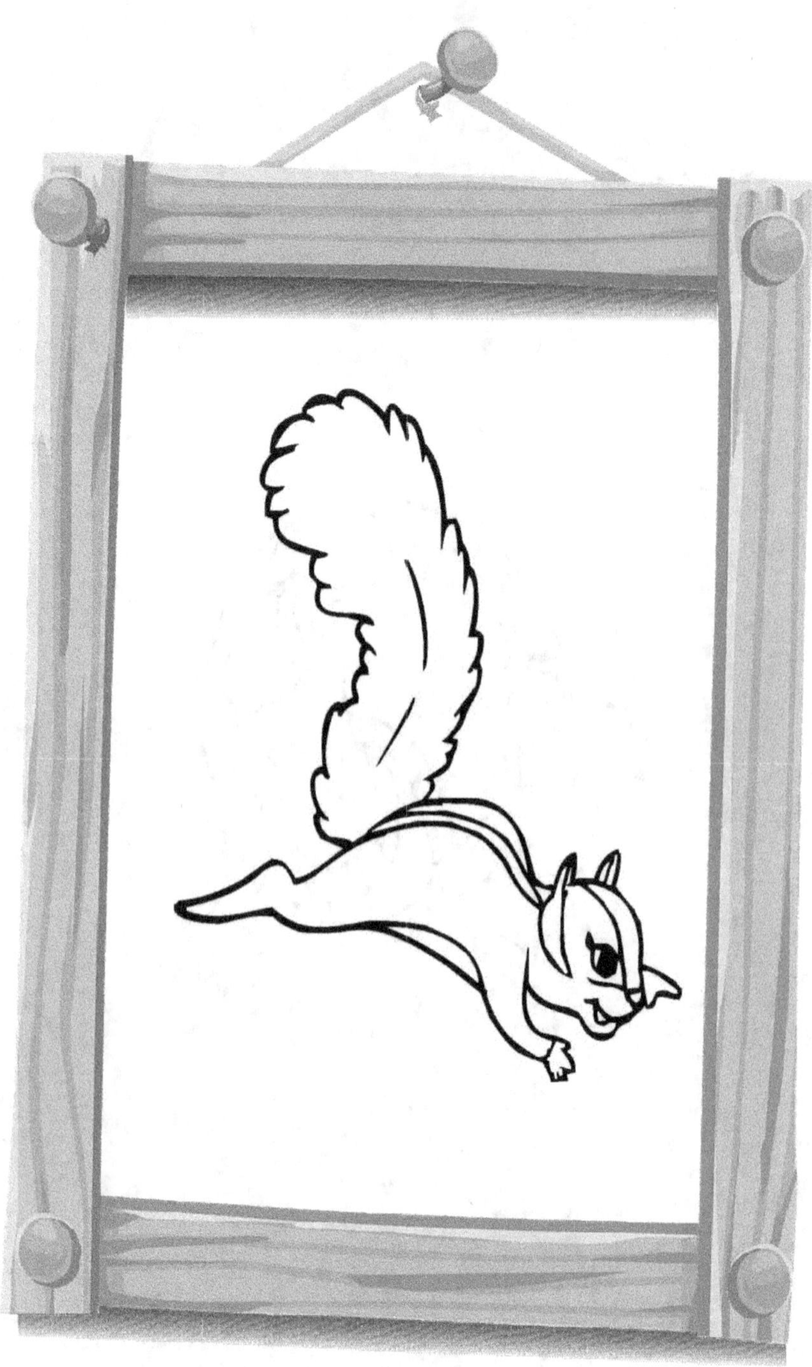

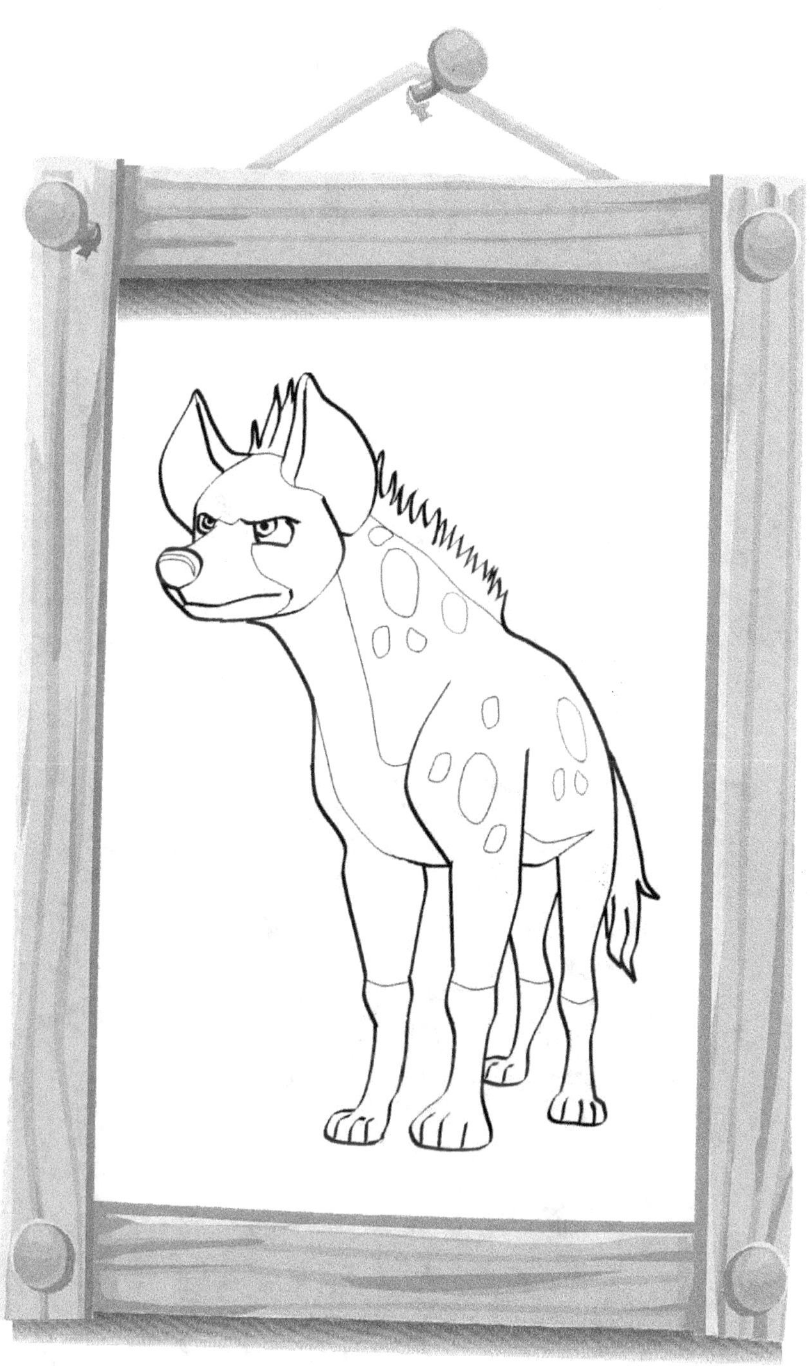

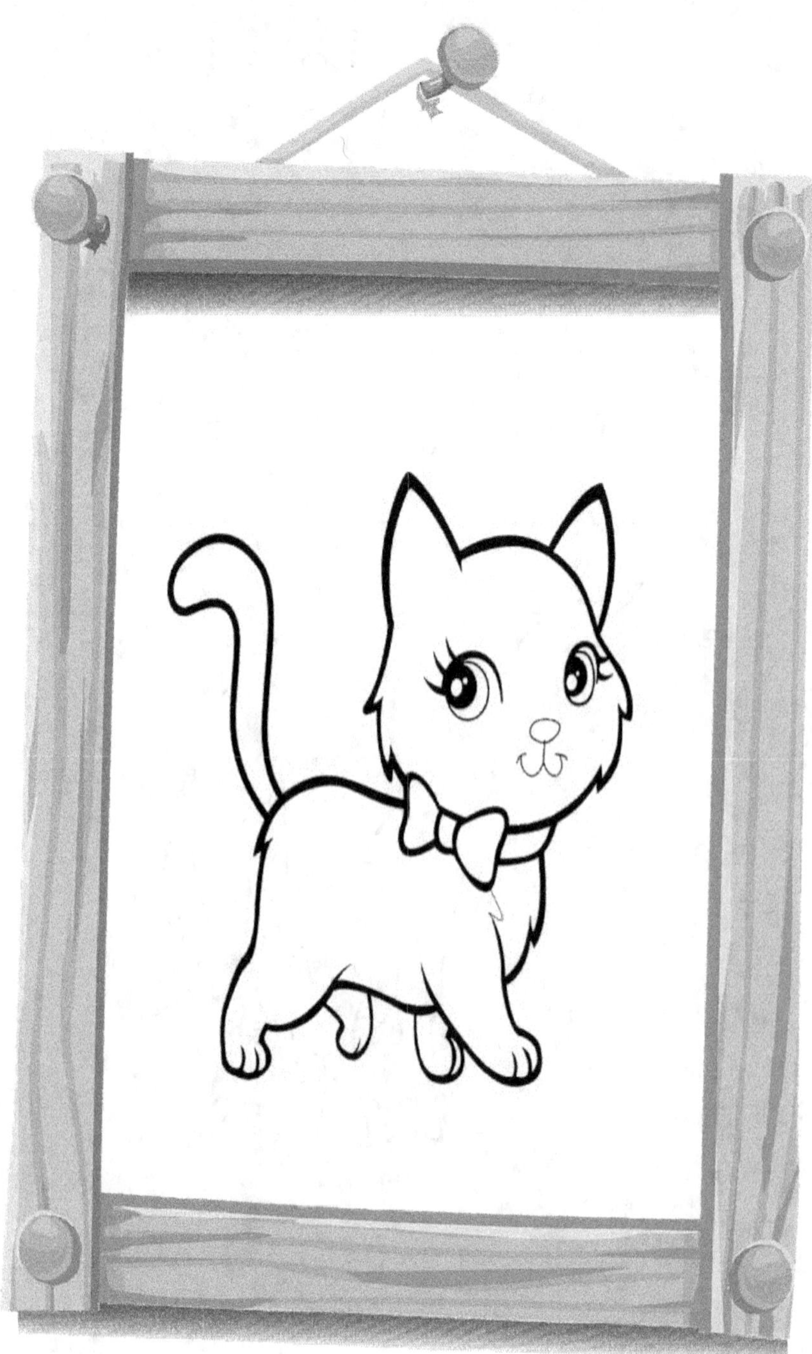

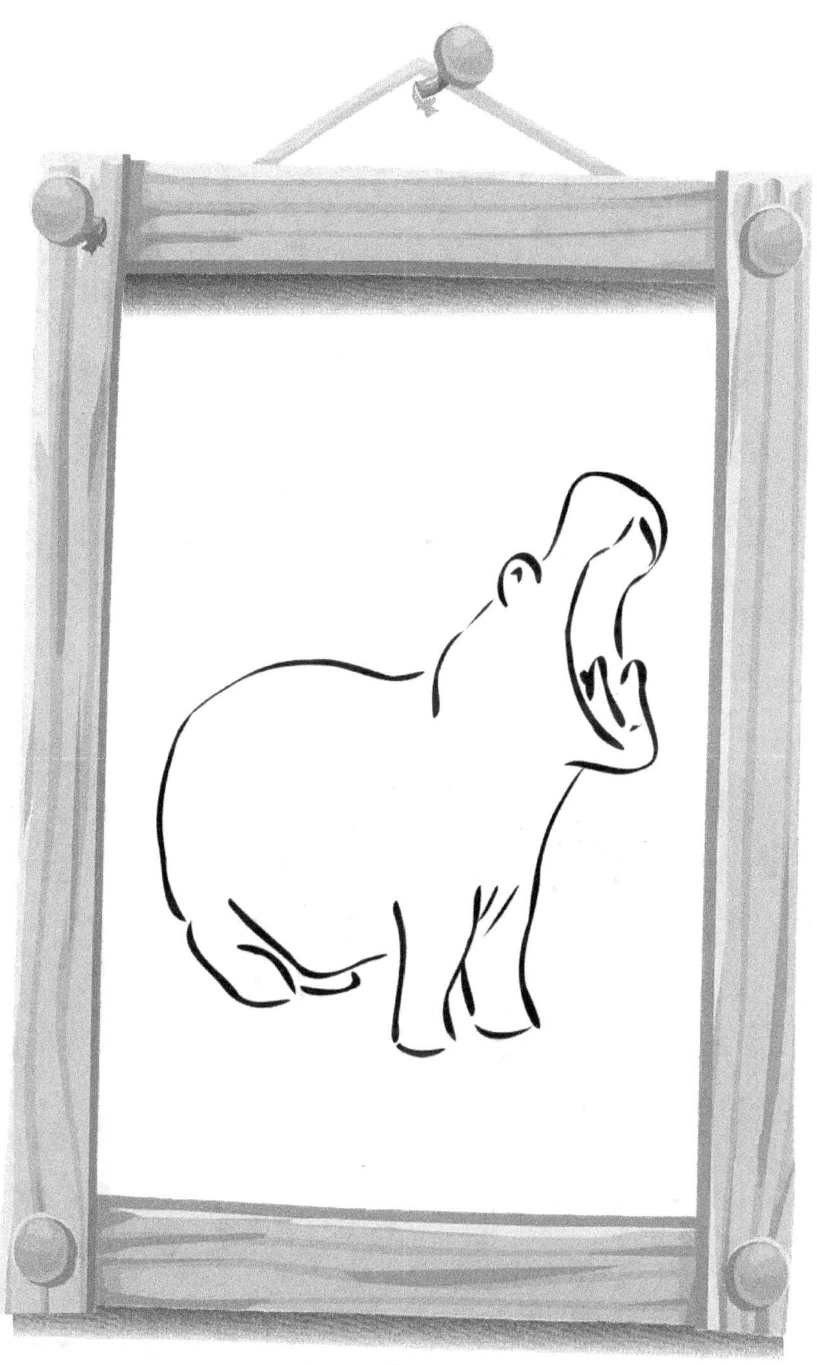

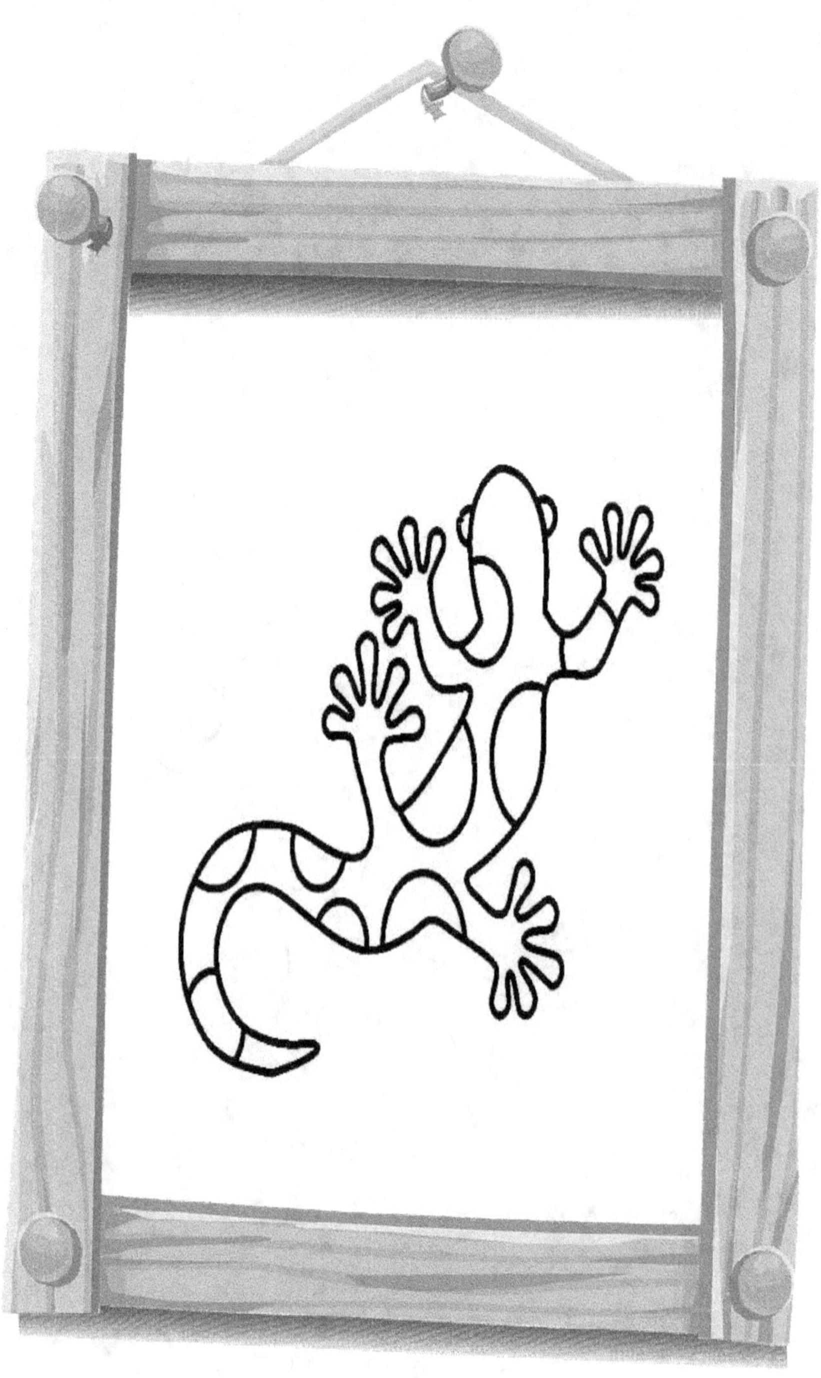

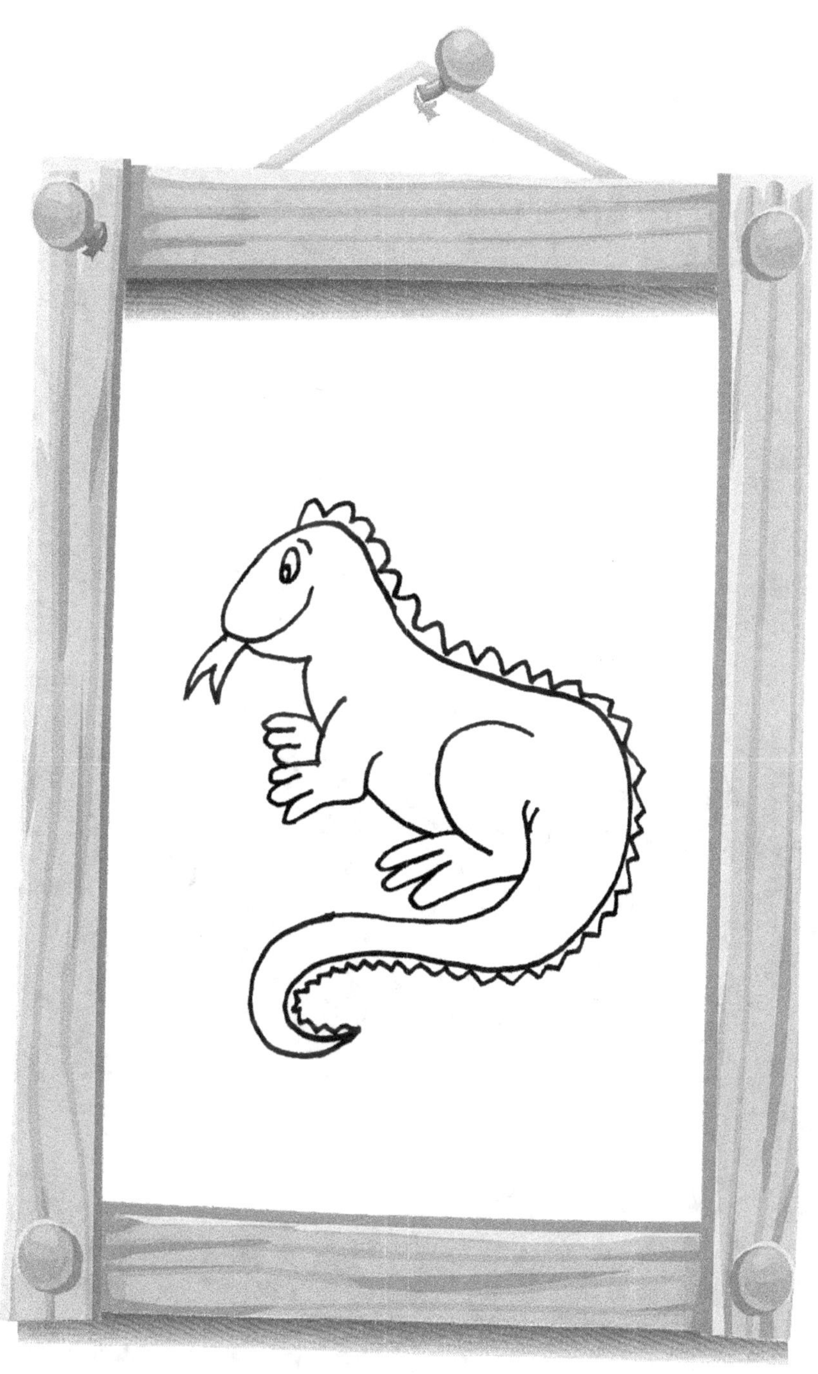

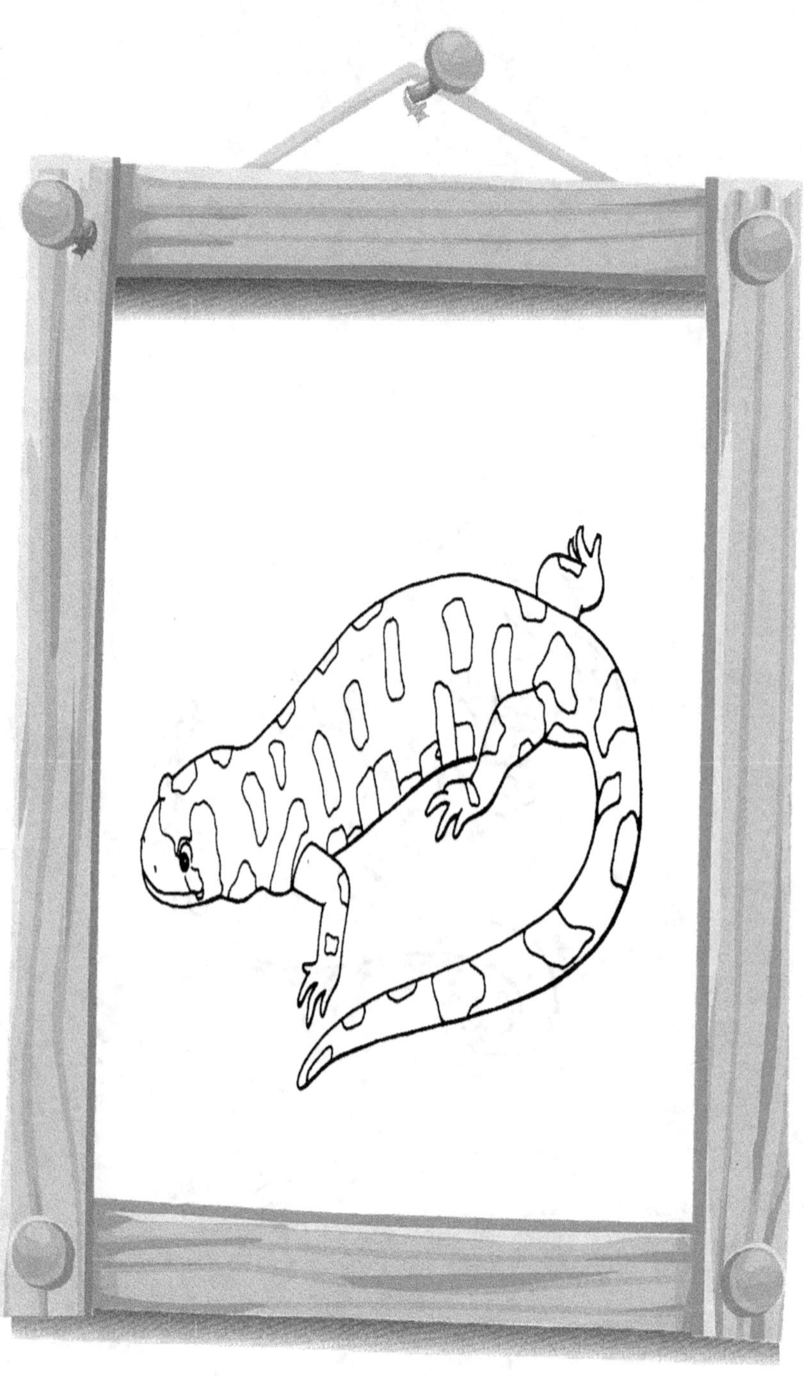

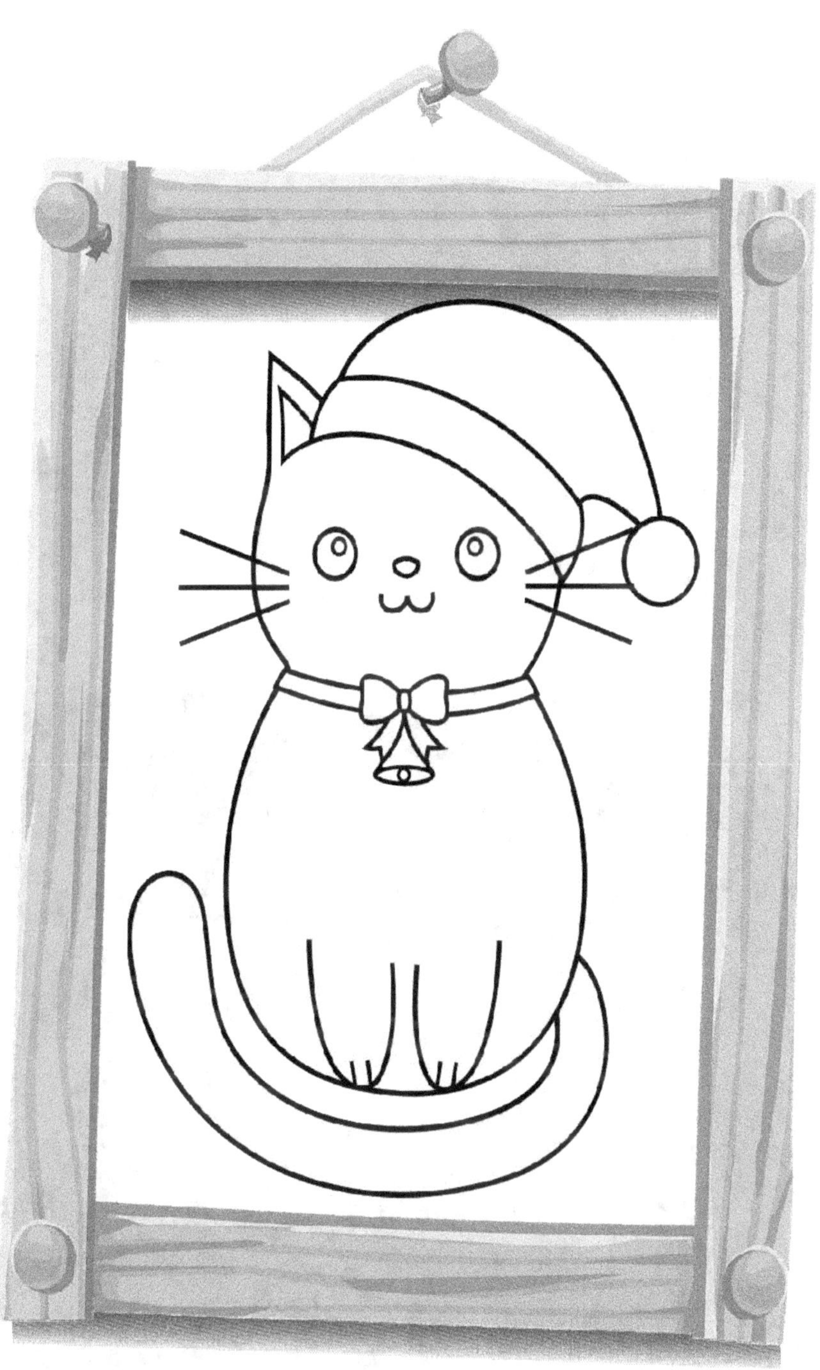

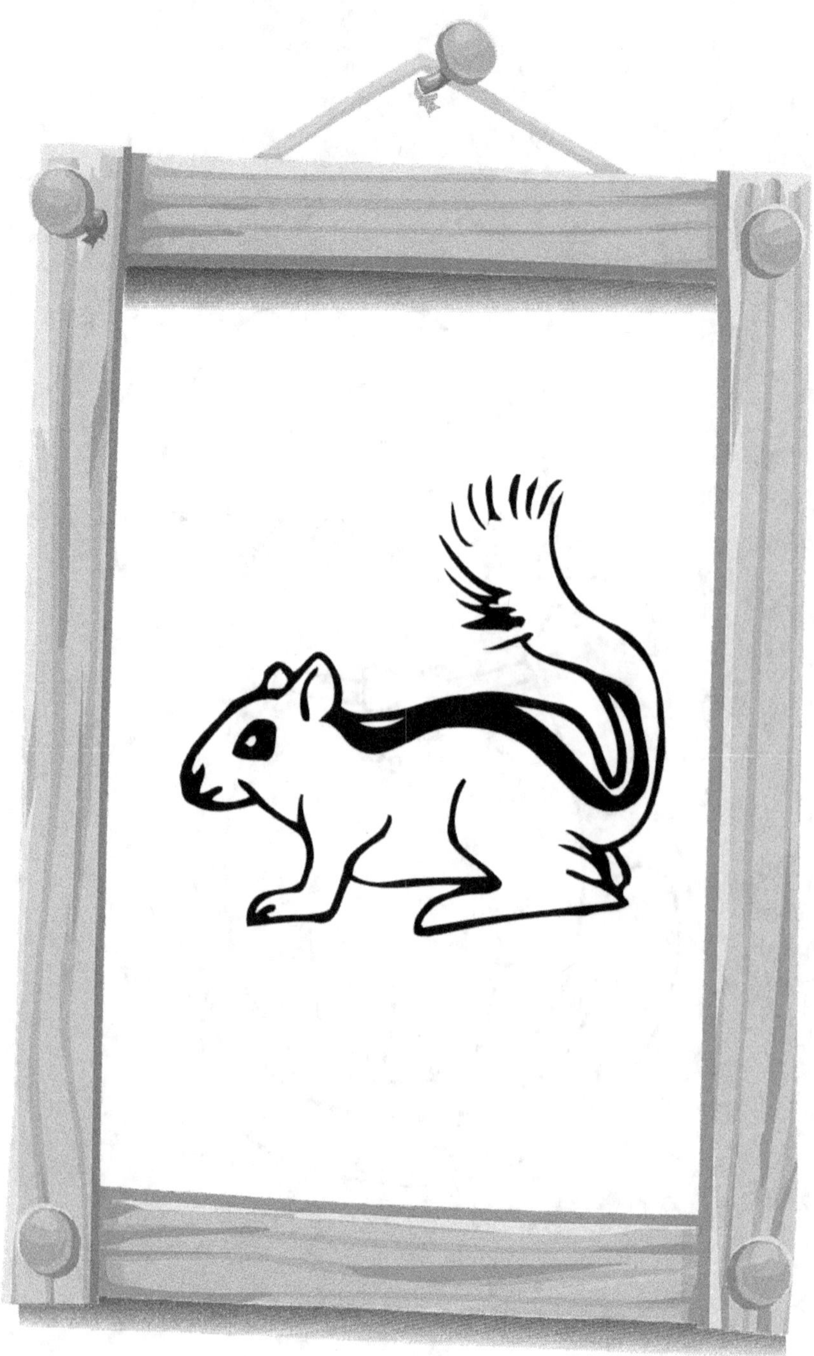

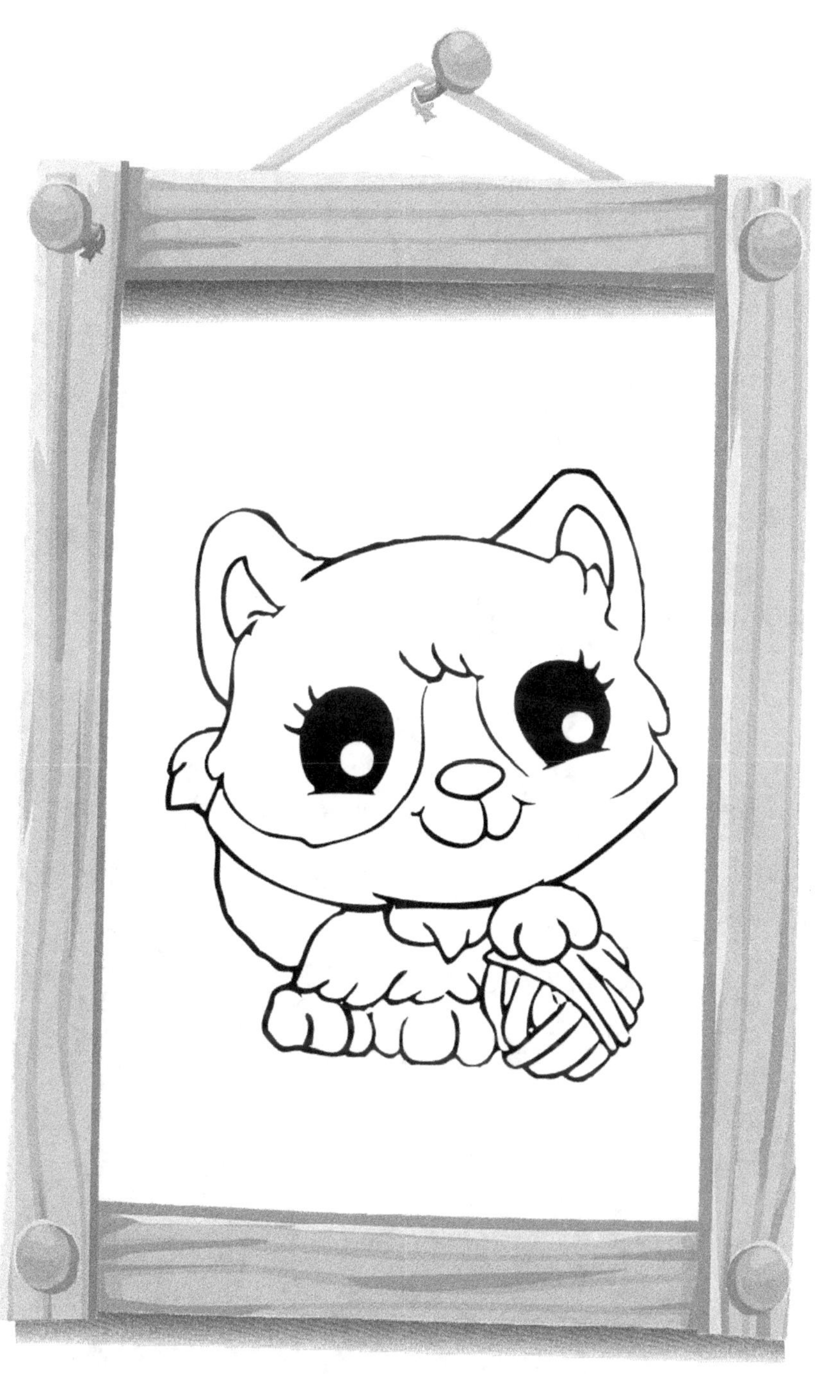

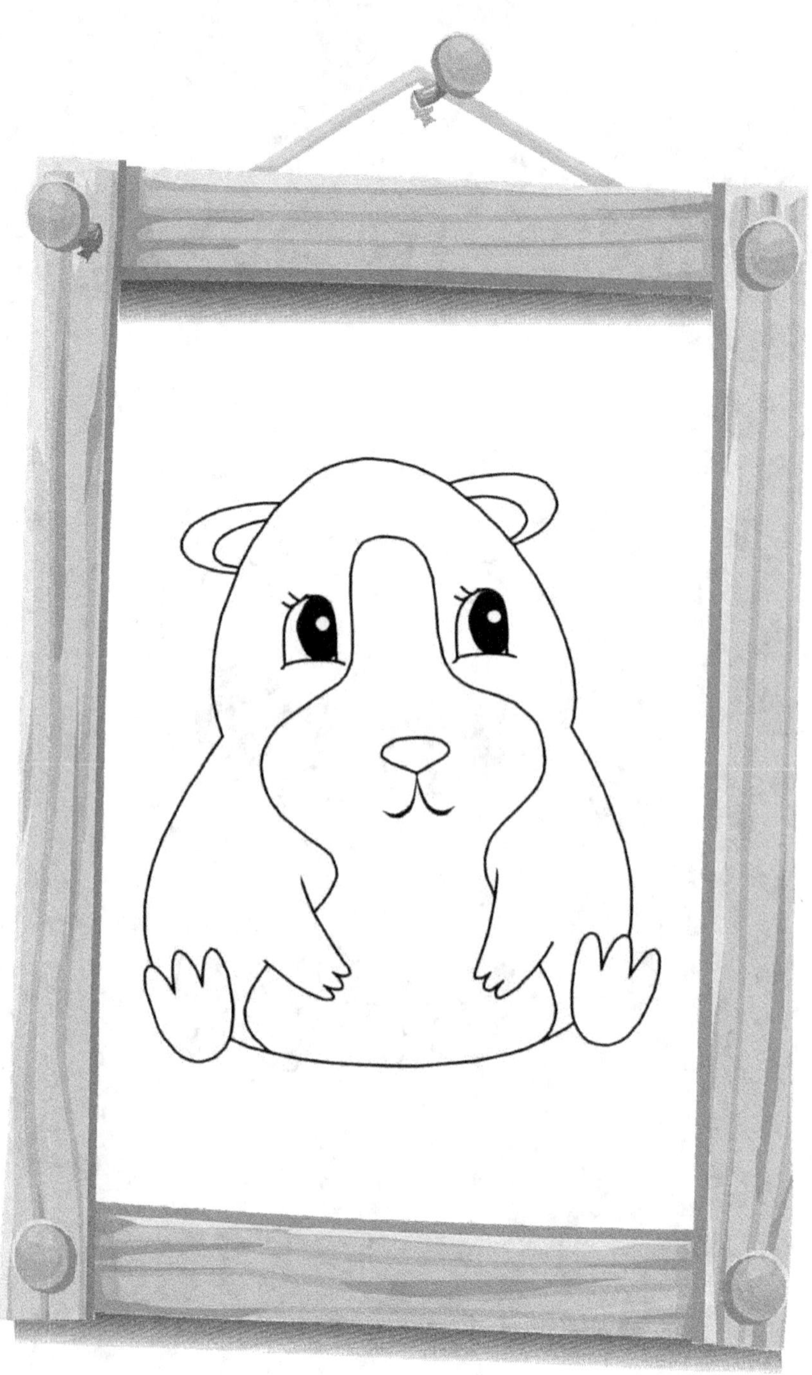

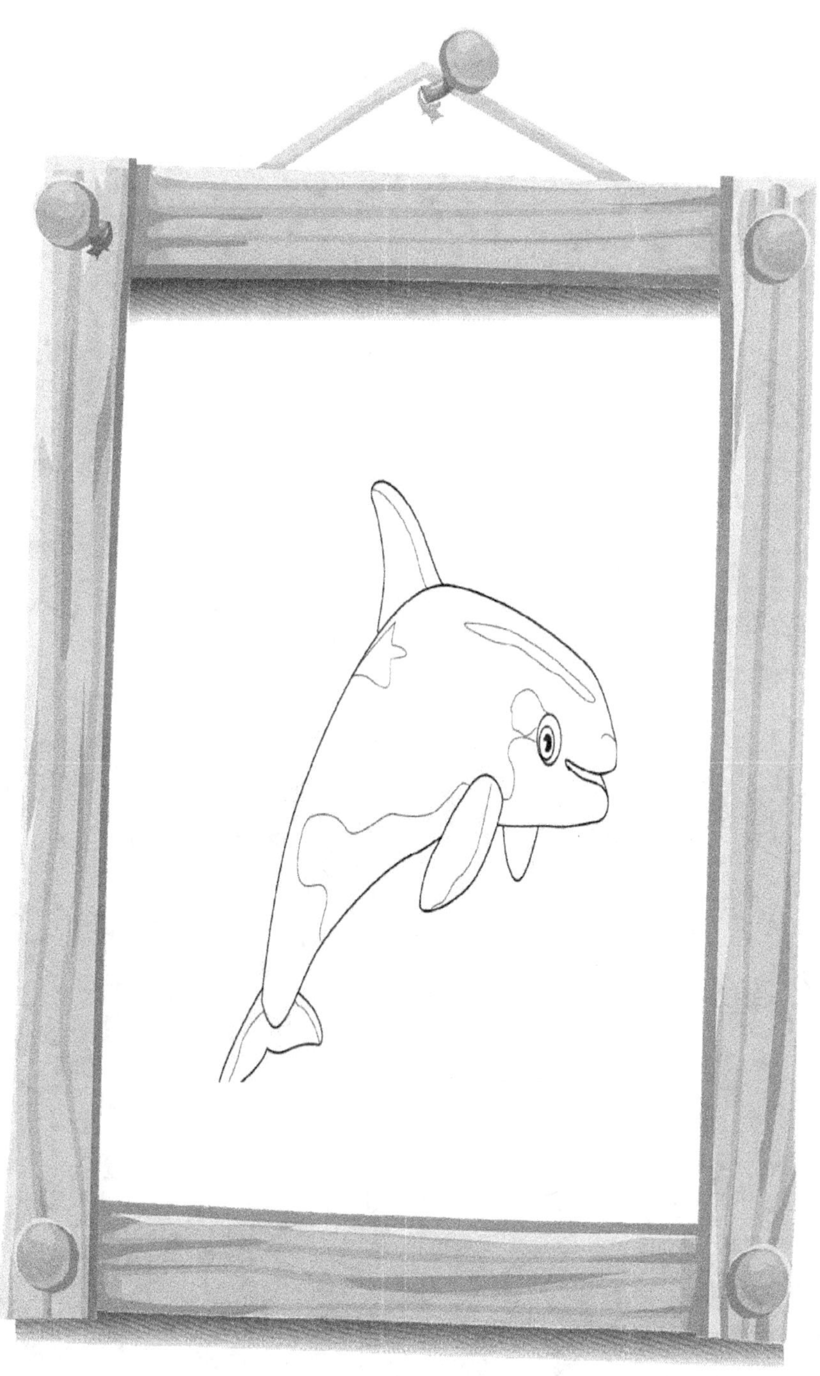

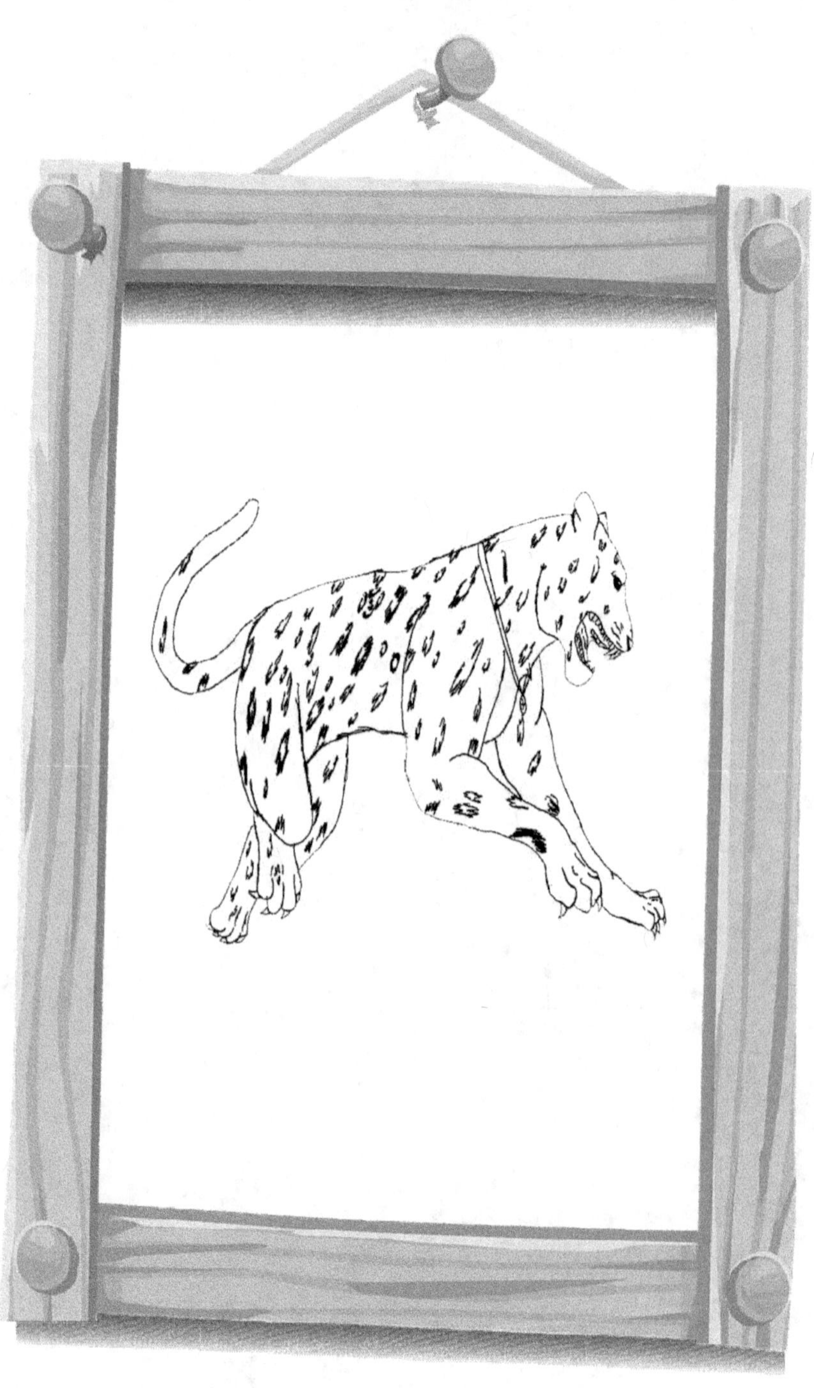

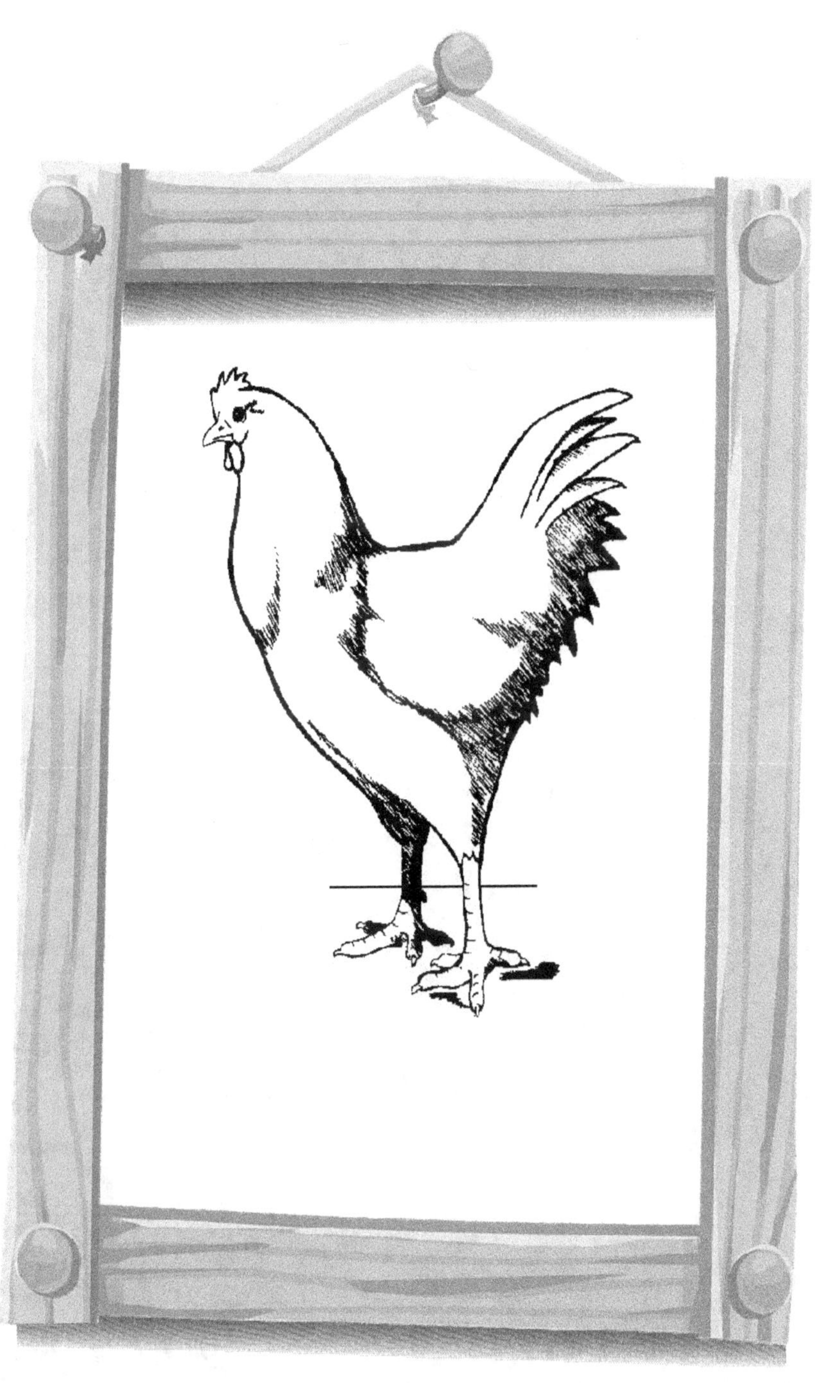

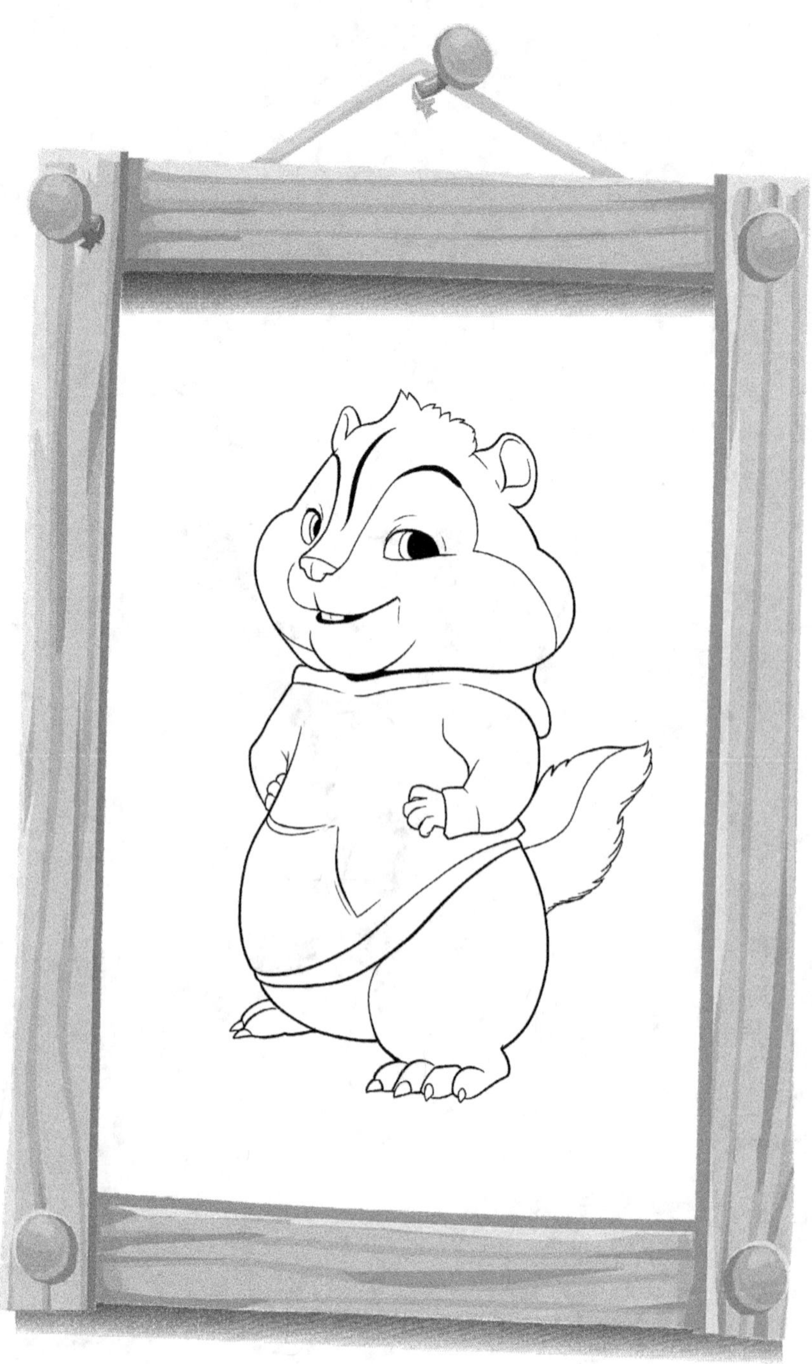

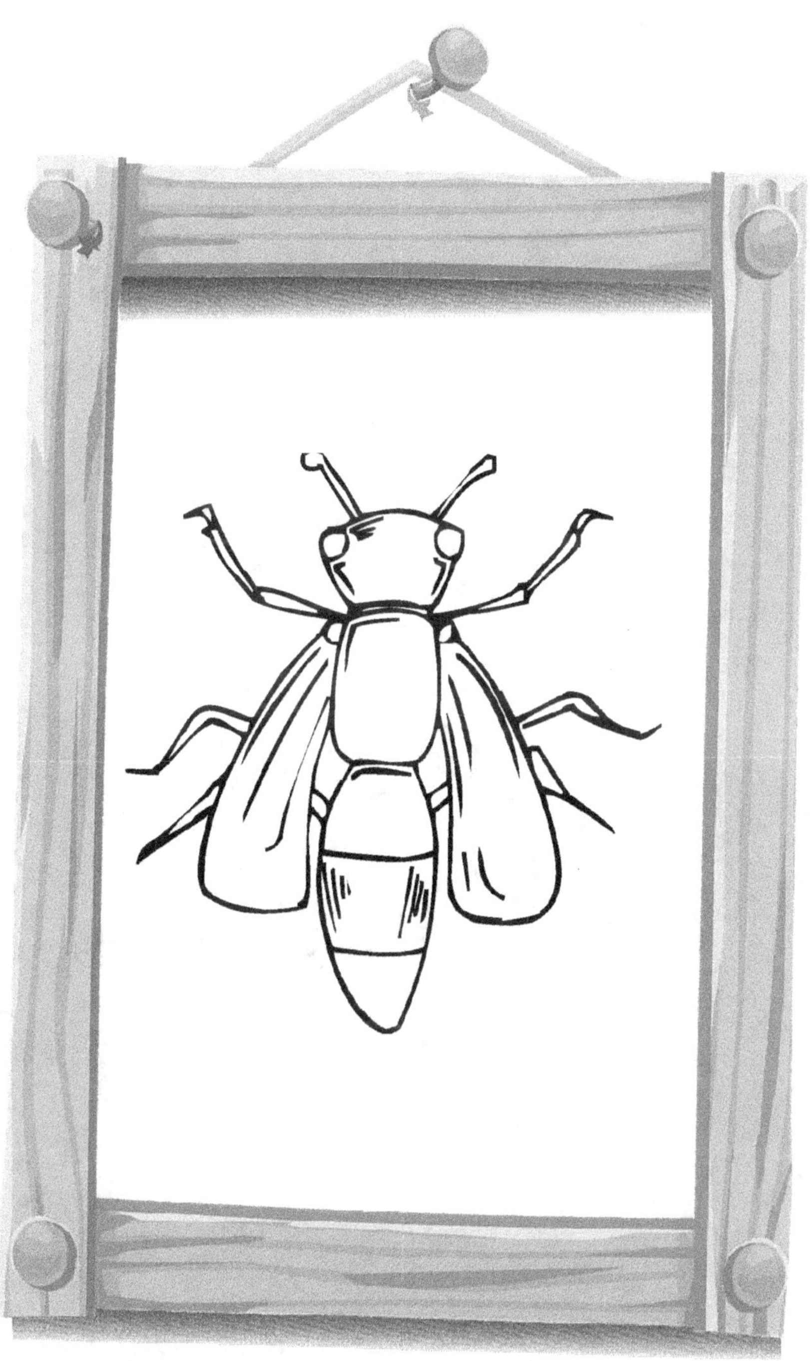

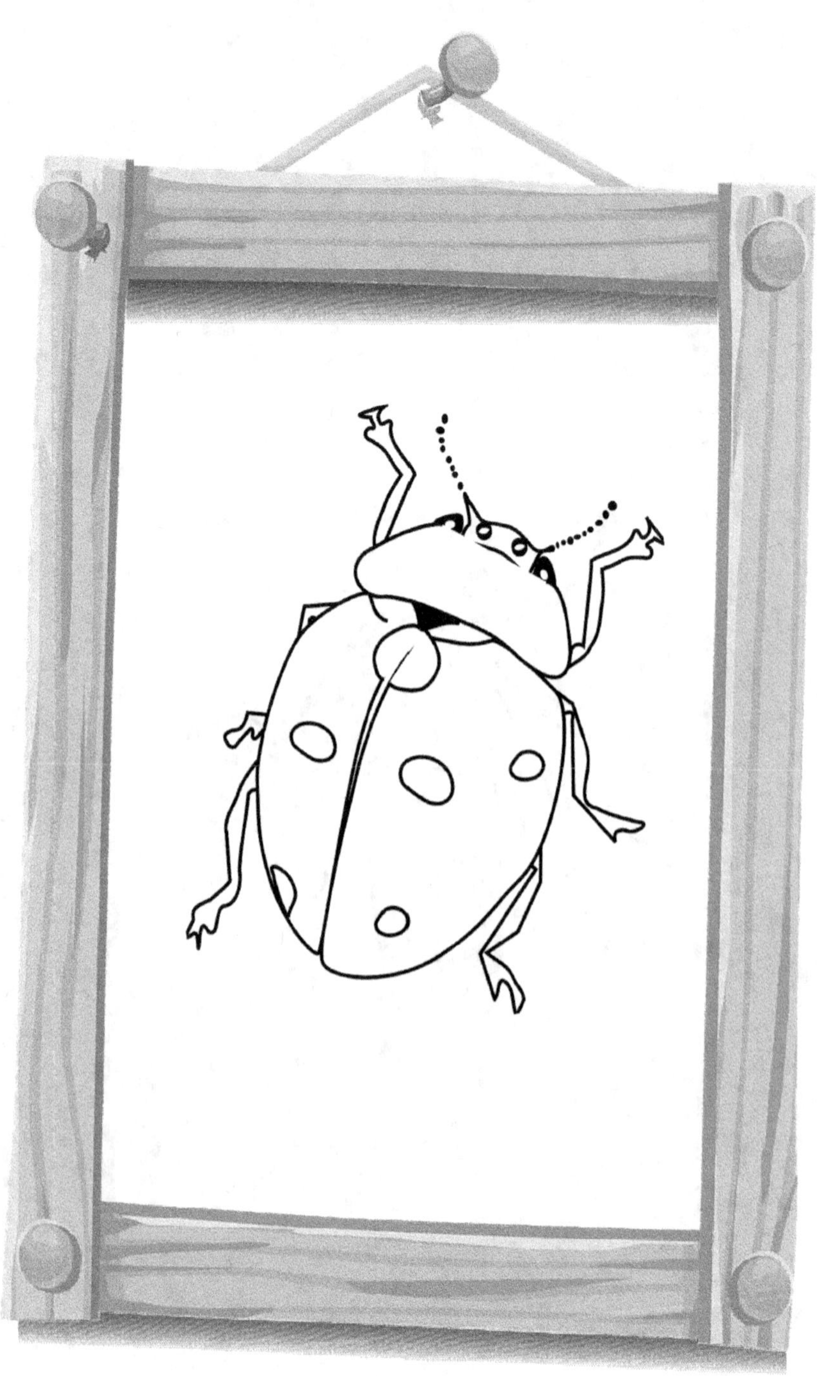

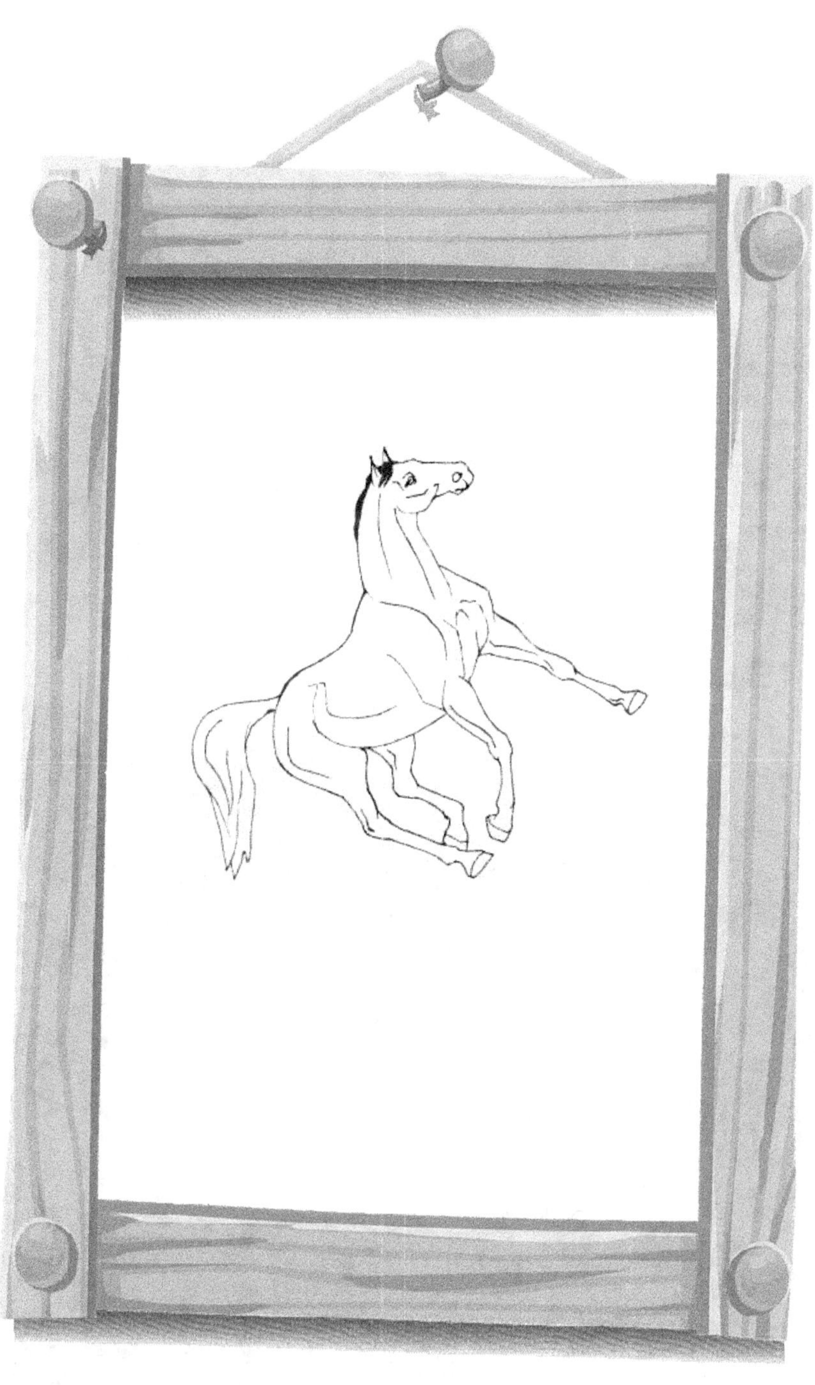

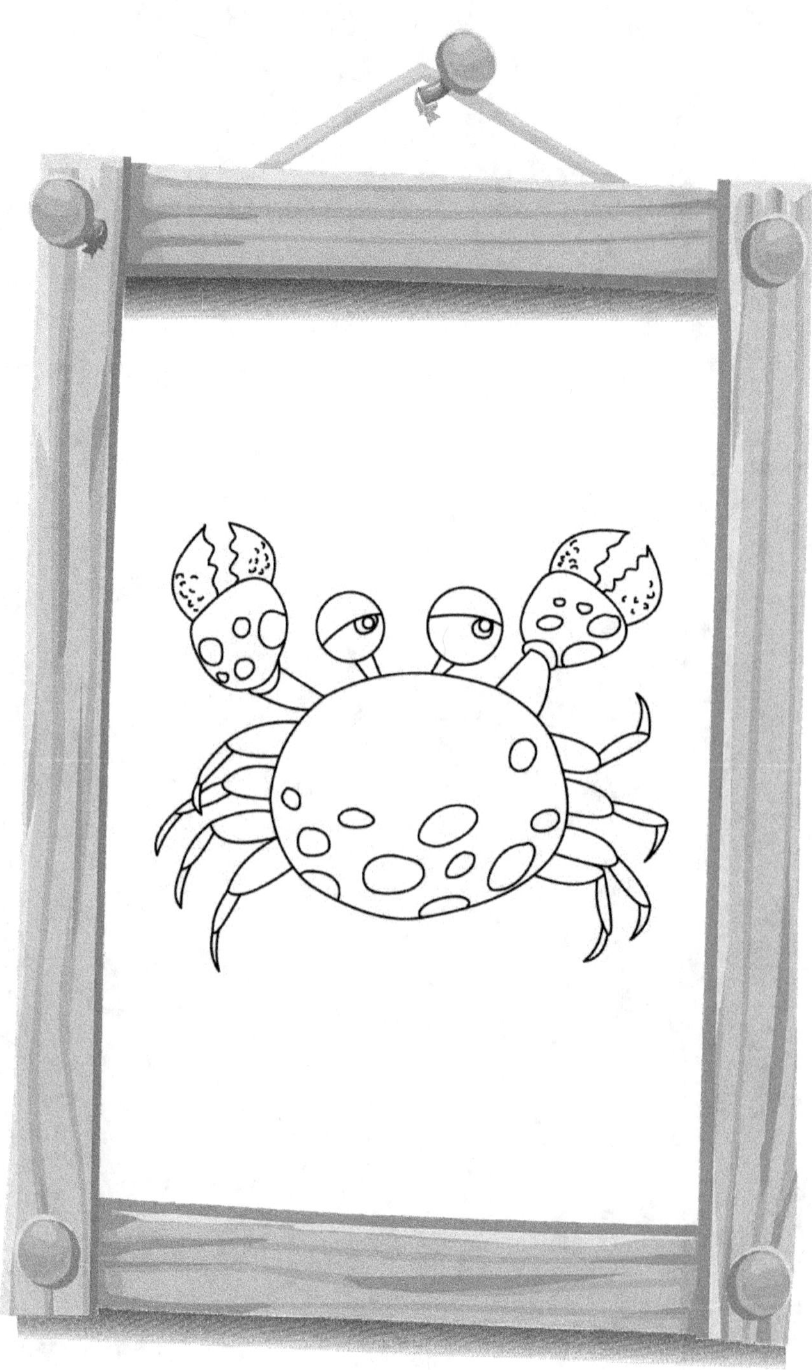

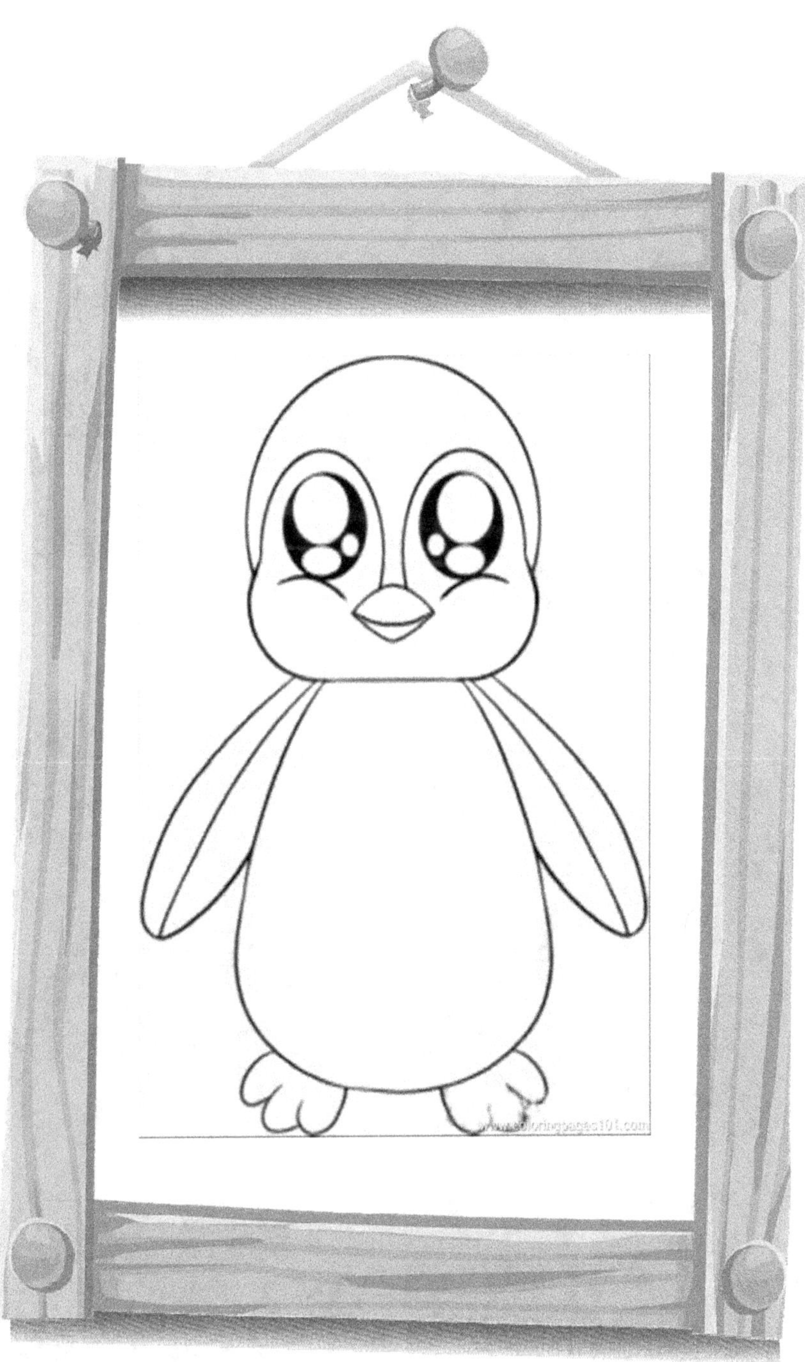
www.coloringpages101.com

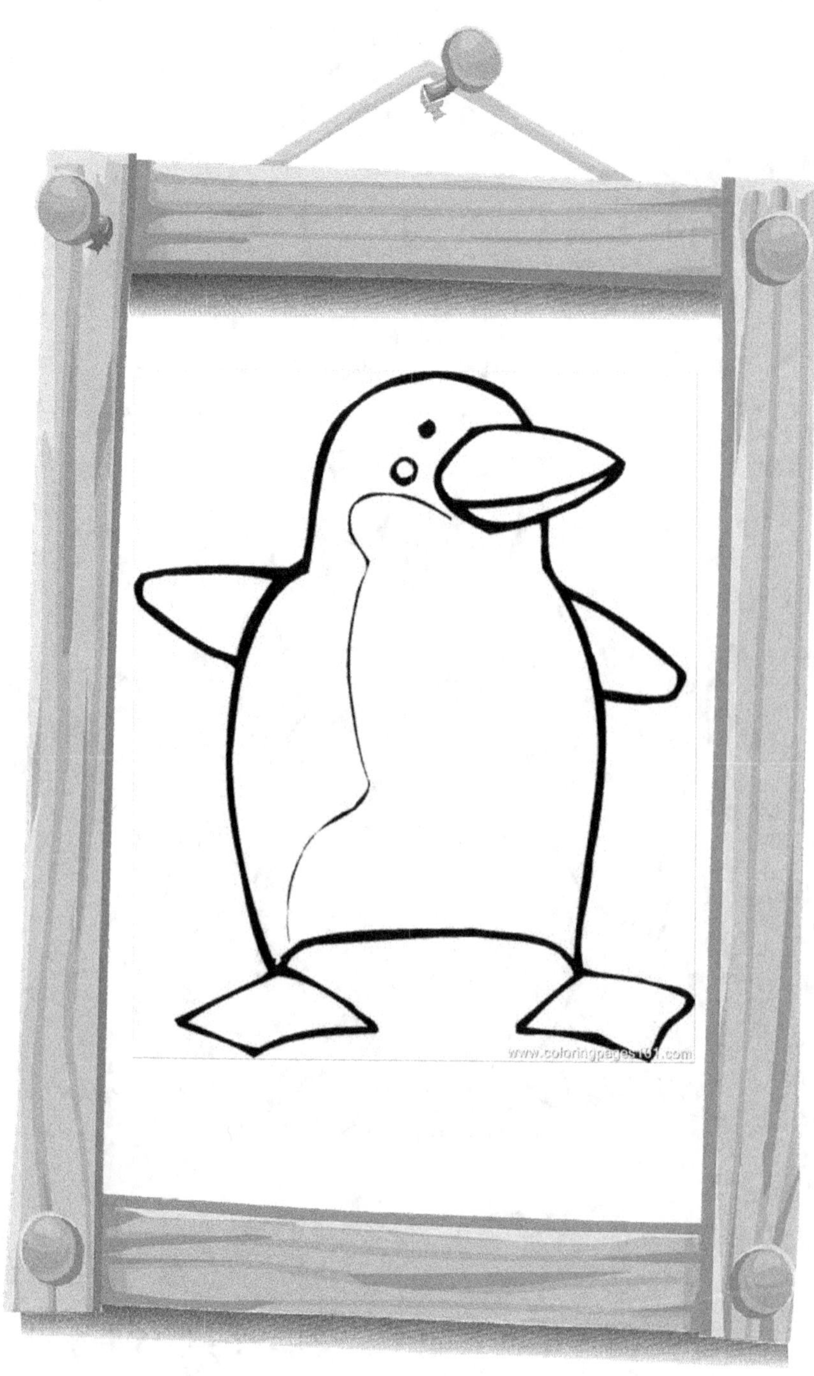
www.coloringpages101.com

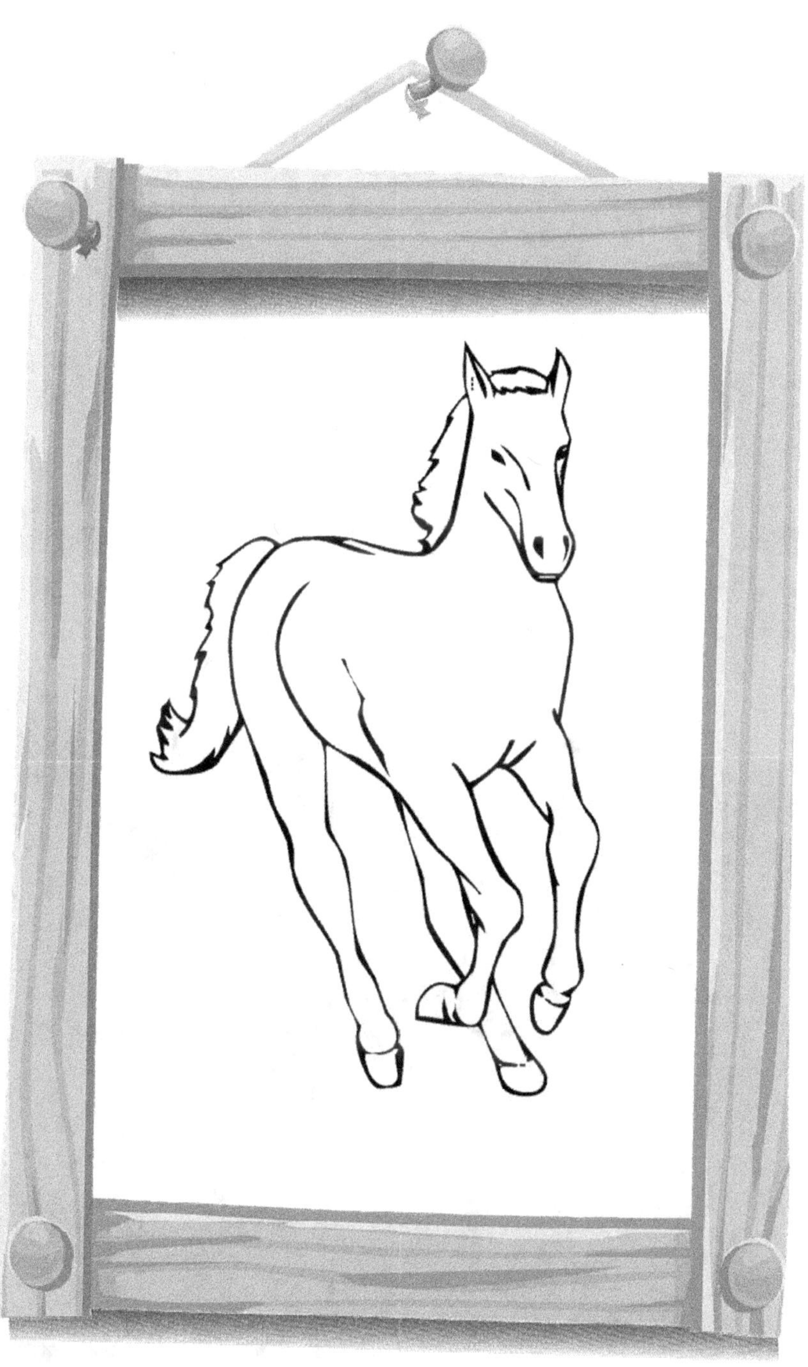

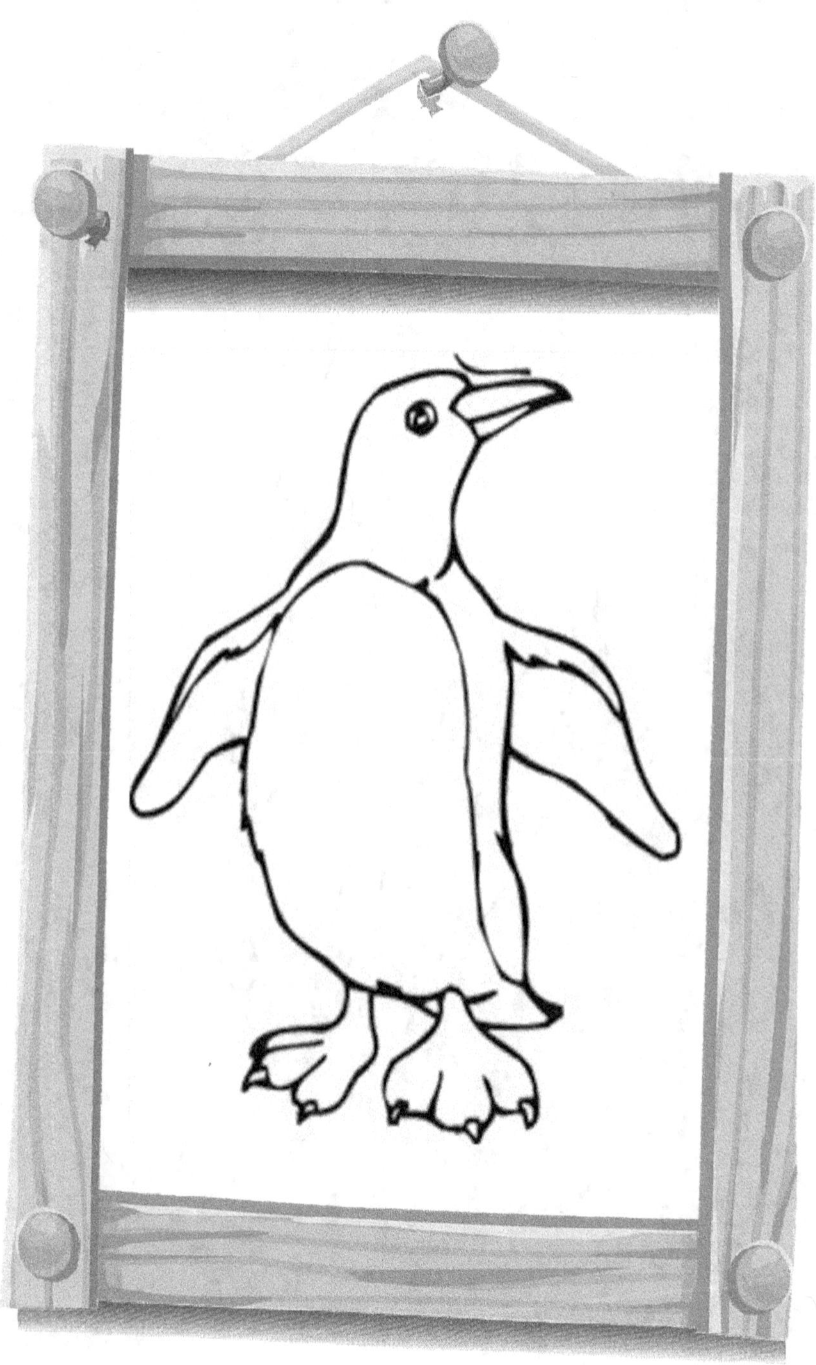

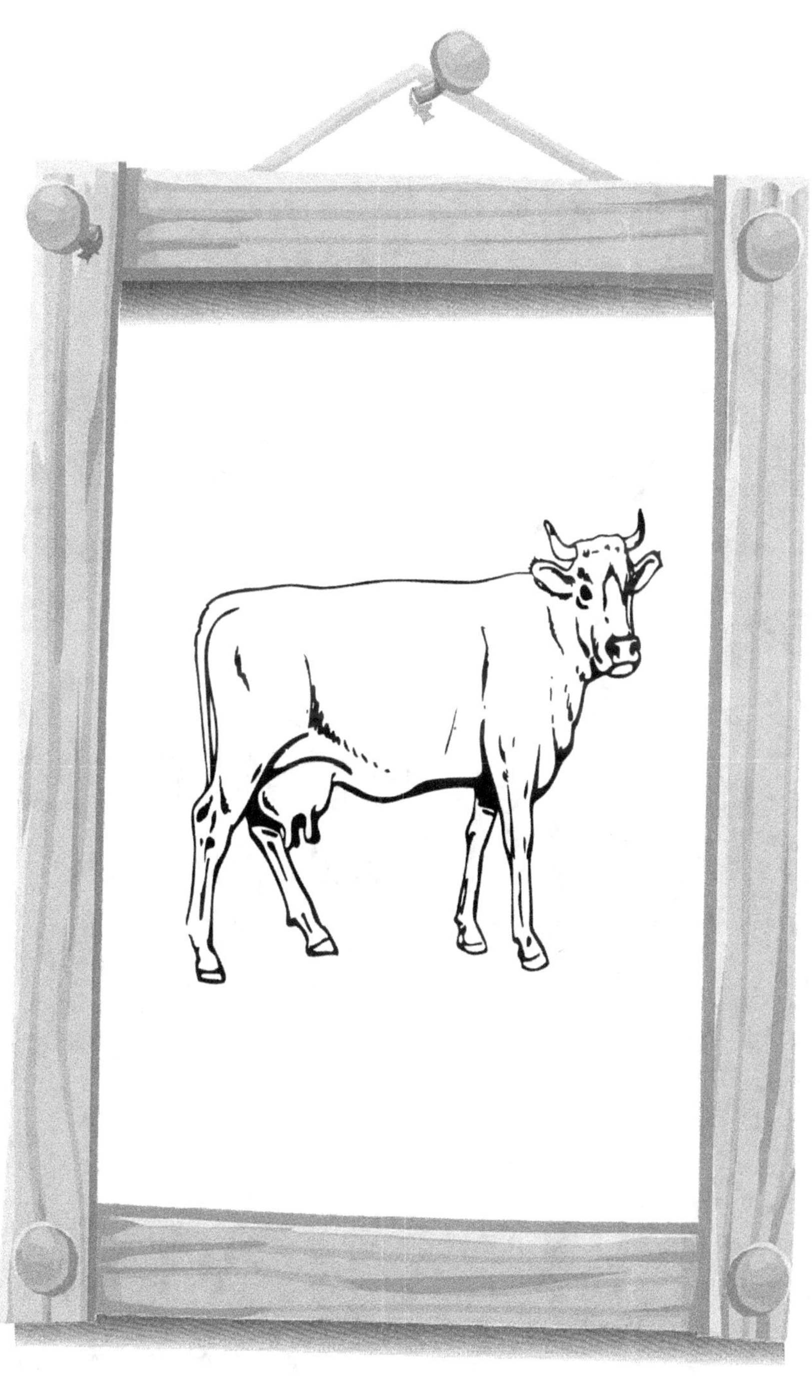

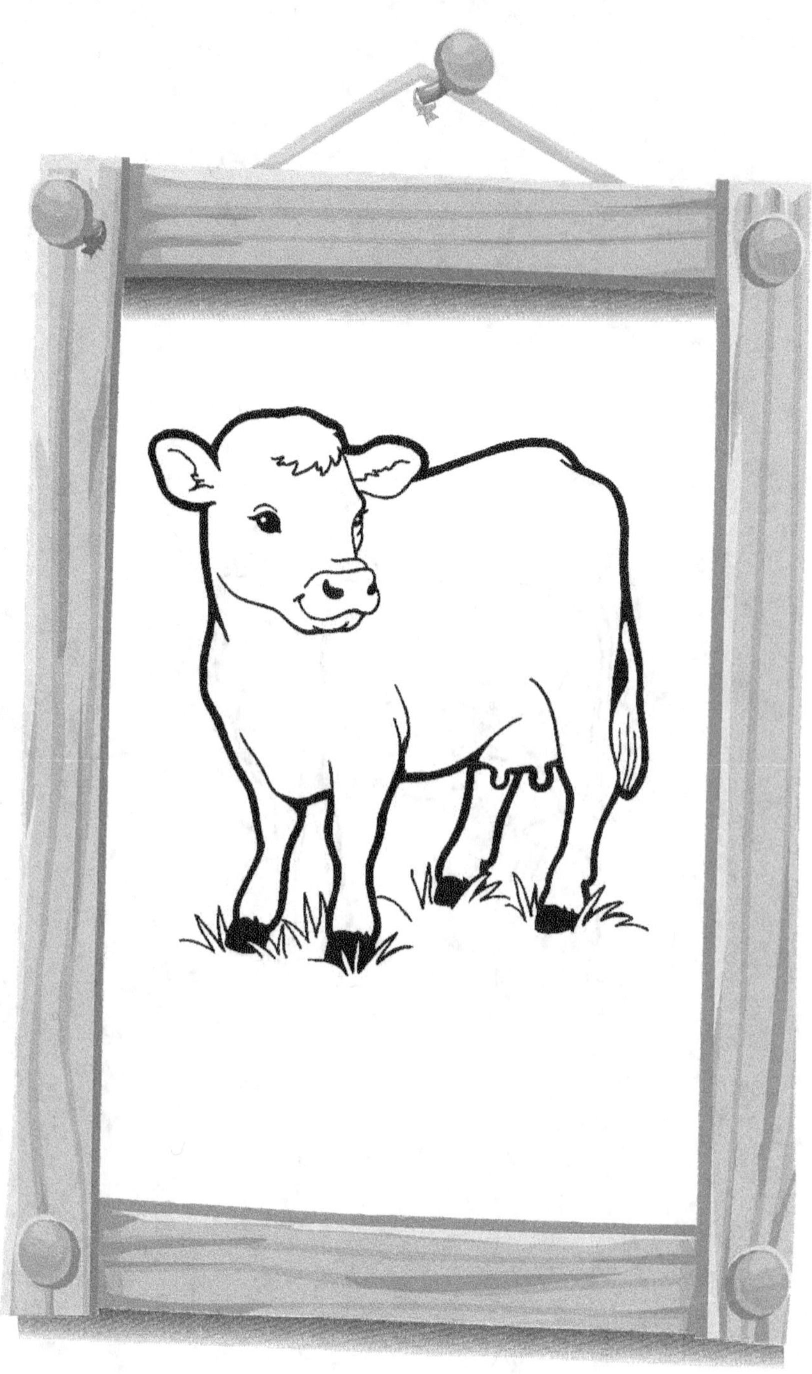

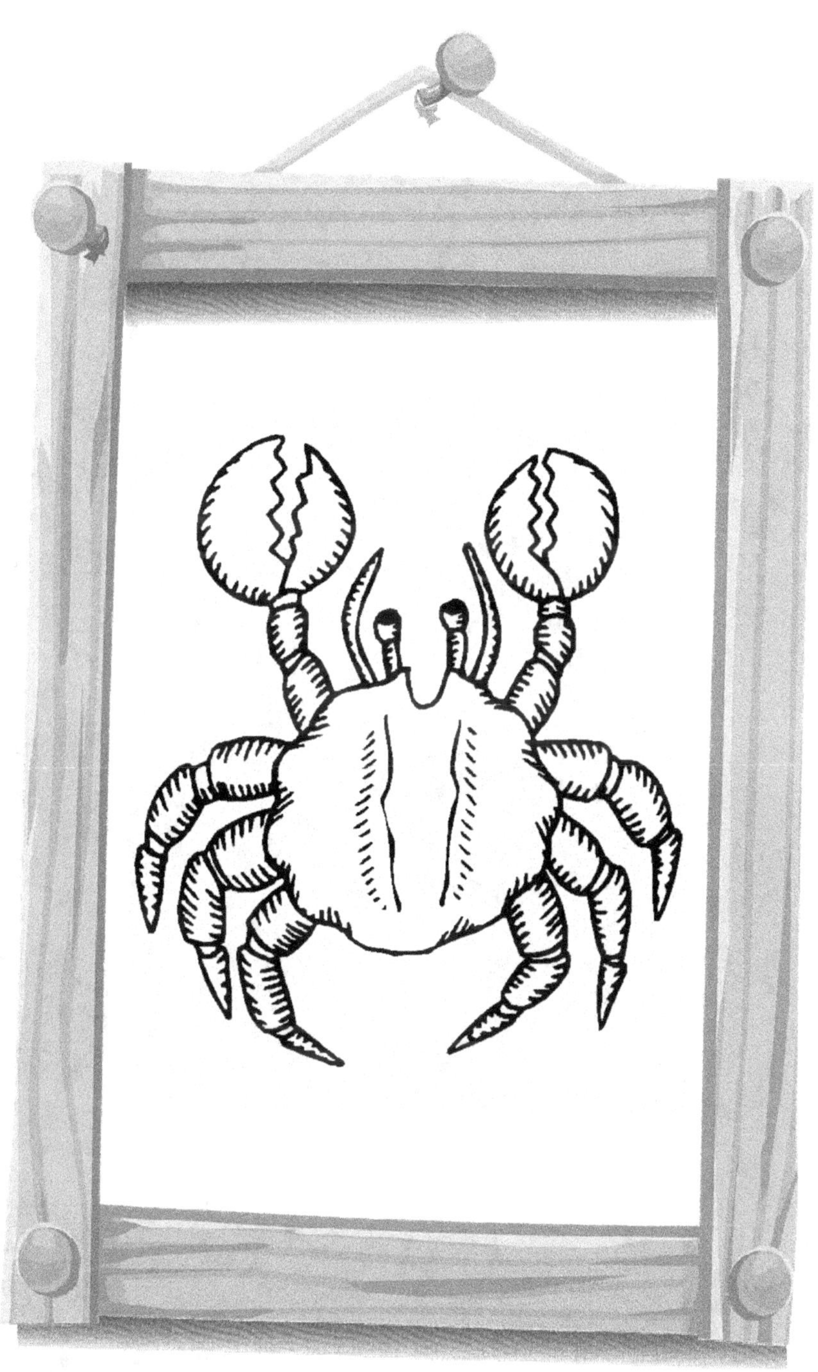

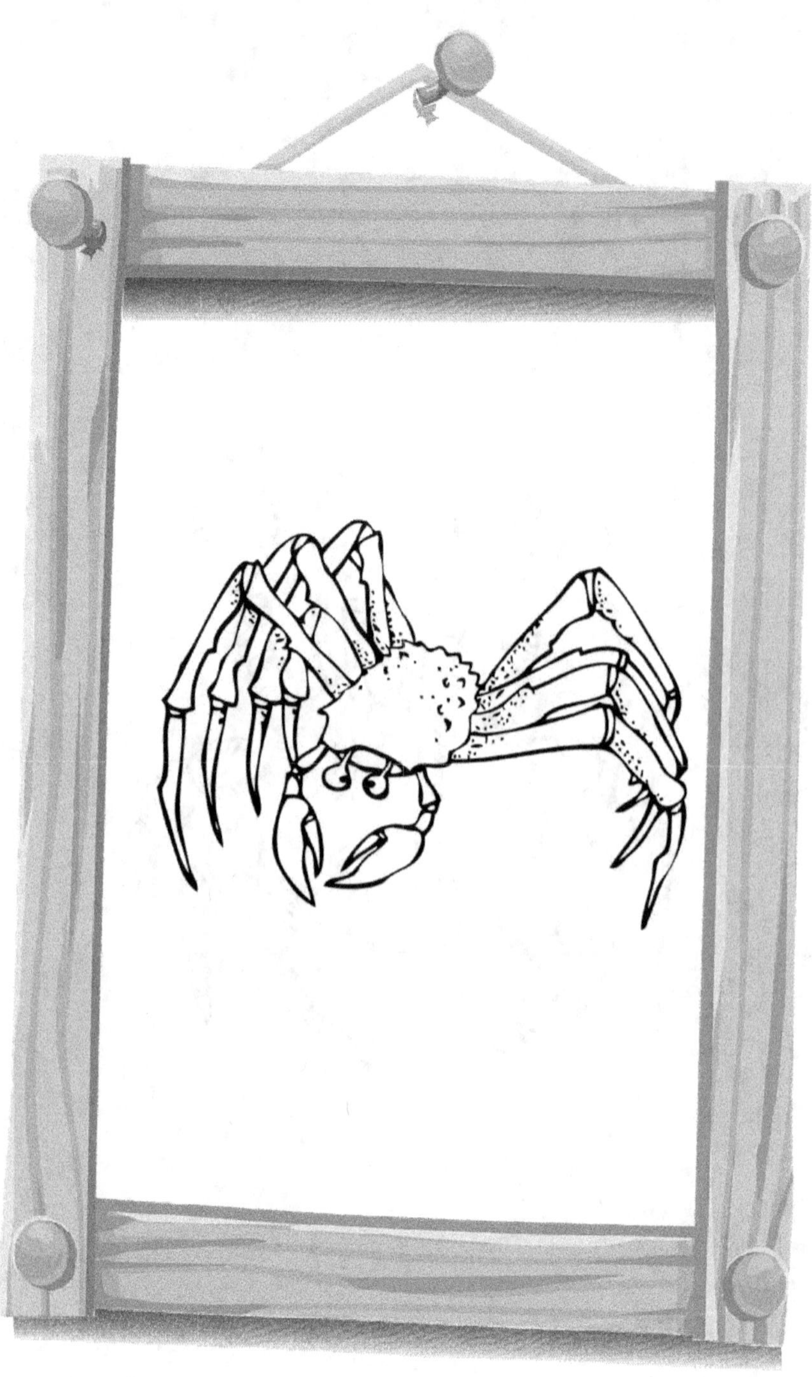

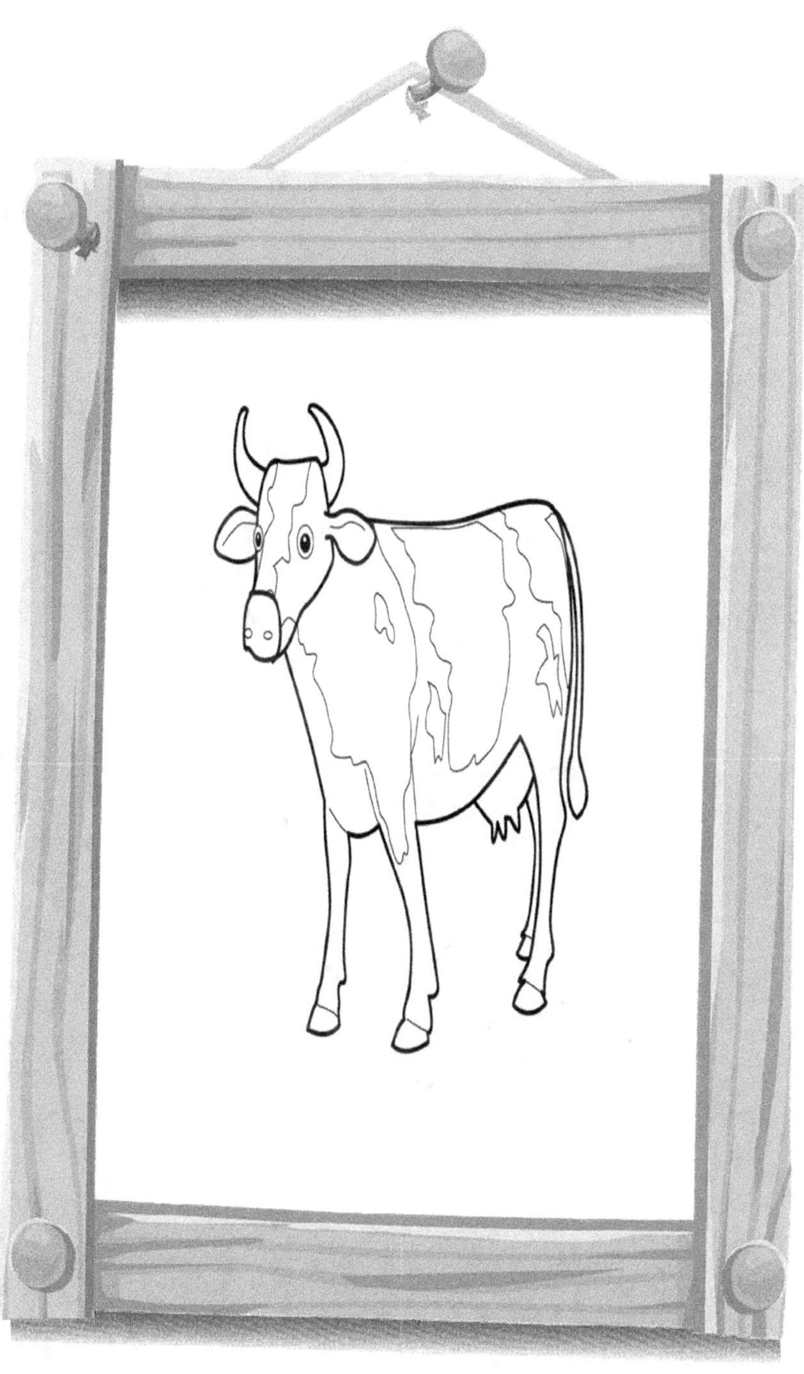

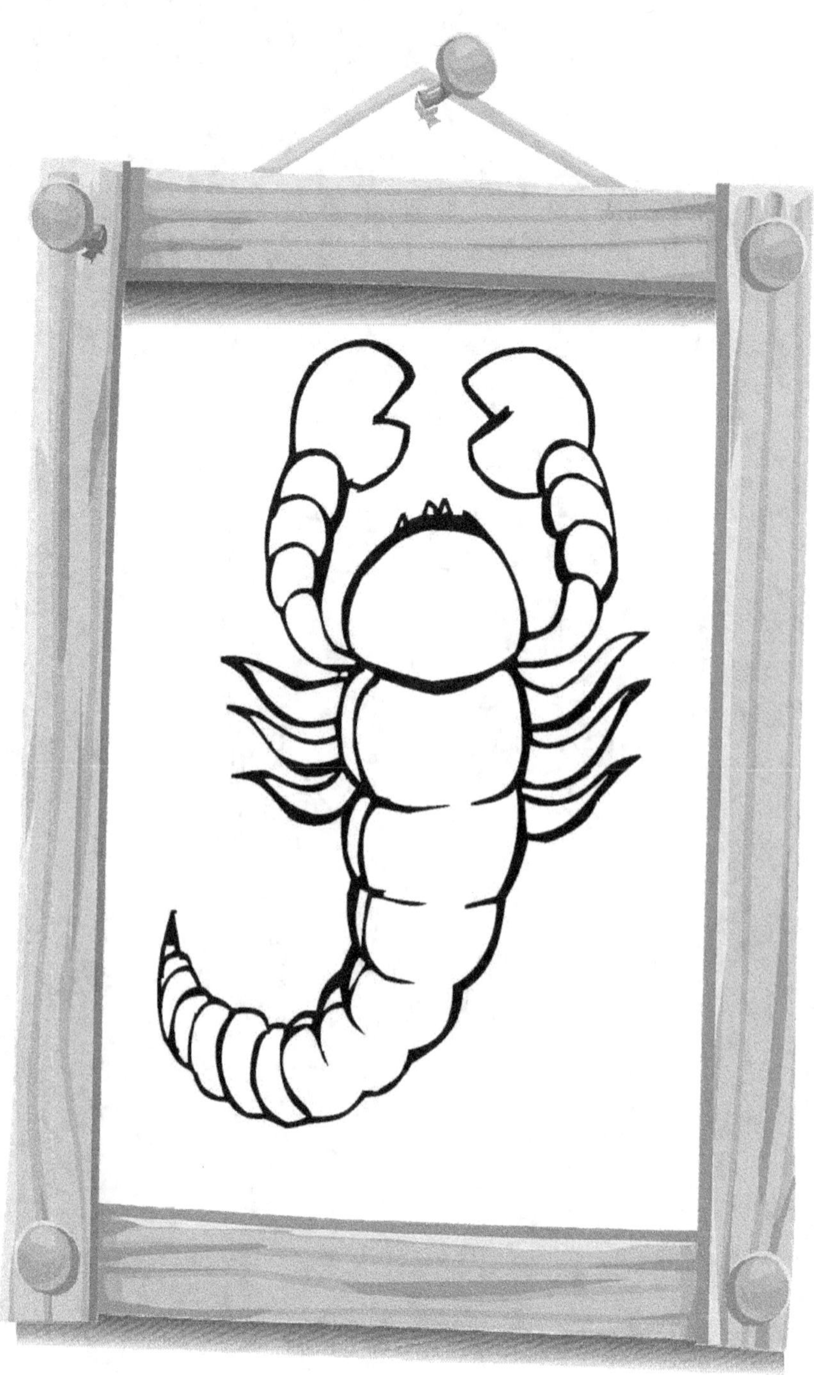

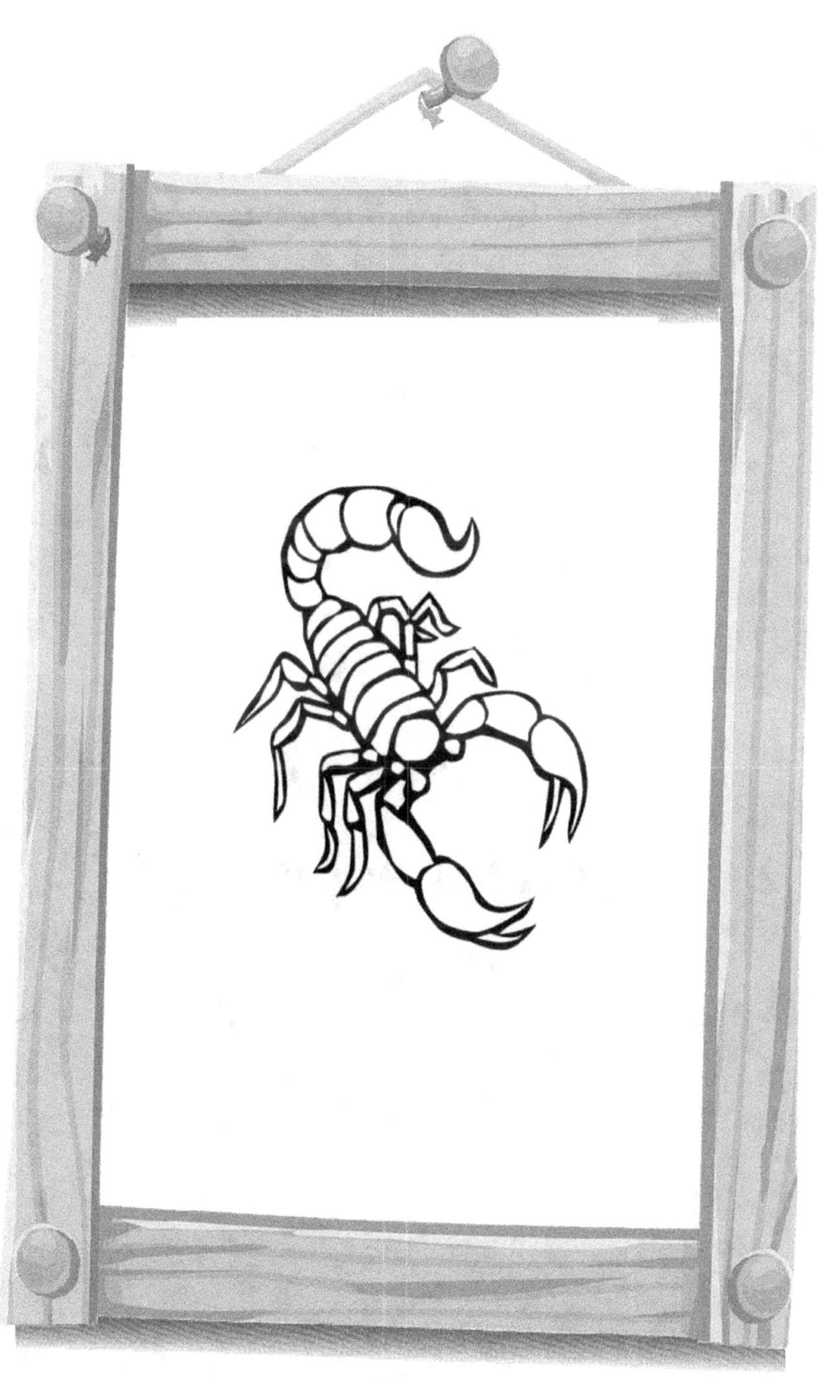

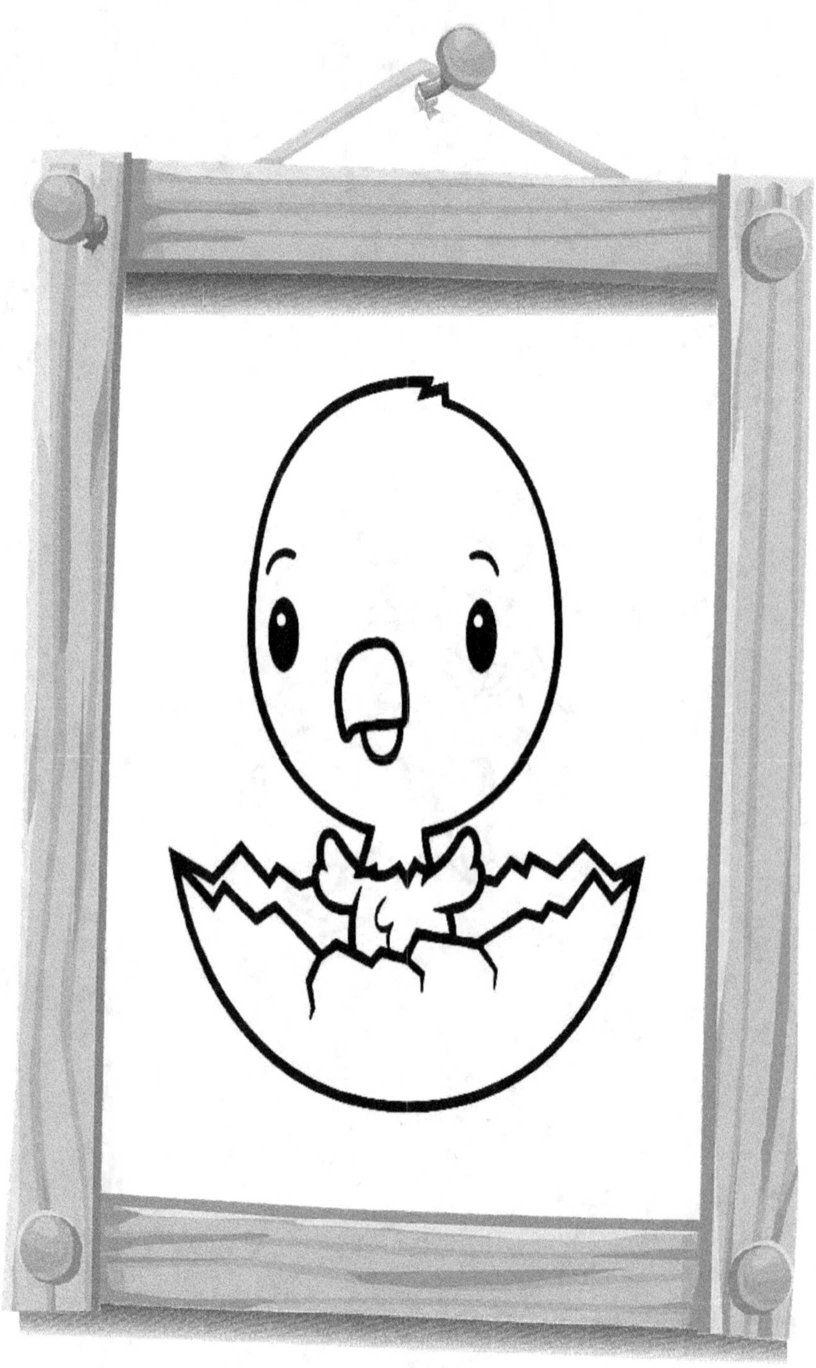

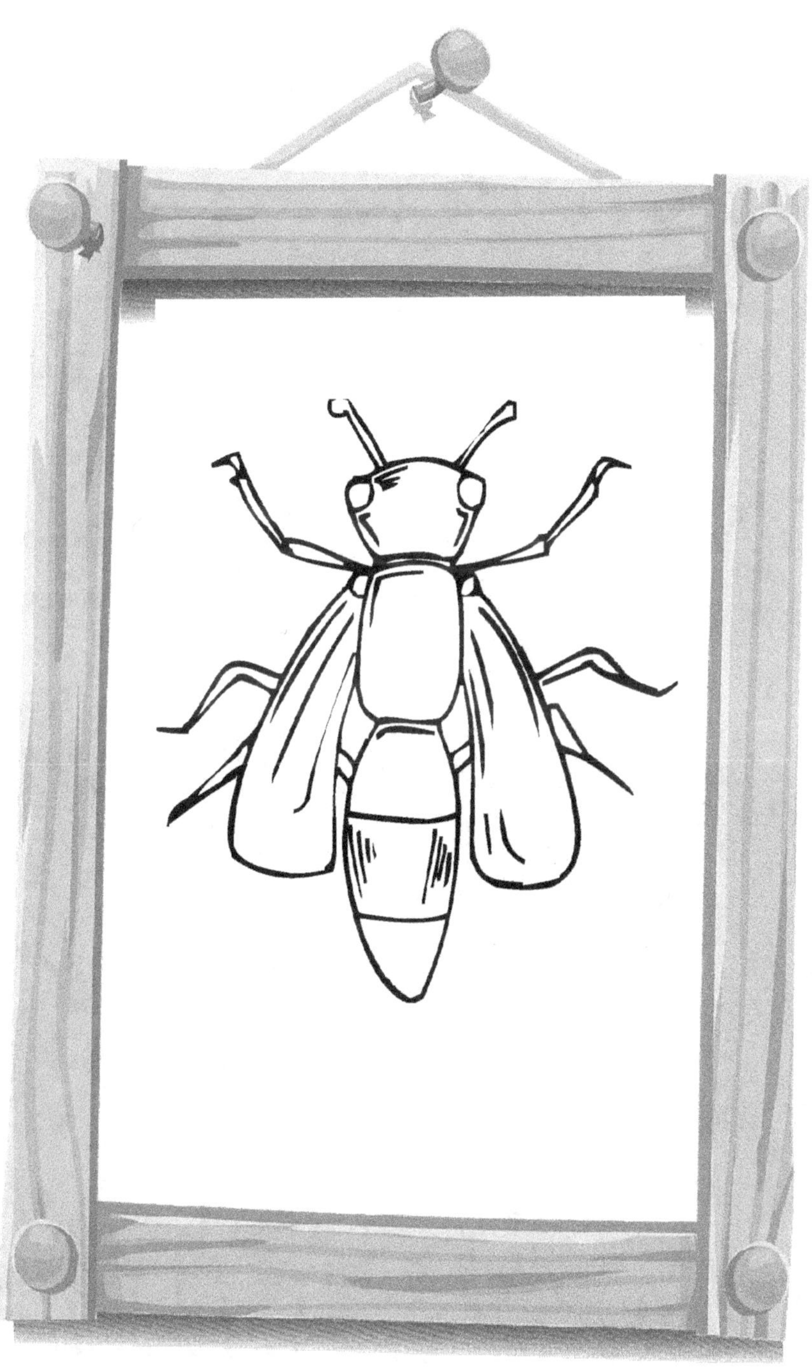

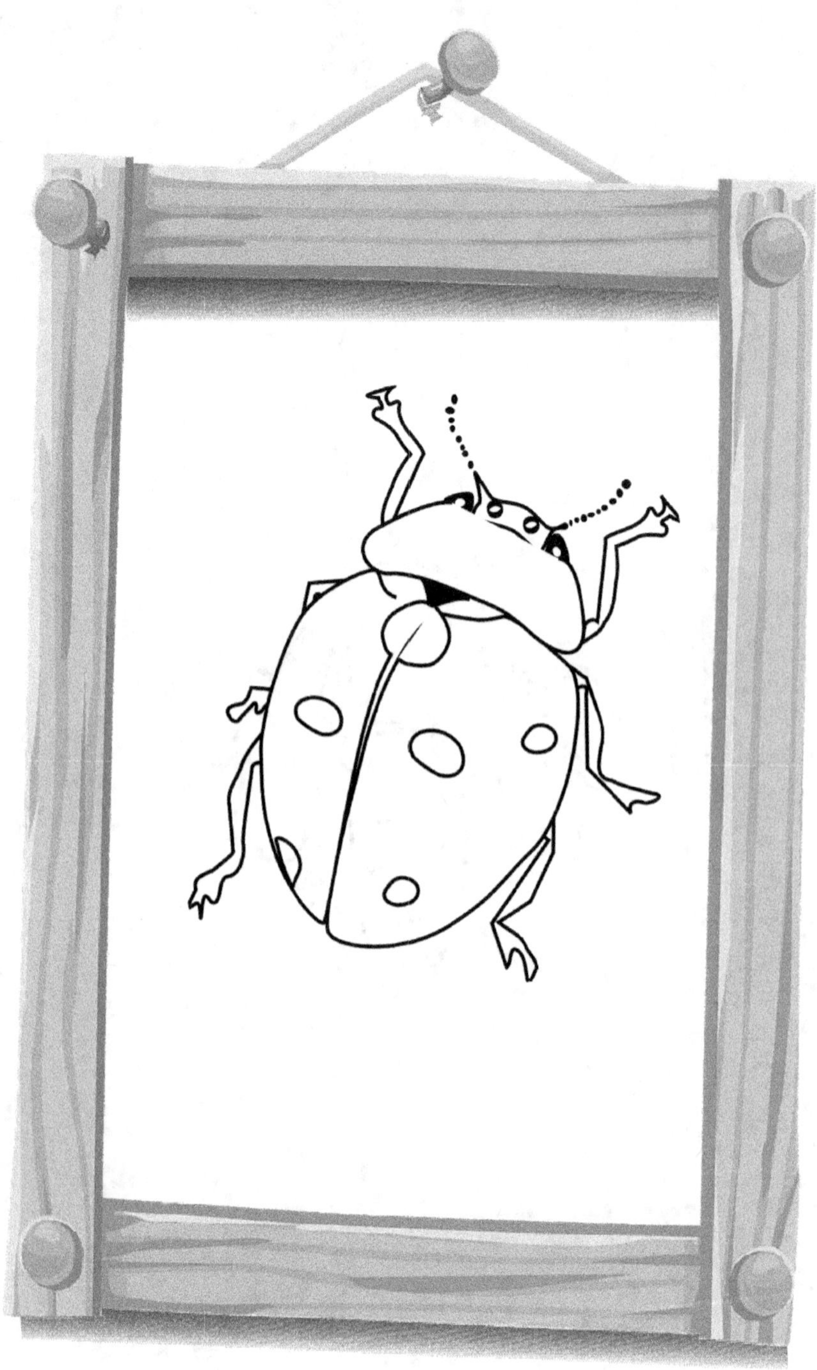

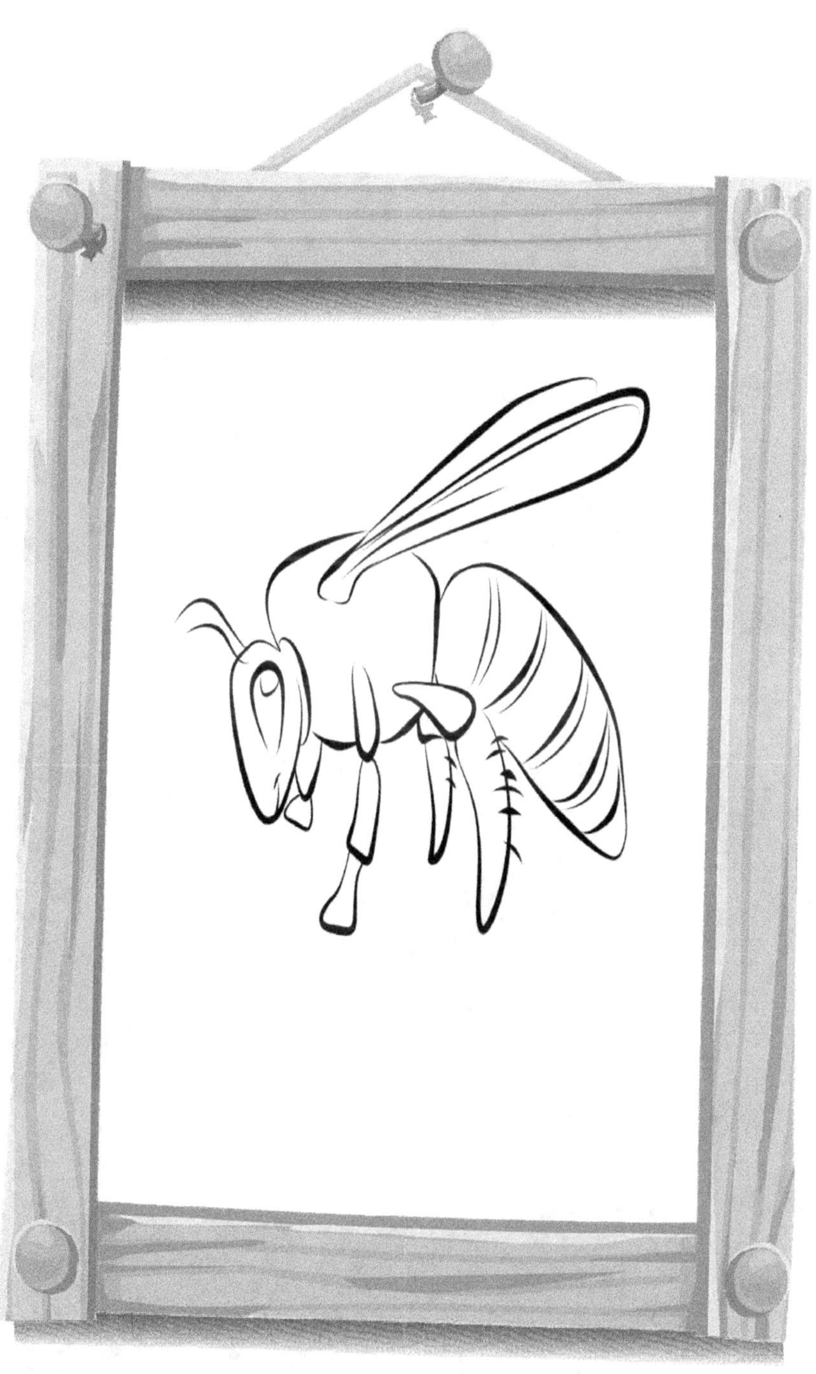

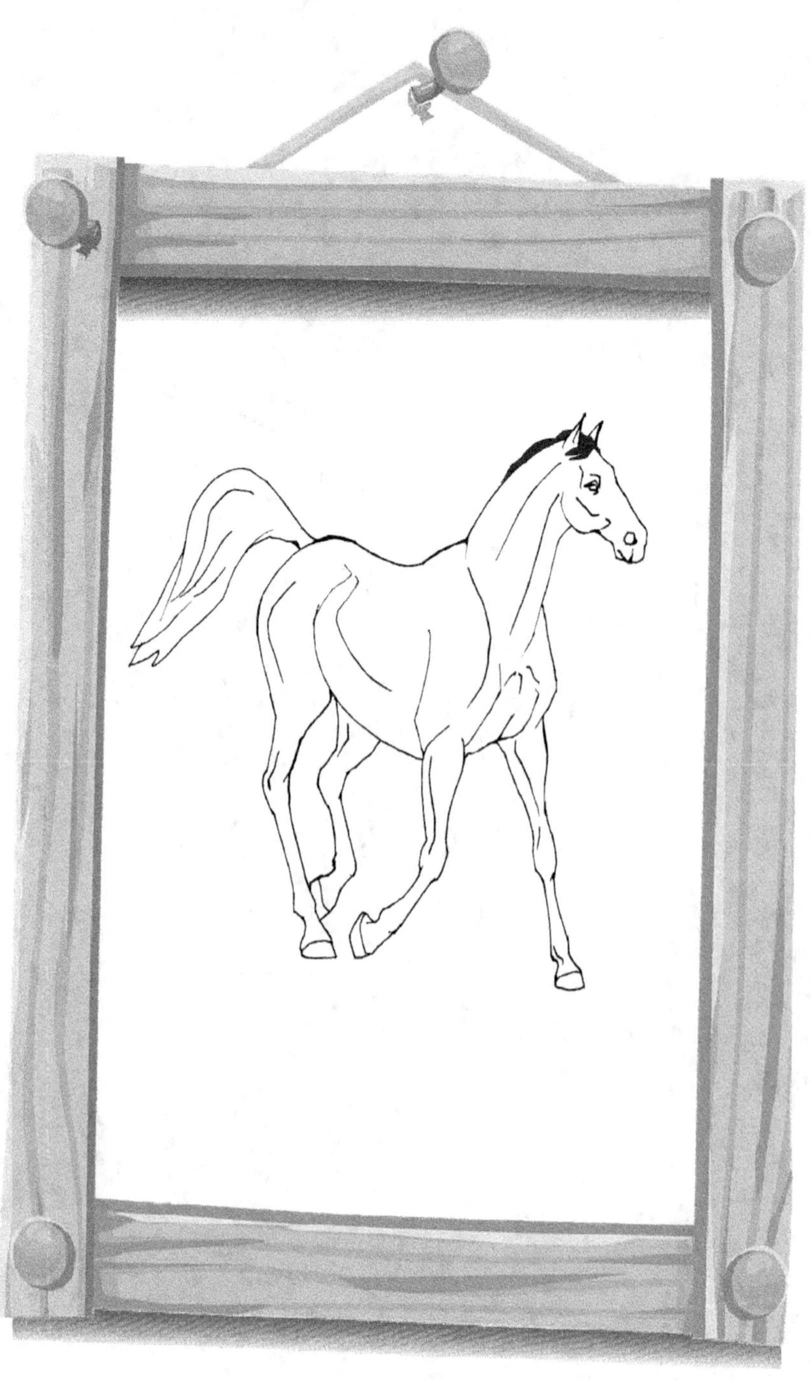

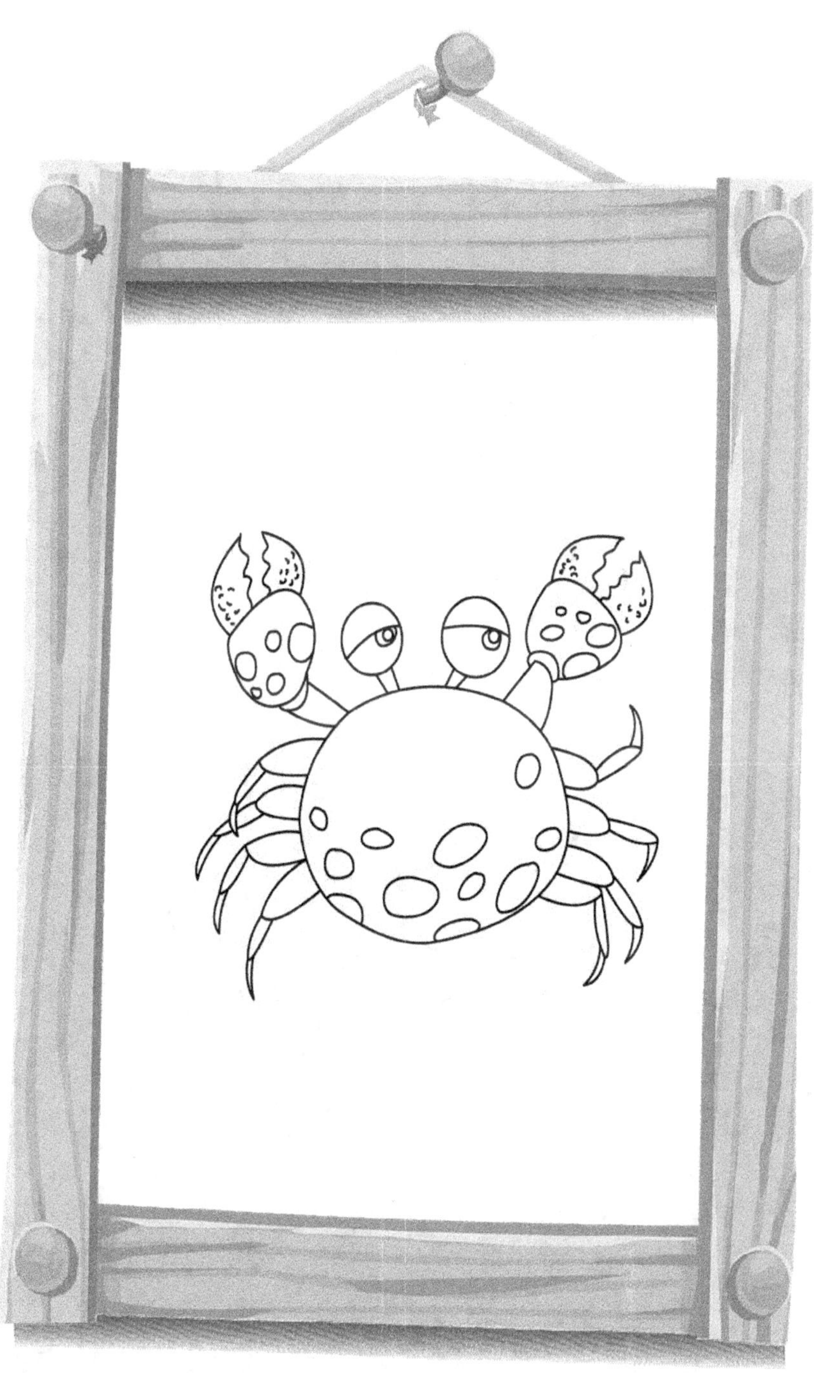

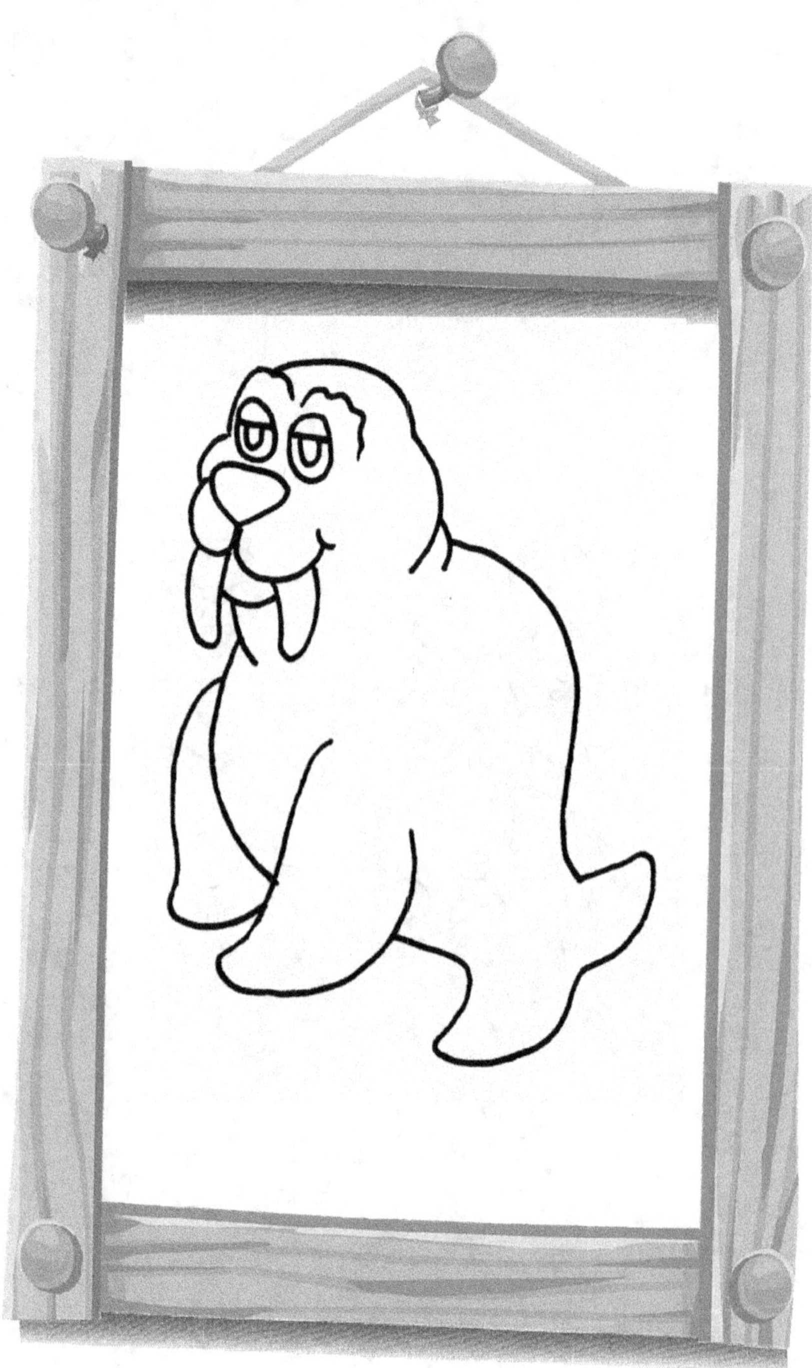

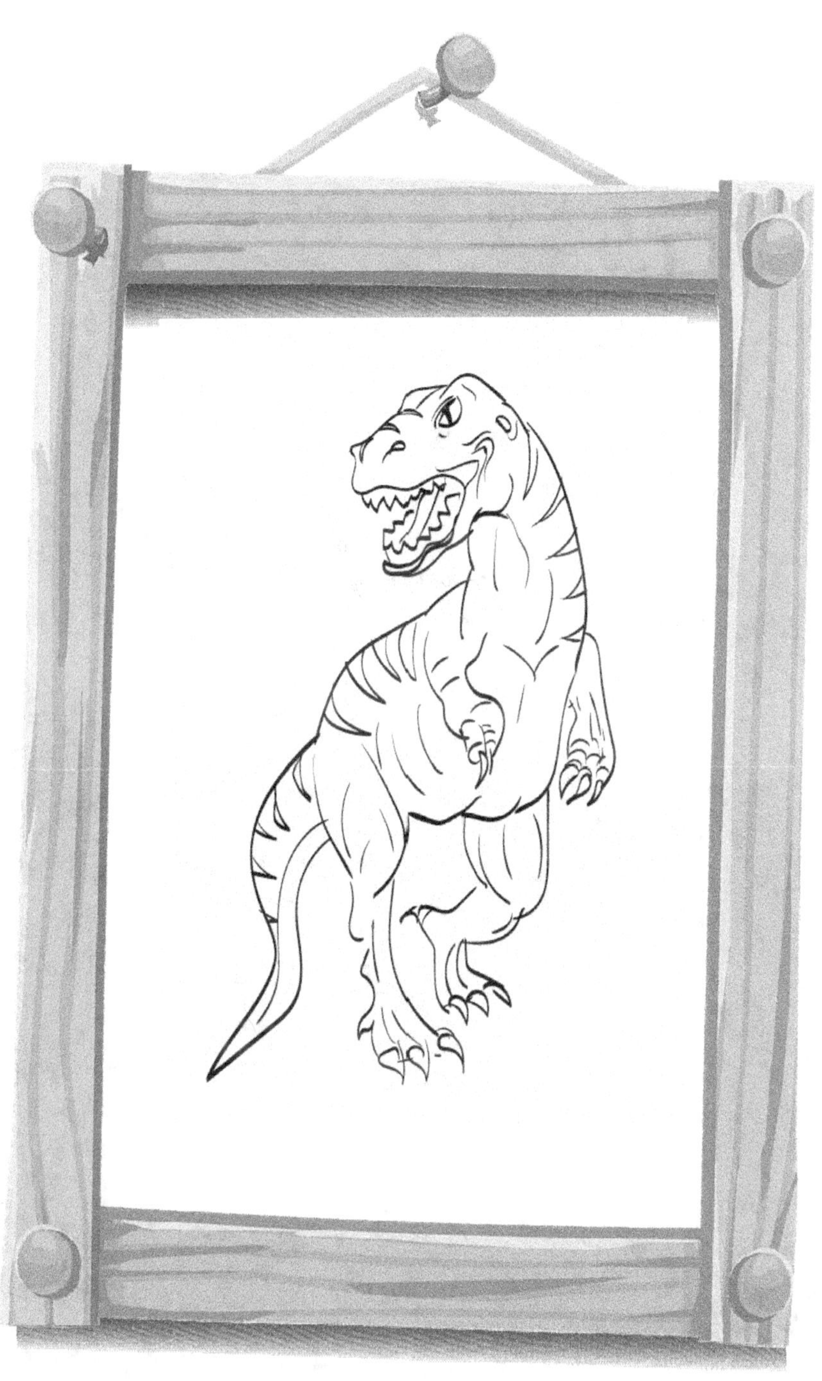

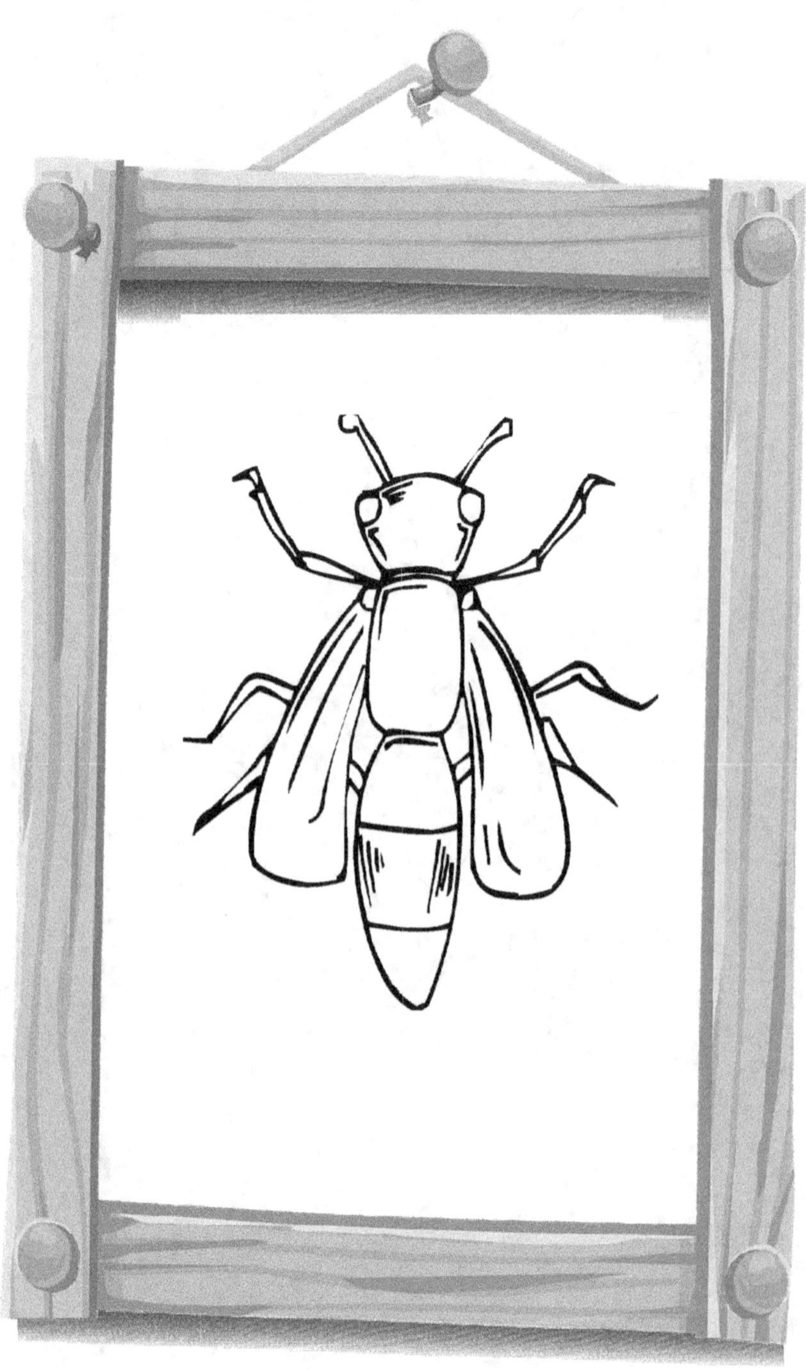